RURAL HEALTHCARE

Rural Healthcare was the first textbook of rural medicine in the UK. In this fully revised second edition, it continues to fulfil the requirement for a resource dedicated to the particular needs of those living and practising in rural areas. Offering an authoritative, informative, evidence-based, practical reference book, it is required reading for undergraduate and postgraduate students of rural healthcare, a foundation for rural healthcare curriculae and an inspirational read.

It is invaluable for both intending and established rural primary healthcare workers, including general practitioners, nurses, midwives, paramedics, therapists, managers and administrators.

Rural Healthcare

Second Edition

Edited by
Jim Cox,
Christopher E. Clark
and Tim Sanders

CRC Press
Taylor & Francis Group
Boca Raton London

CRC Press is an imprint of the
Taylor & Francis Group, an **informa** business

Second edition published 2023
by CRC Press
6000 Broken Sound Parkway NW, Suite 300, Boca Raton, FL 33487–2742

and by CRC Press
4 Park Square, Milton Park, Abingdon, Oxon, OX14 4RN

CRC Press is an imprint of Taylor & Francis Group, LLC

© 2023 selection and editorial matter, Jim Cox, Christopher E. Clark, and Tim Sanders; individual chapters, the contributors

First edition published by CRC Press 1998

ISBN: 978-1-032-29867-2 (hbk)
ISBN: 978-1-032-29866-5 (pbk)
ISBN: 978-1-003-30243-8 (ebk)

DOI: 10.1201/9781003302438

Contents

Figures

Tables

Boxes

Foreword

Many of us live in rural areas and even more of us spend part of our lives in rural settings, for holidays or other personal and professional reasons. This book, whose editors have lived and led as rural GPs, extends the scope of the first edition to embrace a wider audience and content. It will be of interest to healthcare students and trainees, primary healthcare workers and service managers—and probably others too! The chapters cover core concepts related to rurality, strategic opportunities and challenges and practical examples of lives and career opportunities in rural settings. Echoing some of the themes in recent national reports, part of the text draws our attention to sociodemographic tensions—increasing economic divisions due to escalating house prices in desirable retirement and second home venues; centralisation of services and infrastructure, with reduced employment and accessibility in more remote areas; and the biases introduced by training healthcare workers predominantly for and in urban settings. Fortunately, the authors also set out counterarguments and solutions, painting a picture of some of the excitement and stimulation of working and living in rural and remote areas.

The book is also clinically and practically focused. The majority of chapters address key epidemiological and service priorities—diseases with different profiles in rural areas, the need for extended scope of clinical practice (including emergency work) and the adjustments that healthcare teams and service designs can offer their populations.

It also addresses change—many innovations in digital technology used for both clinical care and education were led by those working in rural and remote settings. The push of the COVID-19 pandemic towards better use of remote consultations and supervision of staff and trainees has added to the repertoire of rural practice in a way that urban settings may learn from, and the increasing sophistication of digital apps to investigate and monitor patient well-being without trailing to a hospital outpatient clinic will also be particularly valuable for those with long and complex journeys to secondary care facilities. Although the new digital world will not stop the air ambulance being unable to reach a Scottish island due to fogbound conditions, it should increase the ability of primary care teams to feed out data and get accurate advice and support while the fog clears.

This last example raises a key theme of the book: equity. Whether we are talking of working conditions, training opportunities, modernising infrastructure and technology to support clinical care or recognition of the greater health needs of some rural populations, rural healthcare in the UK shines a light on the need for health service planners (and other government sectors) to conscientiously and consistently consider the rural dimensions of their policies and implementation programmes. I am grateful to the authors for their rich, varied and high-quality contributions from which we can learn much and hope many readers will find this book a real gift of knowledge and insight.

Professor Amanda Howe
University of East Anglia,
Norwich Medical School,
Norwich, United Kingdom

REFERENCE

Whitty C. The Chief Medical Officers Report 2021. Health in Coastal Communities. www.gov.uk/government/publications/chief-medical-officers-annual-report-2021-health-in-coastal-communities.

Contributors

Editors

Jim Cox OBE, DL, MD, FRCP Edin, FRCGP, MICGP, retired rural GP, Cumbria, UK

Christopher E. Clark PhD, FRCP, FRCGP, Clinical Senior Lecturer in General Practice, University of Exeter, UK. Chair, RCGP Rural Forum Steering Group

Tim Sanders FRCGP, FHEA, Clinical Senior Lecturer in Rural Medicine and Urgent Care, University of Central Lancashire, UK. GP and Clinical Training Lead, Cumbria Health on Call, UK

Biographers

Philip Evans FRCGP

Philip J. Sykes OBE, MA, FRCS

Contributors

Helen Atherton PhD, MSc, MPH, University of Warwick, Coventry, West Midlands, GB

Ruth Blundell BN

Andrew Brittlebank FRCPsych

Helen Cheyne PhD, MSc (Med Sci), RM, RGN

Christopher E. Clark PhD, FRCP, FRCGP

Jim Cox OBE, DL, MD, FRCP Edin, FRCGP, MICGP

Rosina Cross MSc, PhD

Miriam Dolan MA, MPH, MSc, FRCGP

Neil Frame MRCVS

Liam Glynn MD, MICGP, FRCSI, FRCGP

Amanda Howe OBE, MA, MD, MEd, FRCGP

Sean Hudson MBE, MSc, MRCGP, FAWM, FEWM

Kate King MPH, PGCMedEd, FRCGP

Jaki Lambert MPH, FHEA, RM

Dan Lasserson MA, MD, FRCP Edin, MRCGP

Sinéad T. J. McDonagh MSc, PhD

Margaret Nelson RGN

Mel Plant MRCGP

Tim Sanders FRCGP, FHEA

Charlie Siderfin MSc, FRCP Edin, FACRRM, MRCGP

Stephen Singleton OBE, FFPH, MRCGP

Natalie Taylor MSc, MRCGP, FEWM

Martin Woodham MBA

Nick Wright MCPara

Venetia Young FRCGP

Acknowledgements

We acknowledge with grateful thanks the contributions, lives and expertise of two rural practitioners now sadly deceased: Dr Iain Mungall, co-editor of the first edition of *Rural Healthcare*, and Dr Michael Cox, whose sketches again illustrate this second edition.

We also thank Hasnain (Hayes) Dalal for the case study in Chapter 17, Kate King for her contributions to Chapter 8 and John Campbell, Jayne Fordham, Karen Clark, Charlie Cox, Laura Sanders, Fiona Cox, Cathy Jackson, Deborah Gaston and members of the RCGP Rural Forum Steering Group for their help and support.

CHAPTER 1

Introduction

....

Jim Cox, Christopher E. Clark and Tim Sanders

Although broadly similar, rural healthcare is different to that in non-rural areas. Why? What are the differences? What does an undergraduate or postgraduate student or practising healthcare professional need to know?

DEMOGRAPHY

Since 1851, the rural population has been a minority compared to the number of people in towns and cities.[1] The Republic of Ireland (36%), Northern Ireland (36%) and Wales (33%) are more rural than England (21%) and Scotland (17%). Scotland is exceptional in that 17% of the population lives in 98% of the land area.[2,3]

Rural communities (and therefore patient populations) are different. Compared to their urban counterparts, rural dwellers are older. The average rural adult age is 58 years, compared with an average urban adult age of 45 years. The more rural the area, the older the population. Educational attainment differs too. Almost a quarter (23%) of all UK rural adults have no qualifications, compared to 9% in urban areas.[4] Fewer adults are in work, and more than twice as many are retired. Average rural household incomes are 15% lower than those of urban households. Rural villages and smaller settlements are changing as young people migrate towards towns and cities, and older people retire to the countryside. Because of escalating house prices, many young people cannot afford to live in the area in which they were brought up, so they move away.

DOI: 10.1201/9781003302438-1

HEALTH AND DISEASE

Rural people are generally healthier than their urban counterparts, but with wide variation. Certain rural occupations, such as agriculture and forestry, carry their own health risks. Some diseases, for example zoonoses, are predominantly seen in the countryside. A working knowledge of animal husbandry and diseases can be invaluable.

ACCESS TO SERVICES

Rural dwellers are often regarded as being stoical. Such fortitude may be a frame of mind or simply an acceptance of the limitations of rural services. It means that some rural patients, particularly those born, bred and working in the countryside, are less demanding of health services. Conversely, such attitudes can lead to delayed diagnosis and treatment.

Health, social and voluntary services are less accessible than they are in towns and cities, particularly in more remote and sparsely populated areas with limited or absent public transport. Increased travel time means more expensive journeys not only in terms of fuel costs etc. but also in time off work or away from home for patients, their family members and carers.

There is a delicate balance between access to healthcare and its quality. For example, morbidity and mortality improve when services are centralised. Specialist teams can focus their attention and gain experience on a small range of problems. Trauma centres and specialist cardiac and stroke units are good examples. On the other hand, members of the public value local services and resist change. They have a sense of 'ownership' and, supported by their political representatives, will fight hard against closure of local hospitals and other health facilities. While healthcare providers often save money when they centralise services, indirect costs for patients and their families increase. For them, longer distances, increased travel costs and more time off work make services less accessible and drain their resources. As ever, those on the lowest incomes are affected the most.

HIDDEN SOCIAL EXCLUSION

The casual observer is easily misled by statistics and by the beauty of much of the countryside: the 'rural idyll'. The relative wealth and high incomes of some rural dwellers, including many retirees to the countryside and second-home owners, compared to the lower incomes of others, are easily hidden by routine statistics. As elsewhere, poverty, deprivation and social exclusion affect health. Particularly in the more sparsely populated areas, wealth and poverty are often found side by side in the same enumeration district or postcode area. Existing indices of deprivation do not adequately define rural deprivation, so there is poor targeting of scarce resources.

Transport is of vital concern in the countryside. Lack of public transport means that many of the poorest members of society must run their own vehicles, thus compounding their poverty.

Service delivery structures and systems developed for urban populations do not necessarily function well in rural areas. However, if they work in rural areas, they may well work in urban settings.

What Is It Like to Be a Rural Health Worker in the UK?

Living in the countryside has its own special joy. Many of us choose to live and work in rural areas and consider ourselves lucky. However, the perfect setting on a fine spring morning can be hideous during a foul winter!

Travelling can be a challenge, sometimes with long drives for schooling, entertainment etc.

Populations tend to be stable with relatively slow turnover, so patients and members of healthcare teams are well known. Because professionals may well be seen as 'community property', some find the lack of anonymity difficult, especially if they are diffident about taking on a wider role within the community.

Colleagues may well be patients, with consequent problems of confidentiality and multi-layered relationships. Meeting and learning can be difficult, engendering a feeling of professional isolation. Digital technology helps.

Education

Having a rural background has been described as being strongly associated with choosing a career in rural practice and has led to educational strategies widely referred to as 'rural pipelines' or 'rural pathways' in which students with a rural background are channelled into rural training programmes, and more students are exposed to rural practice during their training.[5] Such strategies make sense and have been implemented around the world, although, so far, evidence to support them is only moderate.[6]

The Future

Developments in point-of-care investigations, artificial intelligence, machine learning, genetics, robotics and drone technology all offer potential improvements in rural healthcare, some still unimaginable to most of us. Wearable devices such as smart watches are already medicalising everyday life as people routinely monitor their own heart rate and rhythm and the amount of exercise they take. If, as is likely, this leads to patients taking more responsibility for their own health, then the role of healthcare professionals will continue to change as clinicians take a more advisory and supportive role. The benefits for rural residents and those who provide their healthcare are not difficult to imagine.

Conversely, although constructive challenge should be welcomed, trust in public health policies and the health professionals who promote them is increasingly subject to misinformation and hostility in the press and social media. The long-term impact of the COVID-19 pandemic remains to be seen.

The threat of climate change, often better understood by younger people than older generations, affects everyone. Particular issues for rural areas include poor home insulation in older rural houses; fuel costs, particularly heating oil in the many areas without a mains gas supply; and the impact of travel on greenhouse gas emissions. There is an opportunity to reduce travel by embracing some of the developments in healthcare accelerated by the COVID-19 pandemic, including remote consulting and patients' use of phone apps, smart watches etc. to monitor and report their own health.

We draw attention to the inequities of government funding formulae based on historic activity, not patients' needs, but also describe constructive solutions to challenges. For example, see in the next chapter what is being done in Scotland.

We write at a time of both opportunity and uncertainty. Exacerbated by the COVID-19 pandemic, pressure on health and social care services is intense, stress levels high and 'burn-out' a tragedy for individual practitioners, their patients who receive sub-standard care and their employers who prematurely lose them from the workforce.

Our aim is to support undergraduate and postgraduate rural healthcare education in the UK and the Republic of Ireland. We appreciate that, across the globe, rurality and remoteness present many different and often greater challenges, particularly in less well-resourced healthcare systems. We have not attempted to address these issues, but we believe that everyone can and should learn from international experience and the expertise of people who work in other parts of the world.

We hope that you find this book useful and enjoyable and welcome your comments, corrections and suggestions.

REFERENCES

1 Davenport RJ. Urbanisation and mortality in Britain, c 1880–50. *The Economic History Review.* 2020; 73: 455–85. https://doi.org/10.1111/ehr.12964

2 World Bank. https://data.worldbank.org/indicator/SP.RUR.TOTL.ZS?locations= IE [Accessed 18 July, 2022].

3 House of Lords Library. *Factfile: Rural Economy.* London: UK Parliament, 2020. https://lordslibrary.parliament.uk/fact-file-rural-economy/ [Accessed 11 May, 2022].

4 Financial Conduct Authority (FCA). *The Financial Lives of Consumers across the UK: Key Findings from the FCA's Financial Lives Survey 2017, Updated January 2020.* London: Financial Conduct Authority, 2020. www.fca.org.uk/publication/research/financial-lives-consumers-across-uk.pdf [Accessed 11 May, 2022].

5 World Health Organisation (WHO). *WHO guideline on health workforce development, attraction, recruitment and retention in rural and remote areas.* WHO, 2021. www.who.int/publications/i/item/9789240024229 [Accessed 11 May, 2022.]

6 Grobler L, Marais B, Mabunda S. Interventions for increasing the proportion of health professionals practising in rural and other underserved areas. *Coch Database Syst Rev.* 2015;2015(6):CD005314. https://doi.org/10.1002/14651858. CD005314.pub3. https://pubmed.ncbi.nlm.nih.gov/26123126/ [Accessed 11 May, 2022].

CHAPTER 2

What Is Rurality?

....

Rurality is a combination of the physical, psychological and philosophical. For some rural inhabitants, it reflects ways of living and working that span multiple generations, with a connection and interdependence with the land and the environment and a sense of ownership, husbandry and deep responsibility for the community. For others, it is a choice: a scenic place to live and commute from, retire to or retreat from the noise and pace of urban living. For others still, it is a challenge, an inconvenience or worse. Local hub towns cannot be reached on foot, and public transport links, where present, are expensive relative to metropolitan areas. Housing stock tends to be older, lacking the economic advantages of modern insulation and heating systems.

Rurality is a relative concept, dependent upon the remoteness, size and sparsity of the population in the context of the country or region as a whole. A hamlet in the UK might be the same size as a village in Nepal; a village in the southeast of England might be described as a town in the highlands of Scotland. Fortunately, although different in Northern Ireland, there is now a standard definition for most official statistics in Great Britain: the 'rural-urban classification', originally adopted for the 2001 census and revised in 2011, is based upon population size and population sparsity.[1]

This chapter compares Scotland, the Republic of Ireland, Northern Ireland, Wales and England, considering their demography and different definitions of rurality, based on population density and sparsity. It discusses the variations in rural healthcare systems in the UK and Ireland with examples of good practice and imaginative solutions to the challenges of recruitment and providing routine and urgent care in remote, rural, coastal and island communities.

DOI: 10.1201/9781003302438-2

For example, health and social care are integrated in Scotland and Northern Ireland but not elsewhere. Community nurses in Wales, but not routinely in England, are co-located in general practices and there is significant private sector involvement in the delivery of healthcare in the Republic of Ireland.

CHAPTER 2.1

Scotland

....

Charlie Siderfin

Scotland is a rural country of 5.5 million people whose health service is devolved to the Scottish government. Rural areas, which include the sparsely populated Highlands and Islands, account for 98% of the landmass but only 17% of the population.

DEFINITION

Table 2.1.1 summarises the Scottish government's urban-rural classification. The distribution of these areas is illustrated in the map (Figure 2.1.1): 70% of Scotland's landmass is defined as 'remote rural' and 28% as 'accessible rural'.

RURAL HEALTHCARE IN SCOTLAND

The Scottish government has an ambition to be a world exemplar in the delivery of rural, remote and island healthcare. There is an understanding that service delivery structures developed for urban populations do not necessarily work well for rural but that if structures work in rural areas, they are likely to work in urban settings.

Scotland has a long history of rural healthcare innovation. The Dewar Report,[4] published in 1912, described the woefully inadequate provision of medical services to crofters in the Highlands and Islands of Scotland. It recommended the provision of a centrally planned service, resulting in the Highlands and Islands Medical Service, which was widely

DOI: 10.1201/9781003302438-3

TABLE 2.1.1 Scottish Government Urban Rural Classification 2016[2]

Class	Class Name	Description
1	**Large Urban Areas**	Settlements of 125,000 people and over
2	**Other Urban Areas**	Settlements of 10,000 to 124,999 people
3	**Accessible Small Towns**	Settlements of 3,000 to 9,999 people and within a 30-minute drive time of a settlement of 10,000 or more
4	**Remote Small Towns**	Settlements of 3,000 to 9,999 people and with a drive time of over 30 minutes to a settlement of 10,000 or more
5	**Very Remote Small Towns**	Settlements of 3,000 to 9,999 people and with a drive time of over 60 minutes to a settlement of 10,000 or more
6	**Accessible Rural Areas**	Areas with a population of less than 3,000 people and within a 30-minute drive time of a settlement of 10,000 or more
7	**Remote Rural Areas**	Areas with a population of less than 3,000 people and with a drive time of over 30 minutes but less than or equal to 60 minutes to a settlement of 10,000 or more
8	**Very Remote Rural Areas**	Areas with a population of less than 3,000 people and with a drive time of over 60 minutes to a settlement of 10,000 or more

cited in the Cathcart Report of 1936 and contributed significantly to the philosophy of the National Health Service (NHS) in 1948.[5] Over the last two decades, the government has invested in important programmes of rural healthcare service delivery development and research.

NHS SCOTLAND

The central values of NHS Scotland are:[6]

- Care and compassion
- Dignity and respect
- Openness, honesty and responsibility
- Teamwork and quality improvement

NHS Scotland consists of 14 regional NHS boards, each responsible for the protection and improvement of its population's health and the delivery of healthcare services. A further seven special NHS boards and one

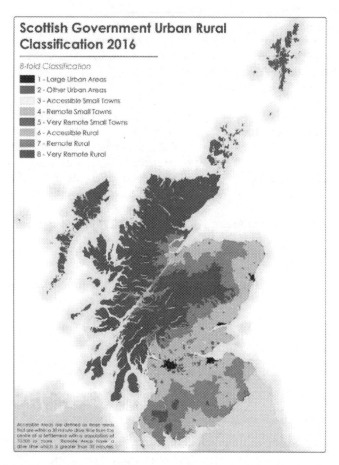

FIGURE 2.1.1 Map showing Scottish government urban rural classification.[3]

public health body provide a range of important specialist and national services (Table 2.1.2).

In the 2019 Scottish Household Survey, the people of Scotland rated themselves as having a good sense of community, with 94% of households saying that their community was a very good or a fairly good place to live, where they felt that they 'belonged', could influence decisions and felt safe at night.[8] This sense of community and belonging is reflected in government policy. NHS Scotland is a collaborative organisation, with a philosophy of working together across Scotland to improve the health of the population and the healthcare experience of individual patients.

TABLE 2.1.2 Special NHS Boards of Scotland[7]

Public Health Scotland	Scotland's lead national agency for improving and protecting the health and well-being of all of Scotland's people
Health Improvement Scotland	Supporting the delivery of high-quality, evidence-based care and scrutinising services to provide public assurance about the quality and safety of healthcare
NHS Education for Scotland	Quality education for a healthier Scotland
NHS National Waiting Times Centre	Ensuring prompt access to first-class treatment
NHS24	Providing health advice and information
Scottish Ambulance Service	Responding to almost 600,000 accident and emergency calls and taking 1.6 million patients to and from hospital each year
The State Hospitals Board for Scotland	Providing assessment, treatment and care in conditions of special security for individuals with a mental disorder who, because of their dangerous, violent or criminal propensities, cannot be cared for in any other setting
NHS National Services Scotland	Supplying essential services, including health protection, blood transfusion and information

SUPPORT FOR HEALTH PROFESSIONALS

For a rural practitioner, the practical day-to-day reality is that advice and support are freely available from primary, secondary and tertiary care colleagues within the same health board or a health board with which a 'service level agreement' has been negotiated. If specialist advice is required outside these areas, advice is usually given free of charge. If formal referral is required, the referring practitioner applies to their health board for funding.

The COVID-19 pandemic accelerated the already ambitious national transformation agenda with organisations such Health Improvement Scotland[9] and the Centre for Sustainable Delivery[10] working with territorial health boards in collaborative forums to develop services together, supporting and learning from each other. The aim was not to deliver a strictly uniform service across Scotland but to provide quality-assured services adapted to the differing needs of local communities. The innovation and ingenuity required to deliver services to rural and remote populations provide a rich source of learning for larger conurbations.

HEALTH AND SOCIAL CARE INTEGRATION, REALISTIC MEDICINE AND QUALITY IMPROVEMENT

Health and social care are integrated. Thirty-one Health and Social Care Partnerships (HSCP)[11] across Scotland are mandated to work with the voluntary sector and local communities to develop localised, joined-up systems to improve the lives of individuals, with an emphasis on anticipatory, preventative and community-based care delivered as close to the patient's home as possible.

The rapid adoption of videoconference technology during the COVID-19 pandemic facilitated the ability of rural areas to deliver specialist outpatient care directly to patients' homes. It also enhanced the ability of rural clinicians and managers to engage as equal partners in the Scottish government's programme of health and social care transformation.

Realistic medicine[12] is an evolving philosophy of professional behaviours and attitudes to deliver personalised care through joint decision making with the patient. It is about continuous quality improvement and innovation, with appropriate management of risk, alongside the reduction of variation to minimise harm and waste, while ensuring that the needs and wishes of the patient are at the centre of what is done. Some say that many aspects of realistic medicine are what rural practitioners have been practising for many years.

'Clusters'[13] of GP practices work collaboratively with HCSPs to improve care. GP clusters replaced the quality and outcome framework (QOF),[14] moving from a quantitative, financially driven mechanism of quality improvement to a more nuanced, locally appropriate, holistic approach based on professionalism, not financial reward. Improved services are achieved by identifying locally important aspects of care and through discussion, structured review of data, the understanding of variation and the utilisation of quality improvement methodology,[15] developing better care for patients.

EXPERT MEDICAL GENERALISTS

The Scottish General Medical Services contract of 2018[16] identified GPs as expert medical generalists who manage complex and undifferentiated medical conditions and lead multidisciplinary primary care teams, in which each team member works towards the top of their license. (See Chapter 3: Role of the Generalist.) Most team members are directly employed by

HSCPs, working in an integrated fashion with independently contracted general practices. Clinicians, social care providers, voluntary organisations and community representatives sit on HSCP decision-making committees, ensuring a local, community-based focus to the delivery of care.

MODELS OF HEALTH AND SOCIAL CARE DELIVERY

General Practice

Across rural Scotland, GP partnerships or salaried GPs work with HSCP-employed multidisciplinary, generalist teams to provide a wide range of services, including dispensing. The out-of-hours (OOH) service in most of rural Scotland is provided by health board–employed teams, with only a small number of practitioners providing 24/7 cover to the most isolated populations.

A wide range of care delivery models have developed across rural Scotland to meet the different needs of individual communities, often driven by healthcare professional recruitment difficulties and challenging geography.

NHS Orkney has practices on ten remote islands, with individual populations ranging from around 50 to 600. The Isles Network of Care (INOC) was established in 2010 after a failure to recruit any single-handed GPs for two years. Following extensive consultation with the island communities, advanced nurse practitioners (ANPs) were recruited to six of the islands, with the other four larger islands having a GP and an island nurse. Individuals are appointed to small teams on specific islands, working in rotation. ANPs work two weeks on and two weeks off, while the GPs tend to work rotations of three-week blocks with three or four GPs appointed to each island. This allows the GPs to undertake a wide range of different work elsewhere. Weekly videoconference meetings bring geographically separated practitioners together to discuss cases, learn together and provide mutual support. Monthly meetings focus on quality improvement. Social media groups allow rapid responses to clinically related questions as well as the exchange of personal news and comment, an important ingredient for mature teams.

Significant work has been invested in the standardisation of emergency care provision through training, protocol development with emergency equipment and medication set out in a proscribed format. This helps build practitioner confidence and supports easy movement of staff between islands when required.

In the Small Isles of Eigg, Rum, Muck and Canna, in 2015, NHS Highland worked with the communities to develop a system where the Broadford practice in Skye provides a weekly visiting service, alongside remote consultations via telephone or videoconference.[17] A supply of medication is kept on each island, accessible to designated keyholders. First responders provide urgent care with evacuation support via helicopter or lifeboat when required.

Following a visit to Alaska by residents and NHS Highland to witness first hand the Nuka System of Care,[18] rural health and social care support workers were appointed to empower and increase community resilience. The support workers undertake tasks such as dressing changes, clinical observations, taking blood samples and delivering home care duties. Each rural support team (RST), composed of nurse and paramedic advanced practitioners (AP), covers large sparsely populated areas of western Highland.[19] Created in part to address difficulties with GP recruitment, teams deliver a wide range of holistic care to remote communities and are an integral part of routine and urgent care provision in healthcare facilities or in the home. RSTs support general practices with GP vacancies and cover leave. They also alternate with GPs to visit the Small Isles. RST members always have access to GP advice and support while they, in turn, have developed 'professional friendships' with the Small Isles support workers.

Developing communities of practice between multi-professional teams providing care to remote communities has been an essential element in ensuring quality of care and in supporting both recruitment and retention. Focusing on the needs of individual patients, learning together and providing emotional support are important ingredients for bringing disparate practitioners together into cohesive, functioning teams, with each professional group bringing their own areas of experience and expertise.

Community Hospitals

Community hospitals across rural Scotland provide a range of intermediary care inpatient beds. Some also provide a minor injuries service. 'Community-plus hospitals', staffed by GPs, nurses and other professionals with extended training and skills, provide more extensive inpatient and emergency services. Situated in remote areas, they are also known as 'no-pass community hospitals', indicating that ambulance crews should not bypass them on the way to more distant specialist units but take critically ill or injured patients either for stabilisation and onward transfer or for definitive treatment.

Rural General Hospitals

There are six rural general hospitals (RGH) in Scotland, all in the Highlands and Islands, located in Wick, Fort William and Oban and on the islands of Lewis (Stornoway, Western Isles), Shetland (Lerwick) and Orkney (Kirkwall). Each provides services to rural populations of 22,000 to 25,000.

Consultant-led medical, surgical, anaesthetic, obstetrics and public health services are delivered through inpatient (including a high-dependency unit) and outpatient facilities. Multidisciplinary teams (MDT) with broad generalist skills include nursing, midwives, physiotherapy, occupational therapy, dietetics, podiatry and speech and language services. Visiting specialist services are provided in outpatient departments or delivered remotely. Strong working relationships between the RGHs and their tertiary referral centres support high-quality care as close to home as possible.

GPs with special interests provide some inpatient and outpatient services while rural emergency physicians may lead emergency departments and provide inpatient support.

Each RGH has a laboratory providing a range of haematology, biochemistry and microbiology investigations and a radiology department providing plain radiographs, CT scanning and ultrasound services. Specialist nurses and advanced practitioners provide both care in the RGHs and outreach into the communities from the hospitals. They work closely with tertiary referral centres, covering specialties such as oncology and palliative care, renal dialysis, diabetes, cardiology, and neurological conditions such as multiple sclerosis, Parkinson's disease and motor neurone disease.

EMERGENCY CARE PROVISION

The Scottish Trauma Network[20] comprises four regional networks (North, East, South and West), each having a major trauma centre. NHS Scotland operates a national retrieval service for critically ill patients across Scotland. Scottish Specialist Transport and Retrieval (ScotSTAR), operated by the Scottish Ambulance Service (SAS), provides two consultant-led teams ready for deployment 24/7 across Scotland, using dedicated fixed-wing aircraft and helicopters to provide inter-hospital transfers and prehospital retrievals. ScotSTAR works from Glasgow Airport, bringing together the adult emergency medical retrieval Service (EMRS),[21] paediatric retrieval service[22] and neonatal retrieval service.[23] ScotSTAR also provides real-time advice and support to hospital and prehospital teams caring for critically unwell patients. Around 40% of calls to the service are from practitioners requesting advice or support about care delivery, thereby avoiding transfer. The teams have strong relationships with RGHs, community hospitals and even some individual general practices. They routinely contact local teams the next day to update them on the patient's condition, provide support and feedback and discuss any immediate learning points arising from cases.

The reality for rural practitioners is that, whether they are in the patient's home, at the roadside, up a mountain or in a community hospital or RGH, they have immediate access to specialist support for the care of their patients. ScotSTAR advice is tailored to the skills, equipment and environment of the practitioner. The service organises the logistics of evacuation, freeing the practitioner to concentrate on patient care. They also provide a strong clinical governance framework, videoconference clinical case reviews and audit between specialists and peripheral practitioner to facilitate learning, outreach training and online clinical guidelines, protocols and standard operating procedures across the country.

Prehospital Emergency Care (PHEC)

Delivery of prehospital emergency care (PHEC) is a source of significant anxiety for rural communities and practitioners alike. Although the responsibility for managing critically ill patients—for example, due to illness, trauma or childbirth—may occur relatively infrequently, it is essential that patients receive a high standard of care each time. BASICS Scotland[24] has become the gold standard provider of PHEC training, delivering a range of face-to-face and online courses. Working with the Sandpiper Trust,[25] they provide course graduates with a Sandpiper Bag which contains all the equipment required to deliver emergency care, as taught on their courses. An additional drug-pod is also available. The BASICS Scotland App contains a suite of emergency protocols (kept up to date by BASICS and ScotSTAR), with a standard electronic patient report form (PRF) used as patient record and handover documentation that can be sent to the receiving unit electronically. PRFs automatically provide anonymised information to the BASICS Scotland database which, with Scottish Ambulance Service (SAS) data, provides a reliable record of PHEC activity across Scotland and acts as an important source for governance, learning, research and policy development.

PRF submission also triggers a follow-up call the next day to provide the responder with a patient update, incident de-brief and welfare support.

BASICS Scotland holds regular online videoconference governance meetings with community responders, SAS personnel and hospital staff providing case review, joint learning and the ongoing development of supportive relationships between widely dispersed practitioners across Scotland.

There is an aspiration to standardise training, protocols (with national governance), equipment and drugs so that PHEC provision will be the same throughout Scotland, with equipment contained and set out identically with more extended standardised equipment available in remote areas. This would mean that GPs, advanced nurse practitioners and paramedics could work in any practice, knowing what drugs and equipment are available and where to find them quickly. It would also mean that, when giving advice, ScotSTAR would know what equipment was available to the practitioner.

TRAINING THE RURAL WORKFORCE

NHS Education for Scotland (NES)

NES[26] and its Remote and Rural Healthcare Education Alliance (RRHEAL)[27] are responsible for the coordination of education and development for rural healthcare workers. Their frameworks guide and help practitioners develop the additional knowledge and skills necessary for rural practice.

The Clinical Skills Managed Educational Network (CSMEN),[28] established in 2007, delivers skills training to rural healthcare staff, fire and rescue, coast guards, mountain rescue, first responders and first-aiders etc. Its mobile skills unit (MSU)[29] is a bespoke lorry providing a classroom/training area, video recording to support scenario de-briefing, hi-fidelity manikins, equipment and educational material to support state-of-the-art skills training and inter-agency working in rural areas. Taking the MSU to the communities allows joint skills training with attention to human factors and effective teamwork, helping develop strong, mutually supportive relationships and effective emergency resilience.

A 'Multidisciplinary Rural Advanced Practitioner Capability Framework'[30] outlines the knowledge, skills and attitudes required of rural advanced practitioners from all health professions. Like the rural fellowship for GPs, it supports practitioners to identify and source the additional training they require to move from urban, often specialised practice to work in rural areas.

Rural Training Pipeline

The effective and efficient delivery of rural healthcare requires well-trained and supported generalists. The concept of a 'rural training pipeline' is helpful in visualising the progression from school leaver to rural generalist practitioner.

As an example, the rural training pipeline for GPs illustrates some of the initiatives in Scotland.

Supporting Rural School Students to Apply to Medical School

There is evidence that individuals brought up in rural areas are more likely to take up rural positions at the end of their training.[31] Encouraging and supporting rural students to apply to medical school is therefore an important element in any long-term rural recruitment strategy. The REACH programme[32] is a national widening-access project which supports school students in the most deprived schools in Scotland and in remote and rural areas apply to medical and other vocational courses. It provides career insight days, application support and mentoring.

Medical Schools

The broad range of undifferentiated problems presents rich opportunities for rural hospital and community placements in both breadth and depth of training experience. The small teams in rural locations allow senior clinicians to provide close supervision while allowing students and trainees to take more responsibility than their urban counterparts. As a result, RGH attachments are highly rated by trainees.

The four-year Scottish Graduate Entry Medicine (ScotGEM)[33] course offered by St Andrews and Dundee Universities trains doctors with a generalist interest, focusing particularly on rural medicine and healthcare improvement. Students live and study in a rural environment from their second year.

Dundee University offers longitudinal integrated clerkships[34] in which fourth-year medical students are placed in rural general practices for 40 weeks. During their placements, they follow patients through their journeys in both primary and secondary care.

Aberdeen University offers remote and rural options for students interested in rural medicine.[35] Students can spend their fourth year at Raigmore Hospital, Inverness, attending remote clinics with attachments to rural general practices. Fifth-year students can spend two of their three clinical attachments in rural locations. All five Scottish universities have active rural medicine societies.

Specialty Training

The Scotland deanery offers a rural-track GP postgraduate speciality training programme in the northern region, with trainees undertaking placements in RGHs and rural practices.[36]

Rural fellowships[37] offer the opportunity for relatively recently qualified
GPs to undertake a further year in either rural general practice or a rural hospital to identify their additional learning needs and develop their skills and experience to equip them for rural practice. The year includes 13 weeks of protected
educational time with a generous educational bursary to support a personal
development plan agreed with the programme coordinator. A survey of GPs
who undertook a fellowship during the first ten years of the programme found
that 71% were working in rural areas or accessible small towns in Scotland.[38]

The standard rural fellowship prepares GPs for work in rural general
practice. The acute care fellowship provides training for GPs who intend to
work in community-plus hospitals and RGHs. Competencies for the acute
care fellowship form the basis of the GMC rural and remote credential[39]
for GPs and non-consultant grade doctors providing extended care in rural
hospitals across the UK.

Continuing Education and Support

Monthly videoconference 'grand rounds' bring the six RGHs together with
each hospital taking it in turn to host the meeting, presenting interesting
and educational cases for discussion, strengthening networks and facilitating the sharing of good practice.

The Viking Surgeons[40] is an important forum for discussion, development and support for rural surgeons in Scotland and the Nordic countries.
It has been meeting since 1973, with an annual conference usually held in
one of the peripheral rural hospitals. The COVID-19 pandemic facilitated
the development of virtual attendance, widening the audience around the
world and vastly expanding the number of attendees.

The Royal College of Surgeons of Edinburgh Faculty of Remote, Rural and
Humanitarian Healthcare[41] brings together the NHS, industry and governmental and non-governmental organisations (NGO) interested in the delivery and development of rural and remote medicine. The Scottish government
runs a global citizen programme[42] which encourages healthcare professionals
to utilise their skills to support the development of healthcare in developing
nations. Some rural health boards offer full-time positions that, for example,
fund clinicians to work two-thirds of their time within their health board
and the other one-third overseas with a development project. There is a recognition that the knowledge, skills and attitudes of practitioners delivering
humanitarian aid are very similar to those required in our rural areas.

The Rural GP Association of Scotland (RGPAS)[43] is a membership organisation to support rural general practitioners. The Royal College of General Practitioners Rural Forum[44] also facilitates discussion, networking and professional development throughout the UK.

RECRUITMENT AND RETENTION

Figure 2.1.2 illustrates a functional framework to support the planning of a sustainable rural workforce.[45]

The Scottish Rural Medicine Collaborative (SRMC)[46] is a programme to support the recruitment and retention of the rural multidisciplinary workforce, promoting the unique challenges and satisfaction of a rural career

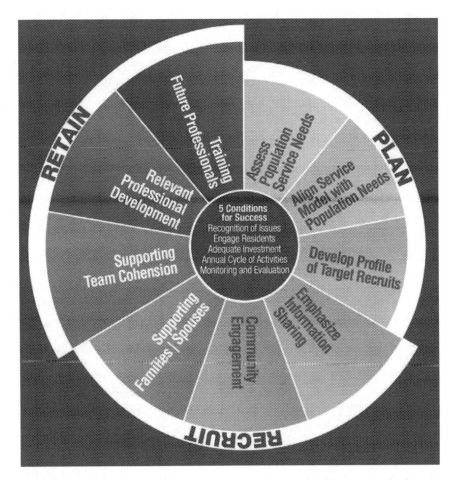

FIGURE 2.1.2 Plan, recruit, retain: a framework for local healthcare organisations to achieve a stable remote rural workforce.

and signposting training pathways and courses. The SRMC promotes rural networks, bringing together practitioners, health boards and other stakeholders to encourage collaborative working and the sharing of experience, knowledge and ideas to address the challenges of rural practice and improve the service to rural patients.

SRMC pioneers recruitment, producing good practice guidelines,[47] developing promotional material for conferences and championing a Scotland-wide recruitment strategy to help individuals find the job that best suits their career and personal aspirations, rural or urban.

Strong clinical leadership is an important element of successful recruitment. Leaders needs to be empowered to facilitate the development of clinical services and education, with practitioners empowered to develop ideas and create supporting structures. Rural organisations benefit from a strong quality-improvement philosophy which encourages curiosity, testing new ideas, the application of experiences from different places and learning through experimentation. Necessity is the mother of invention, and the challenges of delivering healthcare to rural and remote communities provides a rich environment for innovation, not only for rural areas but also for urban environments.

Rediscover the Joy of General Practice

The SRMC recruitment project Rediscover the Joy of General Practice[48] aims to support joy in primary care by promoting:

- Person-centred holistic care
- Jobs that provide a range of opportunities to suit professionals at different career stages and with different personal commitments
- Continuous quality improvement

GPs, who continue to live in their own homes, travel to and around Scotland to undertake rural placements for as many weeks of the year as they wish. Trained in prehospital emergency care (PHEC) and with the support of colleagues, experienced urban and newly qualified GPs work in rural and remote locations for varying periods of time. They also support practices that are struggling, often due to difficulties with recruitment. Working as a team, they promote a shared philosophy of care and, at the request of practices, support quality improvement activity.

They come together through videoconference and social media groups to share their experiences, learn together and consider how they can support practices through holiday cover, short-notice illness or more protracted periods of difficult recruitment to vacant positions. The scheme has been particularly successful in allowing retiring GPs to utilise their experience and extend their working lives by undertaking new, challenging and re-invigorating work in a supported environment.

Centre for Rural, Remote and Island Health and Social Care

The Scottish rural healthcare environment is vibrant but sometimes confusing due to the broad range of activity. In 2021 The Scottish government committed to developing an overarching National Centre for Rural, Remote and Island Health and Social Care to strengthen collaborative learning, development and service delivery to the geographically disparate communities of Scotland by bringing together patients, communities, voluntary organisations, practices, health boards and universities to deliver properly integrated, high-quality, realistic and sustainable care to the people of rural Scotland.

CHAPTER 2.2

Republic of Ireland

....

Liam Glynn

SOCIODEMOGRAPHIC PROFILE

The Republic of Ireland as an independent state was created in 1922 and consists of 26 of the 32 counties on the island of Ireland. The state extends over an area of about five-sixths (70,273 km^2 or 27,133 sq mi) of the island of Ireland (84,421 km^2 or 32,595 sq mi), with Northern Ireland making up the remainder. The population is 4,761,865 according to the census of 2016 and is predicted to exceed 5 million by Census 2022.[49] Average life expectancy in Ireland is 81.8 years, with 80 years for men and 84 years for women.[50] Ireland has the highest birth rate in the EU (16.8 births per 1,000 inhabitants, compared to an EU average of 10.7) and a very low infant mortality rate (3.5 per 1,000 live births).

The Commission for the Economic Development of Rural Areas (CEDRA), established in November 2012 as an independent expert group to examine and report on the medium-term economic development of rural Ireland to 2025, published its report 'Energising Ireland's Rural Economy' in April 2014.[51] This landmark report defined rural Ireland as 'all areas located beyond the administrative boundaries of the five largest cities'. However, this broad definition does not convey the multiplicity and heterogeneous nature of rural areas and communities in Ireland.[52] The census definition of an urban area is a town with a total population of 1,500 or more, and therefore towns with a population of less than 1,500 are included in rural areas.[49]

During the period 1991–2011, the number of people living in the countryside (areas outside the cities and towns) increased by 44% (1.8 million to

DOI: 10.1201/9781003302438-4

2.6 million), i.e. from 51% of the population nationally to 57%, but there was substantial spatial variation over the period, with some areas experiencing very large increases in population while others experienced declines in population. (In general, rural areas close or accessible to the main cities and larger towns experienced substantial and sustained growth in their populations between 1991 and 2011 while more remote areas and those less accessible to towns and cities showed a decline.)[52] High proportions of the population in these more remote areas were in older age cohorts, with many having left school before the age of 18.[49] It is possible that this trend of rural repopulation will be augmented by the flexible and remote working arrangements triggered by the global COVID-19 pandemic.

OVERVIEW OF THE HEALTHCARE SYSTEM

The Department of Health, headed by a minister of health, determines health policy in the Republic of Ireland, and the Health Services Executive (HSE) is then tasked with the delivery of publicly funded healthcare. There is also significant private sector involvement in the delivery of healthcare, ranging from GPs to allied healthcare professionals to private hospitals. The majority of health expenditure (73%) is funded by the government, with the balance funded by private sources, including health insurance (14%) and household out-of-pocket expenditure (12%).[53] Anyone holding a European health insurance card is entitled to free maintenance and treatment in public beds in Health Service Executive and voluntary hospitals and free access to GP care and hospital outpatient services on an emergency basis. Irish citizens are entitled to free maintenance and treatment in public beds in Health Service Executive and voluntary hospitals, but access to GP care is means tested, with approximately 54% of the population paying for GP visits.[54]

RURAL HEALTHCARE DELIVERY

Since the advent of the 'dispensary' model of primary care delivery in the last century, rural communities have been served very successfully by often small general practice–led primary care teams which research demonstrates can deliver both cost-effective and high-quality care to such populations.[55] The continuity of care created by such a system is associated with a reduced need for out-of-hours services and acute hospital admission and is also associated with decreased mortality.[56–58] However, like other developed countries globally, Ireland has a rural GP manpower crisis which is likely to worsen significantly in the next five years, with a large number of the current GP cohort in the Republic of Ireland set to retire. As a result, an increasing number of rural

GP posts remain unfilled, with lists being dispersed or ad hoc and expensive locum arrangements in place with a significant erosion of that principle of continuity of care on which rural healthcare delivery has been traditionally based.[59] A recent examination of GP workload in an Irish setting estimated that rural GPs reported working more than 9.5 hours per day in their practices (excluding breaks), and they spent a greater proportion of their time on house calls than their urban counterparts.[60] However, use of electronic medical records is practically universal, and the majority of practices now operate from purpose-built premises.[61]

In addition, these GP practice teams work in conjunction with publicly funded community-based HSE multidisciplinary primary care teams of nurses, physiotherapists, occupational therapists, social workers etc. in the community. However, the scope and function of these teams varies geographically, and significant problems remain that can disrupt team formation and functioning.[62] Regrettably, mental health services in the community are consultant led and are not integrated into the primary care team structure. Out-of-hours services are delivered to the vast majority of rural communities by GP cooperatives, although some much more onerous out-of-hours rotas remain: for example, covering Island communities such as the Achill Islands and the Aran Islands.

CHALLENGES

In 2015, the Irish College of General Practitioners published a report on the future of Irish rural practice which looked at the challenges and recommendations to improve the provision of care.[63] Again, recruitment and retention of staff were noted as the main concerns, with examples of GPs being asked by the HSE to continue in their posts after their age of retirement because their posts had not been filled after multiple advertisements. Other practices where recruitment has not been possible have simply been subsumed into larger practices based in other locations, leaving communities without a local healthcare service. Other key issues identified in rural areas by this report were a lack of infrastructure support, costs associated with smaller practice lists and difficulty finding adequate out-of-hours or locum coverage, occasionally causing interruptions to service due to lack of available GPs.

CHAPTER 2.3

Northern Ireland

....

Miriam Dolan

Northern Ireland (NI), created as a country within the UK in 1921, is located in the northeast of the island of Ireland. Its population is around 1.8 million. There has been little change in the life expectancy since 2000.[64]

The Northern Ireland Statistics and Research Agency (NISRA) defines all settlements with a population of less than 5,000 and areas of open countryside as rural.[65] The distance to a settlement with a population of 10,000 or more is used as a proxy for accessibility to key services, with rural areas in their vicinity considered to be more likely to thrive. More than a third (36%) of Northern Ireland's population lives in a rural area.[66]

A Department of Agriculture Environment and Rural Affairs (DEARA) report published in September 2020 describes key urban/rural differences and disparities across a range of domains including health, well-being and quality of life. Important findings from the report are:

- The cost of living is higher in rural areas.
- The household income is lower.
- Rural households are twice as likely to be in fuel poverty.
- Travel time to healthcare services and response time of emergency services are often longer.
- Private transport is frequently a necessity in rural areas, with vehicle ownership and running costs consuming a greater share of available household income.

DOI: 10.1201/9781003302438-5

- People living in rural areas report higher happiness levels and life satisfaction.
- Life expectancy is higher in rural areas, and people in rural areas can expect over four years more 'healthy' years.

This DAERA publication is intended to give a robust evidence base to inform the future direction of rural policy in Northern Ireland and to support equitable treatment of rural communities in policies and programmes. Rural policy is reinforced by the Rural Needs Act (Northern Ireland) enacted by the Northern Ireland Assembly.[67]

Since 2016, DAERA has also published an annual monitoring report. Its report for April 2019 to March 2020 describes how health and social care policies and activities were assessed for specific rural needs,[68] but there is no mention of the need for specific attention and support for planning primary healthcare services and the primary care workforce in rural areas.[69]

Differing from Wales and England, health and social care in NI is commissioned as an integrated service by the Department of Health through local commissioning groups.[70]

In March 2021, the Business Services Organisation[71] reported there were 321 GP practices in NI, a reduction of 29 (8%) since 2014, mainly decreasing in the districts of Fermanagh and Omagh, where there was a 30% decrease of GP practices.

These serious issues of recruitment of healthcare workers, particularly GPs, are palpable in Southwest Fermanagh, the most rural area in NI and a beautiful lake district. Faced with the workforce crisis, it is often in rural areas that innovations happen.

Practices are merging, fast-tracking new technologies such as virtual group consulting and e-consulting and developing teamwork. GPs are taking on new roles as managers and mentors in extending primary care multidisciplinary teams whose members are substituting and supplementing tasks and services traditionally provided by doctors. The jury is out on how these new models of general practice will deliver high-quality, safe, efficient, acceptable and sustainable primary care.[72, 73]

Maybe this rapid evolution of rural primary care services will prove to be fundamental, to ensure that the envisioned changes from a hospital-reliant system with incredible long waiting lists[74] to a community-based system[75] materialises.

Within the UK, the geography of NI brings unique additional challenges for rural people with regards accessing healthcare. Parts of the province share a border with the Republic of Ireland. Prior to Brexit, a European directive and cross-border agreements meant that patients living in border areas could access healthcare services on either side of the border, but since Brexit, these arrangements are in jeopardy. Increased travel times and longer waiting lists are impacting accessibility.

The health and well-being of the people of NI, moreover, is affected by the turbulent history of the province and the persistent division within its society, especially within rural border areas.[76] Morbidity, including mental health and addiction issues, is often exaggerated, if not caused by, social deprivation,[77] and the NISRA postcode look-up tool[78] strikingly identifies pockets of rural social deprivation in border areas, where people also experience hurdles to accessing primary or secondary care services due to long travel times and poor public transport.

Looking at the future, it is encouraging that more medical and other healthcare students are coming to rural primary care for their placements; for example, Queens University medical students spend more time in general practice, and the University of Ulster in Derry/Londonderry has opened a graduate-entry medical school in the more rural western area of NI. This is promising as the WHO has found that a positive undergraduate experience in rural practice is a main driver for recruitment to rural areas in the future.[79]

CHAPTER 2.4

Wales

....

Mel Plant

Green rolling hills, majestic mountains, waterfalls, clean air and open spaces create the rural idyll which is Wales. One-third of the population (approximately one million rural inhabitants) are scattered across this expanse of open land and farmland in isolated houses, hamlets and villages with a few larger towns. The remaining two million Welsh inhabitants live in two small, densely populated areas: one in the southeast, containing the capital and devolved parliament, and one in the northeast.

Rural isolation is exacerbated by poor transport infrastructure, with no major road or rail links between north and south Wales. From north and south Wales, the direction of travel is eastwards into England, but mid-Wales, the largest rural area, does not even have that benefit. It is impossible to travel from north to south Wales in one day on public transport without significant detours into England. Healthcare tends to follow travel routes, so rural border areas rely heavily on England for secondary care.

Statistical analysis remains a challenge when assessing very small numbers of people scattered over large areas (see Chapter 16: Rural Social Exclusion), but the Welsh government has made great efforts to assess rural deprivation with a more nuanced assessment: the Welsh Index of Multiple Deprivation.[80] While this still emphasises urban need, it begins to recognise that rural populations not only have more difficulty accessing healthcare but also have differing needs that require different solutions such as access to healthy food options, exercise, education, child support services and the needs of an increasingly elderly isolated population.

DOI: 10.1201/9781003302438-6

With national health leaders such as Aneurin Bevin and Julian Tudor Hart (see box in research Chapter 17, page 227) in the NHS's past, its principles are deeply embedded in the Welsh psyche. The government remains committed to equal healthcare for all. It has not allowed NHS services to be provided by private providers unless there is no other option.

Powys, by far the largest county with the smallest population, epitomises rural healthcare. There are no district general hospitals and very few pharmacies. Local general practices are the hubs of healthcare and the first port of call for any and every health need. Rural practice has always had a broad scope, from pharmaceutical services, minor ailments and minor injuries to acute medical emergency care and stabilisation of patients awaiting transport to a district general hospital.

Care is enhanced by district nurse teams co-located in each practice and good communication with specialist community teams of nurses and therapists.

Community hospitals managed by local practices provide rehabilitation, convalescence and medical treatment, as well as palliative care when this is not possible at home. Fifty percent of Powys residents pass away under the care of their local practice.

Partly in response to the crisis in recruitment, primary care teams have expanded to bringing in clinicians with different skillsets and to develop the roles of all staff to meet demand.

Practice nurses specialise in managing chronic conditions such as asthma, diabetes and hypertension while maintaining their general skills and local knowledge.

Pharmacists, with their in-depth knowledge, improve the care and support for patients after hospital discharge or outpatient appointments and help patients on multiple medications. Rural practices dispense medication to most of their patients, a vital service given the lack of community pharmacies. (See Chapter 10: Rural Pharmacy and Dispensing.) Practice pharmacists support, upskill and mentor dispensing staff who are often the face-to-face contact for patients with their medication queries.

Nurse practitioners work at a high level to diagnose and treat both minor and serious ailments, often in specialist areas of interest. This allows GPs to focus on more unwell patients and those with complex problems and to provide diagnostic support and advice to the clinical team.

Paramedics, now common in practice, manage acute emergencies. They also assess unwell patients at home and discuss their findings with a GP.

Some practices have recruited physiotherapists and mental health workers to their teams, but recruitment in rural areas remains difficult.

Not surprisingly given the complexity of the clinical team, receptionists have become lynchpins, directing patients to the most appropriate service or member of the team. Non-clinical team members shoulder the burden of administration and operations of the team, which is often based in many sites.

GPs and other healthcare professionals, by necessity, still live in their practice areas or next to them; their children go to school in those areas, and they are intimately aware of the problems and difficulties faced by their patients.

While the population over-65s is increasing everywhere, the rate of increase is disproportionately higher in Welsh rural areas as inward migration of retirees continues to increase. This is coupled with a decrease in the 25–50 age group, which provides most of the workforce. The needs of an elderly population are different to those of a young, fit population in terms of improving quality of life and treating illness. Powys and rural Wales are at the sharp end of this challenge to provide care.

Although fragmentation of care is detrimental, particularly for the elderly, frail population, progressively increasing demand in urban practices can be mitigated by directing patients to other services. This is not possible in rural Wales where the continuing traditional approach puts patients and their wishes and needs as the central focus, backed up by trusted relationships, guiding and supporting patients through the choices available and identifying what really matters to them.

Patient and their families must be prepared for a half or whole day away from home or work to access secondary care, whether for an outpatient appointment, imaging or treatment. Having the knowledge, confidence and, most importantly, trust that allows gentle discussion to explore patients' wishes and, together, make responsible decisions as to whether such travel is in patient's best interests relies on health professionals with broad training working at a high skill level who can continue to support the patient in accordance with their wishes. This model of care continues, although overall responsibility no longer belongs to general practitioners but is shared by the team.

Frail patients admitted to district general hospitals with acute illnesses decondition rapidly both mentally and physically and do better if they can be supported at home through the acute phase. To prevent admissions, Powys is developing a practice-based 'virtual ward' model of care to provide a same-day rapid response for acutely unwell frail patients: coordinating the medical care and liaising with carers, community therapists, social services and voluntary sectors. Linking to secondary care, community hospitals and the ambulance services progressively more effectively, the virtual ward improves communication between primary care, specialist therapists and social care, avoiding duplication of work, keeps patients and their wishes firmly at the forefront and leads to fewer 'unanticipated' events.

The increase in older patients also increases the number of patients presenting with and living with cancer. Patients need multiple trips to secondary care to establish a diagnosis and then for treatment. This comes at a high cost for rural patients and their families financially, physically and mentally. When the travel distance is too far or they are too ill, patients need to stay overnight somewhere. When Welsh rural patients access English hospitals (and this applies to half of Powys' population), differences in diagnoses and treatments can take time to understand and resolve.

Welsh rural health boards are actively looking at bringing specialist scans such as heart scans and radiology nearer to patient's homes to alleviate the burden of travel, and successful trials for breast cancer using shorter courses of radiotherapy have been instituted rapidly, to the benefit of the rural patient.

Working in primary healthcare in rural Wales has never been more attractive or supported. The Welsh Assembly government is supportive, recognising both its important contribution to health and the pressures it is under. With increased attention to rural needs in *all* policy making, the Welsh rural idyll may become a reality.

CHAPTER 2.5

England

....

Tim Sanders

DEMOGRAPHICS

In 2020, the estimated total population of England was 56.6 million, of whom 9.7 million (17.1%) lived in rural areas and 46.9 million (82.9%) in urban areas.[81]

The rural population is older, with 21% of the rural population aged over 65 years in 2018, compared with 16% in urban areas.[82] This largely results from an ingress of people retiring to the country, professionals with flexibility in choice of working location as they gain seniority in the middle and latter parts of their careers and an egress of young adults, who move to towns and cities for their educational, employment, social and cultural benefits or because they are unable to afford to buy or rent property in their home area.

Compared to the country as a whole, rural populations are less ethnically diverse: 97.6% of the population is white, in comparison with 81.4% in urban areas. Annual rates of growth of Black, Asian and minority ethnic (BAME) communities is also slower at 0.3% versus 1.4%.[83]

In comparison to urban populations, rural dwellers overall have better indices of employment, unemployment and income. However, this is not distributed evenly. Statistically, 18% of rural town populations sit in the least deprived decile, dropping to 4% in rural villages and less than 1% in the most sparsely populated areas,[83] but much rural deprivation is hidden from routine statistics. Social exclusion, poverty and deprivation are important determinants of health that manifest themselves

DOI: 10.1201/9781003302438-7

differently in rural areas and are the topics of Chapter 16: Rural Social Exclusion.

RURAL VERSUS REMOTE

The association between rurality and remoteness in England is different to other areas of the world with shorter distances between communities and less sparse population densities. Some features of remoteness are associated with urban populations situated in peripheral, often coastal areas, a legacy of bygone eras of shipbuilding, mining and shipping industries. The concept of 'remote urban' brings challenges of unemployment, social deprivation and pursuant poor health outcomes, deserving focus in their own right.

COMPARISON WITH OTHER UK NATIONS

In contrast to Scotland and Wales, where the larger urban populations are confined to relatively small areas of the country (for example, the Scottish 'central band' and the south Wales coast), rural populations in England are distributed more evenly. Such steadier population density gradients may blur the boundaries between 'rural' and 'urban', causing difficulties for policy makers and service planners.

An understanding of what makes rural and remote populations unique and of their differing needs is key to being able to deliver high-quality healthcare. From a raw-numbers perspective, rural populations within the UK are found in their greatest number in England, with, for example, 9.7 million people in England versus 1 million in Scotland. Despite this, as can be seen in the Scottish section of this chapter, Scotland is considerably better advanced in its understanding of and response to the healthcare needs of its rural population and workforce.

DEFINING 'RURAL'

"When you have seen one rural place, you have seen one rural place."[84]

The Department for Environment, Food and Rural Affairs (DEFRA) use the 'rural-urban classification' to determine which parts of the population are 'rural'.[85] The classification defines an area as 'rural' if it sits outside settlements with a more than 10,000 resident population. Settlements are further sub-divided, based on the sparsity of population in the area in which they sit, as either 'not sparse' or 'in a sparse setting', with settlements defined under these categories as one of 'town and fringe', 'villages' and 'hamlets and isolated dwellings'.

Although these definitions, based on population size, density and sparsity, are blunt instruments in terms of their ability to drill down to the needs of individual communities, they are used for decisions about political policy and the distribution of funding and services. Every population is unique and diverse.

For comparison, the population of the London borough of Lambeth is approximately the same as the population of North Cumbria. They both have populations of 325,000. Lambeth packs all these people into just under 27 km^2 and has two major hospitals: Guys and St Thomas's and King's College Hospital. Wherever you are in Lambeth, tertiary healthcare is never more than walking distance away. Conversely, North Cumbria is spread over approximately 3,300 km^2, with its nearest tertiary care hospitals as far afield as Newcastle, Glasgow, Edinburgh or Manchester.

RURAL HEALTHCARE DELIVERY

In response to the challenges of delivering increasingly complex healthcare, difficulties in recruiting healthcare practitioners and a reduction in the number of GPs willing to take on the burden of business ownership, the 2019 NHS long-term plan incentivised groups of practices to form collaborative primary care networks (PCNs).[86]

When they combine practices with similar needs and aims, PCNs have the potential to maximise economies of scale for the benefit of their patients: for example by employing pharmacists, mental health workers and lifestyle coaches across multiple practices or by merging 'backroom' functions such as human resources, finance and recruitment while maintaining smaller teams serving local communities. At the same time, local, easily identifiable practice teams maintain their knowledge, understanding and responsiveness to local communities, benefitting both patients and their practitioners. However, the needs of smaller rural practices risk being sidelined if included in networks with larger urban practices.

Running alongside this, in a push to further improve clinical outcomes as the complexity and technologies required to deliver specialist interventions for myocardial infarction, stroke and major trauma has developed, there has been a move to centralise services, resulting in a reduction of care and treatment options available in local general hospitals and the need to travel farther to access these elements of care.

As demand increases and more health professionals work part time, continuity of care, a key element of effective primary care, is being eroded across the board, with an overall shift towards more episode-based and reactive care.[87, 88]

Patients value good continuity of care,[89] and their outcomes are better.[90] For all patients, especially those with multimorbidity, complex mental health problems or medically unexplained symptoms, a 'lack of choice' can be beneficial as it encourages a patient-clinician partnership approach, reducing harmful over-investigation and facilitating progress through shifting the focus from the biomedical to the psychosocial.

Smaller practices mean that patients have less choice of practitioners, increasing the probability that those who seek continuity will be able to follow up with the same practitioner. It may be tempting to hanker after a 'cradle-to-grave', 'traditional general practice' rural idyll; however, it is probably smaller size rather than rural location, ethos or philosophy that facilitates this effect. This is something to be borne in mind if changes to healthcare delivery lead to increases in practice size.

Despite a wide range of approaches to addressing them,[91] recruitment and retention of primary care staff is a huge challenge, particularly in rural areas.[84] The last decade has seen a change in healthcare worker preferences, with greater mobility from practice to practice rather than settling in one location for life. For doctors, this has included a move towards part-time and salaried working and away from partnership, opening up opportunities for new team members: for example, practice managers, advanced care practitioners and pharmacists. Practices that have responded flexibly, positively and creatively to these shifts have been most successful in recruitment, and the importance of a cohesive team approach is emerging as an important driver of staff retention. Recruitment and retention are discussed further in Chapter 10: Rural Pharmacy and Dispensing.

Ella Joyce Cockram 1899–1975
Bury St Edmunds, Suffolk

Joyce Cockram, the first female doctor in Bury St Edmunds, was inspirational not only for her considerable medical attributes but also for her other local and national contributions.

Born in Bridgwater, Somerset, she attended Oxford High School for Girls and read medicine at St Anne's College, Oxford, and King's College Hospital, London, graduating in 1925 and completing her doctorate in 1937.

Following graduation, she was a research pathologist at King's before becoming a house physician, then resident pathologist in Bury St Edmunds. She initiated the first diabetic clinic at the hospital and set up one of the first blood banks in the country.

She joined Drs Kilner and Ware in 1930 as a partner at the Angel Hill general practice in Bury St Edmunds, where the practice agreement stipulated that if she were ever to marry, she would be deemed to be dead!

During her career of over 30 years, she lived in a delightful large Georgian house in the centre of the market town. Remaining single, she had a staff of a housekeeper/cook and a butler/chauffeur. For home visits in the town and the many surrounding villages, she was driven in her own Bentley. Following retirement, she would only sell her house to another doctor. Nearly 50 years on, her successor is still in residence.

Until the advent of the NHS, it was commonplace that general practitioners fulfilled part-time medical appointments in specialist departments. Throughout the 1930s, she continued as a pathologist at the hospital until a full-time pathologist was appointed in 1942, when Joyce took up the position of honorary physician with an interest in diabetes, which she held until her retirement in 1964.

She became president of the Medical Women's Federation in 1961 at a time when married women doctors seeking to return to part-time practice, postgraduate education and higher qualifications were all important issues.

She was chair of the management committee of West Suffolk Hospital, where a ward is named after her, and president of the local Red Cross Society.

Her interests outside medicine were many: she was a justice of the peace, governor of three local schools, supporter of the cathedral choir and president of the local Bach society. Her devout Christian faith and commitment to service were recognised with her appointment as a lay canon of St Edmundsbury Cathedral.

— Philip Evans

RURAL HEALTHCARE EDUCATION

The profile of the rural practice is slowly rising, with some medical and nursing schools including Aberdeen, Swansea and the University of Central Lancashire, now actively seeking to recruit from rural areas and incorporating student placements in rural locations. There is evidence that access to rural experience leads to better subsequent recruitment to rural areas.[92–94] University remote and rural student societies are emerging, and access for junior clinicians to rural placements, training pathways and academic fellowship posts is increasing.[95–96]

There is clear evidence that clinicians tend to stay in the location where they have trained. For example, approximately 70% of the GP workforce in North Cumbria trained in the local GP training programme. This proportion has remained stable, weathering demographic changes in the intake of trainees. There is international evidence from Australia and North America that recruitment of trainees to train locally has a greater impact on retention than recruiting practitioners who have trained elsewhere.[94, 97]

Being 'sent' to a placement in a rural location can feel like a punishment at any stage of training from undergraduate student through to postgraduate trainee. For those who have chosen to study in a vibrant metropolitan area with its social, sporting and other trappings, being 'sent to the back of beyond', often in very small groups or as a single student, may seem to be an isolating and potentially negative experience. Thankfully, clinical experience in these settings is frequently reported by students as being excellent, and, for many, the reduction in distractions is a positive boost to their studies.

It may be better to ensure that expectations are set correctly from the outset. Students applying to a rurally located university or one with regular rural clinical placements are a self-selected population who apply on the understanding that a proportion of their training will take place in those locations. This self-selection may reflect students' intention to practise in a rural area rather than producing it,[97] but the key to success may be just that: matching up those with an interest to training in their preferred location.

For specialty trainees, rotating away from regional hubs to peripheral locations can be burdensome. Balancing the availability of clinical placements, the need for trainees to gain experience in a variety of clinical settings and their desire to start to settle in an area can be problematic, particularly if distances between settings cannot be safely commuted daily. Owning or renting properties in two locations, a common requirement for trainees whose partners are also developing their careers, is expensive, and the financial burden is borne by the trainees. The availability of suitable rental properties in rural tourist areas, where much of the rental housing stock is given over to holiday letting, is also challenging.

Sharp increases in trainee numbers are resulting in bottlenecks because increased capacity is required to provide clinical placements for medical, nursing, physician associate (PA), non-medical prescribing, advanced nurse practitioner (ANP) and advanced clinical practitioner (ACP) students etc. More appropriately trained clinicians are needed to provide clinical supervision and teaching while continuing to care for their patients, and there is pressure on physical capacity, with surgeries and smaller hospitals lacking sufficient physical spaces where clinical experience can be gained. Space constraints can be mitigated to a degree by creative scheduling, shifting clinical administrative tasks such as referral letter writing and the processing of laboratory results and prescriptions into non-clinical office spaces.

These capacity pressures often occur in the context of recruitment difficulties and staffing shortages, resulting in a 'Catch-22' situation whereby the opportunity to 'grow your own' is lost where training is not provided.

Increasingly, providers are recognising this and giving priority to building capacity and delivering an excellent experience to learners, even when this causes an increase in workload in the short term.

In the more sparsely populated areas, where travel distances are considerably longer than in their urban counterparts, the scope to match trainees to trainers within a manageable commuting distance is also diminished. As the number of postgraduate-entry trainees increases—for example PAs, ANPs and ACPs—the issue is amplified. Older students tend to be more firmly rooted through factors such as long-term relationships, house ownership and family commitments, making staying away from home either unpalatable or unworkable.

Although there is a gradual, small shift towards healthcare education in rural areas, most undergraduate and much postgraduate training continues to take place around urban centres, where several healthcare provider organisations are located in close proximity to each other. This proximity, combined with associations with 'centres of excellence', brings kudos and drives competition between providers to offer innovative opportunities for career development and attractive employment terms and conditions. Training, development and employment options in rural locations are more limited, restricting choice and reducing mobility within the workforce, risking stagnation and loss of the beneficial 'cross pollination' of ideas between providers and potentially stifling innovation. Rural workers and trainees who are unhappy with the setting in which they find themselves may only be able to 'vote with their feet' to find employment and training elsewhere by uprooting their entire lives.

Continuing professional development (CPD) is an essential part of clinical practice in every discipline. In rural areas, long commutes to training events and the lack of a pool of experts within easy reach can be challenging. The relatively small size of clinical specialty teams means that it may be more difficult for specialists to give enough time to meet the multitude of requests for teaching from universities, local GP training programmes, primary care networks, out-of-hours providers etc. Flexible, multi-professional teaching and coordination of specialists as a resource help make best use of scarce resources.

To mitigate time lost to travel to training events, there has been a tendency to provide day- or half-day-long events. However, this is potentially suboptimal as it risks overloading the learner. 'Little and often' better fits an ethos of continuing rather than episodic professional development.

The COVID-19 pandemic stimulated significant development and ubiquitous use of videoconferencing technology. However, webinar-based teaching has limitations and is not a panacea for the delivery of CPD. Rather, it is an important tool in enabling delivery of clinical education updates in ways that fit the demands of day-to-day clinical practice.

Many elements of learning are a social activity. Bringing learners together may be unavoidable when practical skills are being learned, but clinicians also benefit from interacting with each other in person when practical skills are not being learned or refreshed.

However, there has been innovation in practical skills training during the pandemic with, for example, some basic life support (BLS) training providers sending resuscitation mannikins to participants in advance of training sessions to be delivered online. As ever, and particularly in rural practice, flexibility, creativity and the willingness to innovate and collaborate are keys to success.

RECRUITMENT AND RETENTION

While competitive salaries are essential, financial packages alone are an insufficient driver for clinicians to work in rural areas.[98] A wider view that includes flexible job planning and opportunities for professional and career development is necessary for success.[99, 100] Involvement of the local community in the recruitment process has also been successful. Positions with a flexible job plan and funded time set aside for postgraduate study in subjects such as medical and healthcare education, mountain medicine, urgent care and mental health (often referred to as 'fellowship' posts) have resulted in successful recruitment to underserved rural locations. Particularly in rural areas, where the potential pool of applicants to such posts might be limited, a flexible approach that follows the interests of applicants rather than starting with a specific topic or project in mind is more likely to succeed. Investment in individuals through flexible working conditions and professional development opportunities is likely to be most effective.

REFERENCES

1 Office for National Statistics (ONS). 2011. *2011 Rural/urban classification.* London: Office for National Statistics. www.ons.gov.uk/methodology/geography/geographicalproducts/ruralurbanclassifications/2011ruralurbanclassification [Accessed 23 July 2022].

2 Scottish Government Urban Rural Classification. 2016. www.gov.scot/publications/scottish-government-urban-rural-classification-2016/pages/1/ [Accessed 23 July 2022].

3 Scottish Government Urban Rural Classification. 2016. www.gov.scot/publications/scottish-government-urban-rural-classification-2016/pages/2/ [Accessed 23 July 2022].

4 Dewar 2012: A legacy for rural practice. https://web.archive.org/web/20190217015028/http:/ruralgp.com/dewar2012/ [Accessed 23 July 2022].

5 Cathcart Report. www.ournhsscotland.com/history/birth-nhs-scotland/cathcart-report [Accessed 23 July 2022].

6 NHS Scotland Workforce Policies: Principles and Values. https://workforce.nhs.scot/about/principles-and-values/ [Accessed 23 July 2022].

7 NHS Scotland Organisations. www.scot.nhs.uk/organisations/ [Accessed 23 July 2022].

8 Scottish Household Survey 2019: Key Findings. www.gov.scot/publications/scottish-household-survey-2019-key-findings/ [Accessed 23 July 2022].

9 Healthcare Improvement Scotland. www.healthcareimprovementscotland.org/ [Accessed 23 July 2022].

10 NHS Golden Jubilee. Centre for sustainable delivery. www.nhsgoldenjubilee.co.uk/cfsd [Accessed 23 July 2022].

11 Health and Social Care Scotland. About health and social care integration in Scotland. https://hscscotland.scot/integration/ [Accessed 23 July 2022].

12 Realistic Medicine. www.realisticmedicine.scot/ [Accessed 23 July 2022].

13 Scottish Government. Improving together: A national framework for quality and GP clusters in Scotland. www.gov.scot/publications/improving-together-national-framework-quality-gp-clusters-scotland/pages/4/ [Accessed 23 July 2022].

14 Department of Health, Northern Ireland. About the quality and outcomes framework. www.health-ni.gov.uk/articles/about-quality-and-outcomes-framework-qof [Accessed 23 July 2022].

15 Health Improvement Scotland. Methodology toolkit. www.healthcare-improvementscotland.org/about_us/what_we_do/knowledge_management/knowledge_management_resources/methodology_toolkit.aspx [Accessed 23 July 2022].

16 Scottish Government. GMS contract: 2018. www.gov.scot/publications/gms-contract-scotland/documents/ [Accessed 23 July 2022].

17 University of the Highlands and Islands. 2018. Final evaluation of the being here programme. www.srmc.scot.nhs.uk/wp-content/uploads/2020/06/Being-Here-final-report-November-2018.pdf [Accessed 23 July 2022].

18 Southcentral Foundation. 2022. NUKA system of care. https://scfnuka.com/ [Accessed 23 July 2022].

19 The Scottish Rural Medicine Collaborative Bulletin. October 2021. www.srmc.scot.nhs.uk/wp-content/uploads/Newsletters/SRMC-Bulletin-October-2021.pdf [Accessed 23 July 2022].

20 Scottish Trauma Network. www.scottishtraumanetwork.com/ [Accessed 23 July 2022].

21 Emergency Medical Retrieval Service. www.emrsscotland.org/ [Accessed 23 July 2022].

22 ScotSTAR Paediatric Retrieval Service. www.snprs.scot.nhs.uk/ [Accessed 23 July 2022].

23 ScotSTAR Neonatal Transport Service. www.neonataltransport.scot.nhs.uk/ [Accessed 23 July 2022].

24 BASICS Scotland. https://basics-scotland.org.uk/ [Accessed 23 July 2022].

25 Sandpiper. www.sandpipertrust.org/ [Accessed 23 July 2022].

26 NHS Education for Scotland. www.nes.scot.nhs.uk/ [Accessed 23 July 2022].

27 NHS Education for Scotland: The Remote and Rural Healthcare Alliance. https://learn.nes.nhs.scot/786/rrheal [Accessed 23 July 2022].

28 NHS Education for Scotland: Clinical Skills Managed Educational Network. www.csmen.scot.nhs.uk/ [Accessed 23 July 2022].

29 NHS Education for Scotland: Mobile Skills Unit. www.csmen.scot.nhs.uk/mobile-skills-unit/ [Accessed 23 July 2022].

30 NHS Education for Scotland. Multidisciplinary rural advanced practice capability framework—primary and community care. https://learn.nes.nhs.scot/48411/rrheal/rural-teams/multidisciplinary-rural-advanced-practice-capability-framework-primary-and-community-care [Accessed 23 July 2022].

31 Couper ID, Hugo JFM, Conradie H, Mfenyana K. Influences on the choice of health professionals to practice in rural areas. *South African Medical Journal.* 2007; 97(11): 1082–1086. https://pubmed.ncbi.nlm.nih.gov/18250918/ [Accessed 23 July 2022].

32 Universities Scotland. Widening access to medicine. www.universities-scotland.ac.uk/bite-size-briefings/widening-access-to-medicine/ [Accessed 23 July 2022].

33 University of St Andrews. Scottish graduate entry medicine (ScotGEM) MBChB. www.st-andrews.ac.uk/subjects/medicine/scotgem-mbchb/ [Accessed 23 July 2022].

34 University of Dundee School of Medicine. 2017. Longitudinal integrated clerkship. www.scotlanddeanery.nhs.scot/media/79807/seeing-a-patient-as-a-patient-a-more-holistic-view-of-medicine-longitudinal-immersive-clerkship-a-driver-for-change.pdf [Accessed 23 July 2022].

35 University of Aberdeen. Remote and rural placement opportunities. www.abdn.ac.uk/iehms/study-here/remote-and-rural-placement-opportunities-367.php [Accessed 23 July 2022].

36 Scotland Deanery. Trainee information. www.scotlanddeanery.nhs.scot/trainee-information/gp-specialty-training/gpst-educational-opportunities/north/ [Accessed 23 July 2022].

37 Scotland Deanery. GP fellowships. www.scotlanddeanery.nhs.scot/your-development/gp-fellowships/ [Accessed 23 July 2022].

38 MacVicar R, Clarke G, Hogg DR. Scotland's rural GP fellowship: An initiative that has impacted on rural recruitment and retention. *Rural and Remote Health.* 2016; 16: 3550. www.rrh.org.au/journal/article/3550 [Accessed 23 July 2022].

39 General Medical Council. Credentialing. www.gmc-uk.org/education/standards-guidance-and-curricula/projects/credentialing [Accessed 23 July 2022].

40 Viking Surgeons Association. www.vikingsurgeons.net/ [Accessed 23 July 2022].

41 The Royal College of Surgeons of Edinburgh. Faculty of remote, rural and humanitarian healthcare. www.rcsed.ac.uk/faculties/faculty-of-remote-rural-and-humanitarian-healthcare [Accessed 23 July 2022].

42 NHS Scotland Global Citizenship Programme. www.scottishglobalhealth.org/ [Accessed 23 July 2022].

43 Rural GP Association of Scotland. https://ruralgp.scot/ [Accessed 23 July 2022].

44 Royal College of General Practitioners. Rural forum.www.rcgp.org.uk/rcgp-near-you/faculties/rural-forum.aspx [Accessed 23 July 2022].

45 Abelsen B, Strasser R, Heaney D, Berggren P, Sigurðsson S, Brandstorp H, Wakegijig J, Forsling N, Moody-Corbett P, Akearok GH, Mason A, Savage C, Nicoll P. Plan, recruit, retain: A framework for local healthcare organisations to achieve a stable remote rural workforce. *Human Resources for Health* 2020; 18: 63. https://doi.org/10.1186/s12960-020-00502-x [Accessed 23 July 2022].

46 Scottish Rural Medicine Collaborative. www.srmc.scot.nhs.uk/ [Accessed 23 July 2022].

47 Scottish Rural Medicine Collaborative. GP recruitment good practice guide. www.recruitmentsupport.scot.nhs.uk/ [Accessed 23 July 2022].

48 Scottish Rural Medicine Collaborative. Rediscover the joy of general practice. www.srmc.scot.nhs.uk/joy-project-2/ [Accessed 23 July 2022].

49 CSO. 2016. Census 2016 summary results—Part 1. www.cso.ie/en/csolatestnews/presspages/2017/census2016summaryresults-part1/ [Accessed 11 November 2021].

50 OECD. 2021. Life expectancy at birth. https://data.oecd.org/healthstat/life-expectancy-at-birth.htm [Accessed 11 November 2021].

51 Commission for the economic development of rural areas. 2014. *Energising Ireland's rural economy.* Dublin.

52 DRCD. 2018. *Realising our rural potential—Action plan for rural development.* Dublin: Department of Rural and Community Development (DRCD).

53 C.S. Office. 2019. Ireland's system of health accounts, annual results 2017. www.cso.ie/en/releasesandpublications/er/sha/systemofhealthaccounts2017/ [Accessed 3 March 2022].

54 Kennelly B, et al. The COVID-19 pandemic in Ireland: An overview of the health service and economic policy response. *Health Policy and Technology.* 2020; 9(4): 419–429.

55 Starfield B, et al. Contribution of primary care to health systems and health. *The Millbank Quarterly.* 2005.

56 Sandvik H, et al., Continuity in general practice as predictor of mortality, acute hospitalisation, and use of out-of-hours care: A registry-based observational study in Norway. *British Journal of General Practice.* 2021.

57 Pereira Gray DJ, et al. Continuity of care with doctors-a matter of life and death? A systematic review of continuity of care and mortality. *BMJ Open.* 2018; 8(6): e021161.

58 Barker I, Steventon A, Deeny SR. Association between continuity of care in general practice and hospital admissions for ambulatory care sensitive conditions: Cross sectional study of routinely collected, person level data. *BMJ.* 2017; 356: j84.

59 Tammes P, et al. Is continuity of primary care declining in England? Practice-level longitudinal study from 2012 to 2017. *British Journal of General Practice.* 2021; 71(707): e432–e440.

60 Crosbie B, et al. A real-time measurement of general practice workload in the Republic of Ireland: A prospective study. *British Journal of General Practice.* 2020; 70(696): e489–e496.

61 O'Kelly M, Teljeur C, Ni Shúilleabháin A, O'Dowd T. 2016. *Structure of general practice in Ireland 1982–2015.* Dublin: Trinity College Dublin/The Irish College of General Practitioners.

62 O'Sullivan M, Cullen W, MacFarlane A. Primary care teams in Ireland: A qualitative mapping review of Irish grey and published literature. *Irish Journal of Medical Science.* 2015; 184(1): 69–73.

63 O'Riodran M. 2015. *Vision for the future of Irish rural general practice.* Dublin: Irish College of General Practitioners.

64 Data Commons. 2019. Eurostat NUTS 1 place in United Kingdom, Northern Ireland. https://datacommons.org/place/nuts/UKN.

65 NISRA. 2015. Review of the statistical classification and delineation of settlements. www.nisra.gov.uk/sites/nisra.gov.uk/files/publications/review-of-the-statistical-classification-and-delineation-of-settlements-march-2015%20%281%29.pdf.

66 Department of Agriculture Environment and Rural Affairs (DAERA). September 2020. Key rural issues. www.daera-ni.gov.uk/publications/key-rural-issues.

67 Northern Ireland Assembly. 2016. *Rural needs act (Northern Ireland) 2016.* The Stationary Office. www.legislation.gov.uk/nia/2016/19/pdfs/niaen_20160019_en.pdf.

68 DAERA. 2020. *Rural needs: Annual monitoring report 1 April 2019–31 March 2020.* Belfast: DAERA, 37–41. www.daera-ni.gov.uk/sites/default/files/publications/daera/20.21.116%20Rural%20Needs%20Annual%20Monitoring%20Report%20Final%20V2.PDF.

69 World Health Organisation. 2021. *WHO guideline on health workforce development, attraction, recruitment and retention in rural and remote areas.* WHO. www.who.int/publications/i/item/9789240024229.

70 Health and Social Care Board Northern Ireland. Health and social care board, our work, commissioning. www.hscboard.hscni.net/our-work/commissioning/ [Accessed 7th January 2022].

71 Business Services Organisation (BSO). 2021. *Family practitioner services general medical services for Northern Ireland, annual statistics 2020/2021.* Belfast: BSO. https://hscbusiness.hscni.net/pdf/FPS%20General%20 Medical%20Services%20Statistics%20for%20NI%202020-21.pdf.

72 King's Fund. 2018. *Innovative models of general practice.* London: King's Fund. www.kingsfund.org.uk/publications/innovative-models-general-practice.

73 Nelson P, Martindale A-M, McBride A, Checkland K, Hodgson D. Skill-mix change and the general practice workforce challenge. *British Journal of General Practice.* 2018; 68(667): 66–67.

74 Department of Health. 2021. *Northern Ireland waiting time statistics: Outpatient waiting times quarter ending September 2021.* Belfast: Department of Health. www.health-ni.gov.uk/sites/default/files/publications/ health/hs-niwts-outpatient-waiting-times-q2-21-22.pdf.

75 Bengoa R, Stout A, Scott B, McAlinden M, Taylor MA. 2016. Systems, not structures: Expert panel report. Changing health and social care. www. health-ni.gov.uk/sites/default/files/publications/health/expert-panel-full-report.pdf.

76 McLafferty M, O'Neill S. *Policy and practice briefing. Childhood adversities in Northern Ireland: The impact on mental health and suicidal behaviour.* Ulster University. https://docs.wixstatic.com/ugd/198ed6_ f5d6a964d595490f8bd9bc842036d1d0.pdf [Accessed 7 January 2022].

77 Connolly AM. 2020. An introduction to health inequalities. In: Matheson J, Patterson J, Neilson L, editors. *Tackling causes and consequences of health. a practical guide.* London: CRC Press, p. 9.

78 Northern Ireland Statistics and Research Agency (NISRA). 2022. *NI multiple deprivation measures 2017 lookup tool.* Belfast: NISRA. www.nisra.gov.uk/ news/new-ni-multiple-deprivation-measures-2017-lookup-tool [Accessed 29 April 2022].

79 World Health Organisation. 2021. *WHO guideline on health workforce development, attraction, recruitment and retention in rural and remote areas.* WHO. www.who.int/publications/i/item/9789240024229.

80 Stats Wales. *WIMD 2005.* https://statswales.gov.wales/Catalogue/ Community-Safety-and-Social-Inclusion/Welsh-Index-of-Multiple-Deprivation/Archive/WIMD-2005.

81 Statistical Digest of Rural England [Internet]. GOV.UK. www.gov.uk/ government/statistics/statistical-digest-of-rural-england [Accessed 3 April 2022].

82 Ageing in a Rural Place | Centre for Ageing Better [Internet]. https://ageing-better.org.uk/publications/ageing-rural-place [Accessed 22 April 2022].

83 Rural Population and Migration Statistics [Internet]. Gov.uk. www.gov. uk/government/statistics/rural-population-and-migration [Accessed 22 April 2022].

84 APPG Rural Health and Care | NCRHC [Internet]. www.ncrhc.org/news/ appg-rural-health-and-care [Accessed 3 April 2022].

85 Rural Urban Classification [Internet]. Gov.uk. www.gov.uk/government/ collections/rural-urban-classification [Accessed 3 April 2022].

86 Plan NLT. The NHS Long Term Plan [Internet]. www.longtermplan.nhs.uk/ publication/nhs-long-term-plan/ [Accessed 3 April 2022].

87 Continuity of Care [Internet]. The King's Fund. www.kingsfund.org.uk/projects/gp-inquiry/continuity-of-care.

88 Improving Continuity of Care in General Practice: Four Lessons from the Frontline—The Health Foundation [Internet]. www.health.org.uk/news-and-comment/blogs/improving-continuity-of-care-in-general-practice-four-lessons-from-the [Accessed 3 April 2022].

89 Aboulghate A, Abel G, Elliott MN, Parker RA, Campbell J, Lyratzopoulos G, et al. Do English patients want continuity of care, and do they receive it? *British Journal of General Practice*. 2012; 62(601): e567–e575.

90 Pereira Gray DJ, Sidaway-Lee K, White E, Thorne A, Evans PH. Continuity of care with doctors-a matter of life and death? A systematic review of continuity of care and mortality. *BMJ Open* [Internet]. 2018; 8(6). https://pubmed.ncbi.nlm.nih.gov/29959146/ [Accessed 3 July 2022].

91 Marchand C, Peckham S. Addressing the crisis of GP recruitment and retention: A systematic review. *British Journal of General Practice*. 2017; 67(657): e227–e237.

92 Wolstencroft K, MacVicar R. A taste of rural Highlands and Islands general practice: Evaluation of remote placements in GP specialty training. *Education for Primary Care*. 2011; 22(2): 83–89.

93 Crampton PES, Mclachlan JC, Illing JC. A systematic literature review of undergraduate clinical placements in underserved areas. *Medical Education*. 2013; 47(10): 969–978.

94 Kwan MMS, Kondalsamy-Chennakesavan S, Ranmuthugala G, Toombs MR, Nicholson GC. 2017. The rural pipeline to longer-term rural practice: General practitioners and specialists. https://doi.org/10.1371/journal.pone.0180394 file:///C:/Users/tsanders2/AppData/Local/Mendeley Ltd./MendeleyDesktop/Downloaded/Kwan et al.—2017 The rural pipeline to longer-term practice General practitioners and specialists.pdf.

95 General Practice Training for Remote and Rural Areas [Internet]. www.gmc-uk.org/education/hidden-documents/sharing-good-practice/general-practice-training-for-remote-and-rural-areas [Accessed 4 May 2022].

96 GP Fellowship [Internet]. www.scotlanddeanery.nhs.scot/your-development/gp-fellowships/ [Accessed 4 May 2022].

97 Parlier AB, Galvin SL, Thach S, Kruidenier D, Fagan EB. The road to rural primary care: A narrative review of factors that help develop, recruit, and retain rural primary care physicians. *Academic Medicine*. 2018; 93(1): 130–140.

98 Holte JH, Kjaer T, Abelsen B, Olsen JA. The impact of pecuniary and non-pecuniary incentives for attracting young doctors to rural general practice. *Social Science & Medicine*. 2015; 128: 1–9.

99 GP Recruitment Good Practice Guide [Internet]. www.recruitmentsupport.scot.nhs.uk/ [Accessed 22 May 2022].

100 Cross R, McDonagh STJ, Cockcroft E, Turner M, Isom M, Lambourn R, et al. 2022. Recruitment and retention of staff in rural dispensing practice. In: Society for Academic Primary Care Annual Scientific Meeting [Internet]. Preston. https://sapc.ac.uk/conference/2022/abstract/recruitment-and-retention-of-staff-rural-dispensing-practice-retain_1c-6 [Accessed 5 July 2022].

CHAPTER 3

Role of the Generalist

....

Christopher E. Clark and Amanda Howe

GPs are experts in whole person medicine; that is the essence of our discipline, and its future.[1]

'Generalist' is a term most commonly linked to general practitioners (GPs), but it can just as appropriately be used to describe community and practice nurses and other members of the wider multidisciplinary team. This is particularly true in rural settings where (as discussed in Chapter 12: Rural Nursing) smaller teams operate, requiring a broad skillset. Generalism describes the breadth of expertise that a clinician applies in assessing undifferentiated symptoms or conditions, permitting assessment, diagnosis, and management of patients at their first point of contact with healthcare. It sits within the broader faculty of the multidisciplinary primary healthcare team and is relevant to other clinical specialities as well. This chapter focusses on *medical generalism*, a narrower term generally applied to doctors, because that is the clinical discipline about which most has been written. Nevertheless, most of the themes discussed can be seen, by extension, to be relevant to the entire rural healthcare team, and *generalism* is used here in that wider context.

WHAT IS GENERALISM?

A founding ideal of the National Health Service (NHS) was to ensure, as Bevan said in 1945, 'that an equally good service is available everywhere'.[2] In 2011 the Royal College of General Practitioners (RCGP) and the

DOI: 10.1201/9781003302438-8

Health Foundation jointly commissioned an independent Commission on Generalism, leading to the report 'Guiding patients through complexity: Modern medical generalism'.[3] The commission defined medical generalism as

> an approach to the delivery of health care, be it to individuals, families, groups or to communities. Its principles apply wherever and whenever people receive care and advice about their health and wellbeing. The generalist approach applies equally to individuals and to clinical teams'.[3]

The following year, a further RCGP report, 'Medical generalism: Why expertise in whole-person medicine matters', expanded the definition, emphasising attributes such as the holistic approach to patients in the context of their family, wider networks and environment; dealing with undifferentiated illness; taking responsibility for continuity of care over time and across different illnesses; and coordinating care across health and social care organisations. (See Box 3.1.)[4] These definitions establish the complex requisite skillset needed to meet the core task of general practice, which is summarised in the NHS England GP contract as 'to offer services to those who are, *or who believe themselves to be,* ill or suffering from chronic disease'. (5, emphasis added)

As well as illness management, generalism encompasses a holistic approach to health promotion, which extends beyond the individual to communities and society at large.

BOX 3.1: THE RCGP DEFINITION OF THE ETHOS OF MEDICAL GENERALISM[5]

Medical generalism is an approach to the delivery of healthcare that routinely applies a broad and holistic perspective to the patient's problems. Its principles will be needed wherever and whenever people receive care and advice about their health and well being, and all healthcare professionals need to value and be able to draw on this approach when appropriate. The ability to practise as a generalist depends on one's training and on the routine use of skills that help people understand and live with their illnesses and disabilities, as well as helping them get the best out of the healthcare options that are available and appropriate for their needs.

It involves:

1   Seeing the person as a whole and in the context of his or her family and wider social environment
2   Using this perspective as part of one's clinical method and therapeutic approach to all clinical encounters
3   Being able to deal with undifferentiated illness and the widest range of patients and conditions
4   In the context of general practice, taking continuity of responsibility for people's care across many disease episodes and over time
5   Also in general practice, coordinating patient care as needed across organisations within and between health and social care.

WHY DEFINE GENERALISM?

All clinicians' training begins with a broad curriculum. To practise in rural areas, healthcare professionals need to retain their generalist knowledge and skills because patients often present with symptoms or signs that overlap specialist disciplines and individual scopes of practice. Clinicians need to retain sufficient breadth and depth of knowledge and skills to be able to assess undifferentiated conditions, manage uncertainty and care effectively for people in primary care with multiple health requirements. Recognition of potentially conflicting needs may have a direct bearing on specialist management choices or, alternatively, lead to onward referral for further assessment. (1) This is much more complex than providing 'hospital medicine outside hospital'.[6]

Historically, generalism has not been recognised as a medical or nursing speciality in its own right, with a long-running perception of general practice and community nursing being inferior to 'specialists'.[7] GPs were excluded from established Royal Colleges until they established their own College the RCGP, in 1952.[8] Unlike in many other European countries, the UK General Medical Council (GMC) does not recognise GPs as specialists but maintains their names on a separate GP register. This may change, but at the time of writing, the necessary amendments to the law are still awaited.[9] The Nursing and Midwifery Council registers both 'specialist practitioners' and 'general practice nurses'.

WHY IS MEDICAL GENERALISM IMPORTANT?

Increasingly, as the population ages, people are living with multimorbidity.[10] Managing multiple long-term conditions simultaneously does not sit easily within the paradigm of single-condition clinical guidelines, pathways and specialist-led care. For example, there may be competing imperatives such as stroke prevention (lower the blood pressure) and falls prevention (don't lower the blood pressure too much).[11] In the presence of multimorbidity (defined as the presence of two or more chronic conditions), National Institute for Health and Care Excellence (NICE) guidance leaves blood pressure target setting to 'clinical judgement'.[12] Consequently, the guideline's blood pressure targets apply to only 22% of people with hypertension in the UK.[10, 13]

The holistic approach of the generalist also needs to recognise patient preferences and relational support as important elements of individual risk assessments.[6] These are hard to classify neatly yet have a direct bearing on health, well-being, disease outcomes and survival. Furthermore, approximately half of primary care recommendations are based on expert opinion alone.[14] It is clear, therefore, that the skills of the generalist need to extend far beyond evidence-based practice.

New concepts such as *interpretive medicine*, defined as 'the critical, thoughtful, professional use of an appropriate range of knowledges in the dynamic, shared exploration and interpretation of individual illness experience' attempt to summarise the holistic approach to the patient.[15] Such skills are essential for safe and effective management of the complexity of chronic diseases: for example, in older age.[16] Continuity of care, now included in the definition of generalism, is important in addressing complexity across multiple consultations. Multimorbidity is generally managed by multidisciplinary practice and community teams, including nurses, pharmacists, physiotherapists, occupational therapists, community mental health teams and doctors, emphasising the importance of continuity across teams. Continuity of care is discussed further later in this chapter, under "What Are the Barriers to and Facilitators of Generalism?"

Efficient and appropriate use of resources is important in any healthcare system. Resource use is maximised if patients see the right people in the right place at the right time. Therefore, the first point of contact where undifferentiated illness or concern for illness is encountered is the logical setting for the medical generalist. Starfield, comparing data across countries, influentially demonstrated the importance of a robust primary healthcare system for reducing health inequality and mortality and also in promoting cost-effective care.[17, 18] As an example, GPs working within accident and emergency departments manage non-emergency accident and emergency attenders safely and use fewer resources than usual accident and emergency staff.[19] The practice-based primary care model of universally available care free at the point of access remains astonishingly good value, delivering per capita an entire year of primary healthcare for less than the cost of two accident and emergency attendances in England.[20]

Innovations such as telephone triage and remote consultations have improved access for patients, but they also add to workload, which may destabilise practices working under extreme pressures.[21, 22] The trend towards expansion of multidisciplinary team members' roles, thus increasing patient access to generalists, has benefits. However, it is also driven in part by difficulties in recruitment of GPs, an issue which disproportionately affects rural areas.[23] Such shifts are not necessarily cost saving; lower allied health professional salaries are counterbalanced by longer consultation times when compared with general practitioners.[24–27]

William Penny Brookes 1809–1895
Much Wenlock, Shropshire

A Shropshire country doctor and the inspiration behind the modern Olympic Games.

William Brookes was born in Much Wenlock, Shropshire, where his father was the local doctor. He studied medicine at St Thomas' Hospital, London, and undertook postgraduate studies in France and Italy before returning to Much Wenlock and succeeding his father.

In addition to practising medicine, he was active locally as a justice of the peace (JP) for over 40 years and involved in a wide range of civic projects, including the town library, museum, gasworks, corn exchange and railway.

His experiences as a doctor and JP caused him to promote self-improvement, particularly for young people. An admirer of ancient Greek ideals, in 1850 he planned and organised the first Wenlock Olympian Games, a mixture of sports, including athletics, cricket, football and quoits. Celebrated with pageantry, banners with Greek inscriptions and the presentation of laurel leaf garlands to the winners, the games were conducted with an ethos of fair play. Brookes's philosophy was part of the 19th-century idea that 'rational recreation'—organised, competitive, physical exercise—promoted a disciplined and healthy workforce and population.

The games were popular, leading to the formation, in 1861, of the Shropshire Olympian's Games, which included a broader range of sports including a three-mile penny-farthing bicycle race, a wheelbarrow race and 'putting the stone', a throwing competition between two local quarries which continued into the 21st century.

In the 1860s, Brookes went on to create a National Olympian Association to encourage local competition in cities throughout Britain. Further expanding his ideas, he organised a national Olympic Games in 1866 at the Crystal Palace, London, where the cricketer W G Grace won the hurdles event. In due course he developed links with the Greek government, seeking a revival of international Olympic Games. Nearer home, he campaigned for the inclusion of physical education in the national school curriculum, finally implemented in 1895.

In 1890 Baron Pierre de Coubertin, who later founded the International Olympic Committee, published a letter asking for information regarding initiatives in different sports. He accepted Brookes's invitation to attend the Wenlock Olympic Games, where Brookes, aged 81, and Coubertin, 27, discussed and shared their love of sport. Brookes suggested that the Olympic games might be revived as an international competition staged in Athens. Coubertin enthusiastically developed the idea, writing in *La Revue Athletique*, 'If the Olympic Games that modern Greece has not yet been able to revive still survives today, it is due, not to a Greek but to Dr W P Brookes'.

The Wenlock Olympian Society continues to this day, as do the international Olympic Games.

— Philip Evans

WHY IS GENERALISM IMPORTANT IN RURAL CARE?

Generalist expertise is desirable in any primary care setting. However, the generally smaller structures and list sizes of rural practices, distances from secondary care and restrictions to the size and professional breadth of primary healthcare teams make it particularly important in rural and remote areas where the population is older, with an even greater need for competence in managing multimorbidity.[28] This is most important for patients. Fewer than 20% of rural patients live within a 20-minute walk of their general practice, so driving time is a more accurate measure of access to care.[29, 30] Journeys for tests, preventive measures or specialist opinions are more time consuming for patients than they are in urban settings. Alternatives such as pharmacies or minor injury units are usually even more distant, meaning that patients in rural areas with undifferentiated symptoms usually present first to general practice.[31]

Another aspect of rural generalism is the need to provide early management of acute emergencies. Rurality dictates longer waiting times for land or air ambulance transfer. Consequently, as discussed in Chapter 9: Emergencies, the rural generalist may have more frequent calls on their immediate medical care skills and may need to stabilise acutely ill patients for longer than in urban settings. Many rural generalists offer their services to the British Association for Immediate Care (BASICS), Mountain Rescue or similar organisations, which benefit from their generalist expertise and, in return, offer opportunities to maintain and update urgent care skills.

Almost 80% of community hospitals in England are found in rural areas. They are highly valued as part of the local fabric of isolated rural communities.[32] They are run by teams including GPs, nurses and other advanced care practitioners who value the extension of roles and skillsets that this demands.[33]

Health professionals are more personally visible in rural areas where social networks inevitably cross work/life boundaries. This is seen as a positive in some settings where rural staff often live in proximity to their work.[30, 34] The rural health professional thus requires the highest levels of expert generalism and compassion in addressing potential cross-boundary issues such as healthcare for staff and their families.[35, 36]

Generalism is not specific to clinicians in rural practice but is relevant to all primary healthcare teams. However, many rural team members have multiple roles, requiring a generalist perspective. For example, receptionists are pivotal to the smooth running of a practice. They support patients in navigating to appropriate sources of care including, increasingly, digital resources.[37] They are key to successful uptake of remote technologies in general practice, which are potential facilitators of clinical encounters without the need to travel.[38] Practice staff members in rural settings may also have additional expertise as trained dispensers, giving them greater insight into, and opportunities to promote, medication adherence, possibly contributing to better clinical outcomes. (See Chapter 10: Rural Pharmacy and Dispensing.)[39] Opportunities for career progression by developing additional skills such as dispensing also appear to help retention of staff in rural dispensing practices.[36] Receptionist performance, better continuity of care and longer duration of consultations are all better for practices with smaller rather than larger list sizes.[40]

WHAT ARE THE BARRIERS TO AND FACILITATORS OF GENERALISM?

Continuity of care—the taking of responsibility, acting and seeing through episodes of care—is a defining feature of generalism and valued by patients.[41, 42] Importantly, it is also associated with improved outcomes such as reductions in mortality rates.[43, 44] However, it is in decline.[45] Continuity of care has several facets: Haggerty et al. identified *informational continuity*—awareness of medical history and personal circumstances in planning care—*manage-ment continuity*—a consistent and coherent approach to management of a health condition that is tailored to a patient's changing needs—and *relational continuity*, which perhaps is the most commonly considered aspect—an ongoing therapeutic relationship between a patient and one or more providers.[46] Job satisfaction for doctors providing continuity and out-of-hours rural care is offset by the time commitment, loss of anonymity and infringement on family life and time.[47] The shift to 'small team', relational continuity may be compatible with the definition of generalism and with current trends, but its effectiveness requires further study.[41]

Teams can only function to their full potential if they can overcome rural recruitment and retention difficulties; otherwise, excessive hours and risk of burnout can lead to a vicious circle with ever more people leaving due to the additional demands of the rural setting. Barriers to recruitment and retention recently highlighted by the UK National Centre for Rural Health and Care (NCRHC) include the higher costs of healthcare delivery in rural settings than in urban ones.[48] Other barriers, including migration of younger people away from rural areas, high employment rates and absence of 'rural proofing' in workforce planning, also require governmental and agency response beyond that within control of health services alone.[49] Attempts to improve working quality of life are not always successful. For example, out-of-hours co-operative participation has not improved GPs' mental health or job stress in comparison to traditional on-call in some rural areas[50]; therefore, an openness to revision and to reviewing what works best, coupled with effective rural proofing of policy, is needed.[51]

WHAT IS THE FUTURE FOR GENERALISM IN PRIMARY CARE?

Emphasis on patient-centred care is a recurring theme of health service reforms. To deliver such care, an holistic approach to every individual patient is essential, encompassing their comorbidities, relationships, environment and, increasingly, their genome. This will require skilled generalist contributions from health professionals in all primary healthcare disciplines as well as a change in ethos in the hospital sectors.[52] It will necessitate full recognition of the distinct skills of the expert generalist within healthcare systems.[53] Attitudinal changes and a rebalancing of the holistic versus the reductionist models of undergraduate medical education are still needed.[54] In the 30 years since, in *Tomorrow's Doctors*,[55] the GMC emphasised the importance of community-based learning and an understanding of the full breadth of health and illness, there has been a shift towards more teaching about and exposure to the skills of the generalist, with a substantial increase in community-based placements at both the undergraduate and postgraduate levels.[56] The introduction of longitudinal integrated clerkships, which extend medical students' participation in comprehensive patient care over longer periods of time than in traditional teaching blocks, may prove important. Students enter into a continuous learning relationship with their patients' clinicians, which brings a new focus on patient-centred care and emphasises continuity of care. It remains to be seen what impact this innovation will have on healthcare.[57, 58]

The quantity of clinical GP teaching at medical school is positively corelated with the likelihood of entering specialist GP training.[59] However, more progress is still needed in both undergraduate and postgraduate curricula to encourage interest in working in rural settings.[60] The 2022 UK government's 'All Party Parliamentary Enquiry into Rural Care' calls for mandatory rural work experience in every general practice, geriatric and nursing course and specific rural content in all undergraduate medical courses.[23, 61] This detailed enquiry also calls for urgent review of all core healthcare pathways such as cancer, cardiovascular and mental health care to better meet rural needs, emphasising the need for generalist skills. Should the report's findings be enacted, the future of medical generalism in rural UK primary care could be positive.

REFERENCES

1. Howe A. What's special about medical generalism? The RCGP's response to the independent Commission on Generalism. *Br J Gen Pract*. 2012;62(600):342–3.
2. Watt IS. Health needs of rural residents. In: Cox J, editor. Rural general practice in the United Kingdom: Occasional paper 71. London: Royal College of General Practitioners, 1995, pp. 5–9.
3. Brindle D, Commission on Generalism. Guiding patients through complexity: Modern medical generalism, 2011. www.health.org.uk/publications/guiding-patients-through-complexity-modern-medical-generalism?gclid=EAIaIQobC hMIsKTQy_Kf9wIVRe7tCh3YPQqQEAAYASAAEgIQE_D_BwE [Accessed 19 April 2022].
4. Howe A. Medical generalism: Why expertise in whole person medicine matters. London: Royal College of General Practitioners, 2012.
5. NHS England, NHS Improvement. Standard general medical services contract. London: NHS England, 2020. www.england.nhs.uk/publication/standard-general-medical-services-contract/ [Accessed 19 April 2022].
6. Pereira Gray D. The scientific basis of medical generalism. *Educ Prim Care*. 2017;28(6):344–5.
7. Reeve J, Irving G, Freeman G. Dismantling Lord Moran's ladder: The primary care expert generalist. Br J Gen Pract. 2013;63(606):34–5.

8. Shorvon SD, Luxon LM, Beckwith J. 500 years of the Royal College of Physicians. London: Third Millennium Publishing, 2018.

9. Royal College of General Practitioners, British Medical Association, General Medical Council. General practitioners: Specialists in general practice, 2019. www.rcgp.org.uk/policy/rcgp-policy-areas/gps-as-specialists.aspx [Accessed 21 April 2022].

10. Barnett K, Mercer SW, Norbury M, Watt G, Wyke S, Guthrie B. Epidemiology of multimorbidity and implications for health care, research, and medical education: A cross-sectional study. Lancet. 2012;380(9836):37–43.

11. National Institute for Health and Care Excellence. Falls: Assessment and prevention of falls in older people. London: National Institute for Health and Care Excellence, 2013.

12. Hypertension in Adults: Diagnosis and Management (NG 136) [Internet], 2022. www.nice.org.uk/guidance/ng136 [Accessed 28 August 2019].

13. Guthrie B, Payne K, Alderson P, McMurdo ME, Mercer SW. Adapting clinical guidelines to take account of multimorbidity. BMJ. 2012;345:e6341.

14. Ebell MH, Sokol R, Lee A, Simons C, Early J. How good is the evidence to support primary care practice? Evid Based Med. 2017;22(3):88–92.

15. Reeve J. Interpretive medicine: Supporting generalism in a changing primary care world. Occas Pap R Coll Gen Pract. 2010;(88):1–20.

16. Atmore C. The role of medical generalism in the New Zealand health system into the future. N Z Med J. 2015;128(1419):50–5.

17. Starfield B, Shi L, Macinko J. Contribution of primary care to health systems and health. Milbank Q. 2005;83(3):457–502.

18. Park B, Coutinho AJ, Doohan N, Jimenez J, Martin S, Romano M, et al. Revisiting primary care's critical role in achieving health equity: Pisacano scholars' reflections from starfield summit II. J Am Board Fam Med. 2018;31(2):292–302.

19. Murphy AW, Bury G, Plunkett PK, Gibney D, Smith M, Mullan E, et al. Randomised controlled trial of general practitioner versus usual medical care in an urban accident and emergency department: Process, outcome, and comparative cost. BMJ. 1996;312(7039):1135–42.

20. NHS England. General practice forward view. London: Department of Health, 2016.

21. Campbell JL, Fletcher E, Britten N, Green C, Holt TA, Lattimer V, et al. Telephone triage for management of same-day consultation requests in general practice (the ESTEEM trial): A cluster-randomised controlled trial and cost-consequence analysis. Lancet. 2014;384(9957):1859–68.

22. Hobbs FD, Bankhead C, Mukhtar T, Stevens S, Perera-Salazar R, Holt T, et al. Clinical workload in UK primary care: A retrospective analysis of 100 million consultations in England, 2007–14. Lancet. 2016;387(10035):2323–30.

23. Annibal I, Sellick J, Turner JR, Haseldine J, Morris AM, Parish R. APPG rural health & care: Parliamentary inquiry. Lincoln, NE: National Centre for Rural Health and Care, 2022.

24. Hollinghurst S, Horrocks S, Anderson E, Salisbury C. Comparing the cost of nurse practitioners and GPs in primary care: Modelling economic data from randomised trials. Br J Gen Pract. 2006;56(528):530–5.

25. Van Der Biezen M, Adang E, Van Der Burgt R, Wensing M, Laurant M. The impact of substituting general practitioners with nurse practitioners on resource use, production and health-care costs during out-of-hours: A quasi-experimental study. BMC Fam Pract. 2016;17(1):132.
26. Simpson SH, Lier DA, Majumdar SR, Tsuyuki RT, Lewanczuk RZ, Spooner R, et al. Cost-effectiveness analysis of adding pharmacists to primary care teams to reduce cardiovascular risk in patients with Type 2 diabetes: Results from a randomized controlled trial. Diabetic Med. 2015;32(7):899–906.
27. Venning P, Durie A, Roland M, Roberts C, Leese B. Randomised controlled trial comparing cost effectiveness of general practitioners and nurse practitioners in primary care. BMJ. 2000;320(7241):1048–53.
28. Lowe P, Speakman L. The ageing countryside: The growing older population of rural England. London: Age Concern, 2006.
29. Todd A, Copeland A, Husband A, Kasim A, Bambra C. Access all areas? An area-level analysis of accessibility to general practice and community pharmacy services in England by urbanity and social deprivation. BMJ Open. 2015;5(5):e007328.
30. Jordan H, Roderick P, Martin D, Barnett S. Distance, rurality and the need for care: Access to health services in South West England. Int J Heal Geogr. 2004;3(1):21.
31. Watson MC, Ferguson J, Barton GR, Maskrey V, Blyth A, Paudyal V, et al. A cohort study of influences, health outcomes and costs of patients' health-seeking behaviour for minor ailments from primary and emergency care settings. BMJ Open. 2015;5(2).
32. Davidson D, Ellis Paine A, Glasby J, Williams I, Tucker H, Crilly T, et al. Analysis of the profile, characteristics, patient experience and community value of community hospitals: A multimethod study. Health Serv Deliv Res. 2019;7(1), ISSN 2050-4349.
33. Seamark D, Davidson D, Ellis-Paine A, Glasby J, Tucker H. Factors affecting the changing role of GP clinicians in community hospitals: A qualitative interview study in England. Br J Gen Pract. 2019;69(682):e329–e35.
34. Pohontsch NJ, Hansen H, Schafer I, Scherer M. General practitioners' perception of being a doctor in urban vs. rural regions in Germany—A focus group study. Fam Pract. 2018;35(2):209–15.
35. Garside R, Ayres R, Owen M, Pearson VA, Roizen J. Anonymity and confidentiality: Rural teenagers' concerns when accessing sexual health services. J Fam Plann Reprod Health Care. 2002;28(1):23–6.
36. Cross R, McDonagh STJ, Cockroft E, Turner M, Isom M, Lambourn R, et al. Recruitment and retention of staff in rural dispensing practice. Preston: Society for Academic Primary Care Annual Scientific Meeting, 2022.
37. Leach B, Parkinson S, Gkousis E, Abel G, Atherton H, Campbell J, et al. Digital facilitation to support patient access to web-based primary care services: Scoping literature review. J Med Internet Res. 2022;24(7): e33911.
38. Brant HD, Atherton H, Bikker A, Porqueddu T, Salisbury C, McKinstry B, et al. Receptionists' role in new approaches to consultations in primary care: A focused ethnographic study. *Br J Gen Pract.* 2018;68(672):e478–e86.

39. Gomez-Cano M, Wiering B, Abel G, Campbell J, Clark C. Medication adherence and clinical outcomes in dispensing and non-dispensing practices: A cross-sectional analysis. Br J Gen Pract. 2021;71(702):e55–e61.

40. Campbell JL, Ramsay J, Green J. Practice size: Impact on consultation length, workload, and patient assessment of care. Br J Gen Pract. 2001;51(469):644–50.

41. Murphy M, Salisbury C. Relational continuity and patients' perception of GP trust and respect: A qualitative study. Br J Gen Pract. 2020;70(698):e676–e83.

42. Iqbal I, Thompson L, Wilson P. Patient satisfaction with general practice in urban and rural areas of Scotland. Rur Remote Heal. 2021;21(4):6634.

43. Pereira Gray DJ, Sidaway-Lee K, White E, Thorne A, Evans PH. Continuity of care with doctors—a matter of life and death? A systematic review of continuity of care and mortality. BMJ Open. 2018;8(6):e021161.

44. Baker R, Freeman GK, Haggerty JL, Bankart MJ, Nockels KH. Primary medical care continuity and patient mortality: A systematic review. Br J Gen Pract. 2020;70(698):e600–e11.

45. Tammes P, Morris RW, Murphy M, Salisbury C. Is continuity of primary care declining in England? Practice-level longitudinal study from 2012 to 2017. Br J Gene Pract. 2021;71(707):e432–e40.

46. Haggerty JL, Reid RJ, Freeman GK, Starfield BH, Adair CE, McKendry R. Continuity of care: A multidisciplinary review. BMJ. 2003;327(7425):1219–21.

47. Cuddy NJ, Keane AM, Murphy AW. Rural general practitioners' experience of the provision of out-of-hours care: A qualitative study. Br J Gen Pract. 2001;51(465):286–90.

48. Palmer B, Appleby J, Spencer J. Rural health care: A rapid review of the impact of rurality on the costs of delivering health care. London: National Centre for Rural Health and Care; 2019.

49. Green A, Bramley G, Annibal I, Sellick J. Rural workforce issues in health and care. Lincoln, NE: University of Birmingham & Rose Regeneration, 2018.

50. Mc Loughlin M, Armstrong P, Byrne M, Heaney D, O'Brien N, Murphy AW. A comparative study on attitudes, mental health and job stress amongst GPs participating, or not, in a rural out-of-hours co-operative. Fam Pract. 2005;22(3):275–9.

51. Department for Environment Food and Rural Affairs. Rural proofing Report 2020: Delivering policy in a rural context. London: UK Government, 2021. https://assets.publishing.service.gov.uk/government/uploads/system/uploads/attachment_data/file/982484/Rural_Proofing_Report_2020.pdfgov.uk

52. Ahluwalia S, Tavabie A, Alessi C, Chana N. Medical generalism in a modern NHS: Preparing for a turbulent future. Br J Gen Pract. 2013;63(610):e367–9.

53. Reeve J, Dowrick CF, Freeman GK, Gunn J, Mair F, May C, et al. Examining the practice of generalist expertise: A qualitative study identifying constraints and solutions. JRSM Short Reports. 2013;4(12).

54. Grumbach K. Chronic illness, comorbidities, and the need for medical generalism. Ann Fam Med. 2003;1(1):4–7.

55. General Medical Council. Tomorrow's doctors: Recommendations on undergraduate medical education issued by the Education Committee of the General Medical Council in pursuance of Section 5 of the Medical Act 1983. London: General Medical Council, 1993. ISBN: 9780901458360.

56. Howe A, Campion P, Searle J, Smith H. New perspectives—approaches to medical education at four new UK medical schools. *BMJ.* 2004;329(7461):327–31.

57. Hudson JN, Poncelet AN, Weston KM, Bushnell JA, Farmer E. Longitudinal integrated clerkships. *Med Teach.* 2017;39(1):7–13.

58. Richards E, Elliott L, Jackson B, Panesar A. Longitudinal integrated clerkship evaluations in UK medical schools: A narrative literature review. *Educ Prim Care.* 2022;33(3):148–55.

59. Alberti H, Randles HL, Harding A, McKinley RK. Exposure of undergraduates to authentic GP teaching and subsequent entry to GP training: A quantitative study of UK medical schools. *Br J Gen Pract.* 2017;67(657):e248–e52.

60. Albritton W, Bates J, Brazeau M, Busing N, Clarke J, Kendel D, et al. Generalism versus subspecialization: Changes necessary in medical education. *Can J Rural Med.* 2006;11(2):126–8.

61. Fleming J, Patel P, Tristram S, Reeve J. The fall and rise of generalism: Perceptions of generalist practice amongst medical students. *Educ Prim Care.* 2017;28(4):250–1.

CHAPTER 4

Rural Diseases

....

Tim Sanders

In this chapter, we provide a summary of the main environmental illness and injuries, arthropod-borne diseases, bites stings, zoonoses and skin conditions that are encountered in UK rural practice.

ENVIRONMENTAL

Blackthorn (*Prunus Spinosa*) Injury

Blackthorn or sloe, a perennial shrub commonly found in hedgerows and undergrowth, has sharp, narrow thorns which easily penetrate the skin and break off, leaving embedded fragments. Injuries, most frequently to the hand and forearm, usually occur during hedge-cutting.[1]

Symptoms, which often follow a delay of weeks, include pain, tenderness and swelling, sterile and bacterial abscess formation, joint and tendon synovitis and septic arthritis.[2]

Injuries from other thorny plants such as roses may present similarly.

Treatment is by thorough surgical exploration to ensure that all fragments of the foreign body are removed.[1]

Blue-Green Algae

While commonly described as algae, 'blooms' (visible scum layers or floating mats) in lakes or ponds, particularly during warmer weather, are caused by cyanobacteria in the presence of high levels of nutrients. Cyanobacteria

DOI: 10.1201/9781003302438-9

toxins are harmful to humans, livestock, domestic pets and fish,[3] causing skin rashes, vomiting, abdominal pain, fever, headache and, more rarely, central nervous system complications.[3, 4]

Most symptoms are self-limiting. Exposure avoidance is recommended. There is no specific antidote, so treatment, if required, is supportive.

Musculo-Skeletal

Farming is associated with an increased incidence of osteoarthritis, especially of the hips and knees. Heavy lifting, particularly in awkward positions when handling animals, results in common complaints of back and neck pain.

Large animal vets report shoulder and wrist pain associated with repetitive tasks, often in awkward positions: for example, ultrasonography and internal examination of pregnant cattle.

Because cattle often weigh 700–1,000 kg, reports such as 'trapped between cow and gate', 'knocked over by a cow' or 'stepped on by a cow' should be treated seriously.

Other rural occupations are associated with industrial diseases. For example, the use of chainsaws in forestry work is associated with vibration disease.

Non-Freezing Cold Injury

Sustained and repeated exposure to cold can result in damage to peripheral tissues and frostbite. Most cases involve the lower limbs; 25% of cases involve the hands.[5] The pathophysiology is poorly understood, but symptoms, which include abnormal sensations in the extremity and abnormal sensation when touching hot or cold things or during sleep, can be debilitating.

Treatment options are limited. Prevention is by appropriate protective equipment, particularly insulated gloves and footwear to limit exposure.[6]

Oily Vaccine Inoculation Injury

Animal vaccination usually takes place at a high pace, frequently in a cold environment where manual dexterity is reduced, and livestock can make sudden movements. These factors increase the risk of needlestick injury with or without accidental inoculation, mostly involving the non-dominant hand, forearm or thigh.

Complications include finger pulp and tendon-sheath infection and the pharmacological effects of the injected substance. For example, mineral oils, particularly when injected into a closed compartment such as the finger pulp, cause both local damage and significant pain. Sequelae include compartmental pressure, ischaemic necrosis, loss of a digit, sterile abscess formation and chronic granulomatous inflammation. Self-inoculation with mineral oil containing vaccines should be treated seriously and urgently by debridement, irrigation and, where necessary, decompression.[7,8] Oxytocin, used to promote milk letdown in dairy cattle, can induce premature labour in a pregnant woman.

ARTHROPODS

Wasp and bee stings are common. Local effects are caused by injection of amines and peptides and other locally active substances such as histamine, dopamine, noradrenaline and GABA. Reactions, which normally last only a few hours, are characterised by pain, swelling, erythema and pruritus. Treatment is with oral antihistamines and local application of ice, crotamiton or 1% hydrocortisone cream.[9]

Wasp stings are retained by the wasp. Bee stings should be removed by gentle scraping as quickly as possible to prevent continuing envenomation.

Systemic reactions to stings because of hypersensitivity include flushing, urticaria, angioedema, faintness, shortness of breath, nausea, vomiting and palpitations.

In severe cases, potentially fatal anaphylaxis, which usually begins within a few minutes of the sting, is characterised by the sudden onset of airway oedema, bronchospasm and shock.[10]

Treatment is based on basic and advanced life support principles with prompt treatment with intramuscular adrenaline and specialist follow-up in an allergy clinic.[10]

Adrenaline auto-injections such as EpiPen, Jext or Emerade may be prescribed for patients to carry with them. NICE recommend a prescription for two auto-injectors with training in their use pending referral and assessment at an allergy clinic for desensitisation.[11,12]

Horse Fly Bites ('Clegs') (Tabanidae Species)

Horse fly bites cause painful, itchy local skin reactions, often with oedema and urticaria. Oral antihistamines, topical crotamiton or 1% hydrocortisone cream may be helpful.

Ticks (Ixodes Species)

Ticks are carried by many animals, particularly sheep and deer. Transmitted to human hosts either directly or via vegetation such as bracken, they feed on blood and can transmit diseases such as Lyme disease, Q fever and typhus. They are easily recognised, particularly when they swell with ingested blood.

For advice on how to remove a tick, see Box 4.1.[9]

BOX 4.1: TICK REMOVAL

TO REMOVE A TICK

Use a pair of tweezers that will not squash the tick (such as fine-tipped tweezers) or a tick removal tool (available from pet shops or vets).

- Grip the tick as close to the skin as possible to ensure the tick's mouth parts are not left in the skin and to avoid regurgitation of parasitic organisms into the host.
- Rotating gently, pull steadily away from the skin without crushing the tick.
- Wash with soap and water and apply antiseptic cream.
- Do not use a lit cigarette end, a match head or substances such as alcohol or petroleum jelly to force the tick out.

Tick attachment may be prevented by insect repellents such as icaridin or DEET.[13]

Secondary Bacterial Infection of Insect Bites

A rapid-onset skin reaction from an insect bite or sting is most likely to be inflammatory or allergic. Antibiotics should only be offered to people with evidence of infection—for example, erysipelas or fever—and those with underlying conditions (e.g. diabetes).[14]

REPTILES

Adder Bites

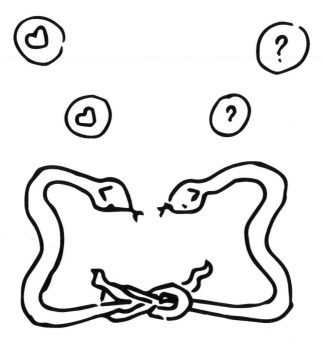

Adders or common vipers (*Vipera berus*) are the only indigenous venomous snakes in the United Kingdom. Most adder bites occur during June, July and August, usually in the foot or, as a result of the victim attempting to pick up the snake, the hand.[15] A variable volume of venom, a complex mixture of high-molecular-weight proteins, proteases, peptide hydrolases, hyaluronidase and phospholipases, is delivered.

Most adder bites result in trivial symptoms, and there may be bites without envenomation; 70% of reported adder bites result in either no or very mild effects.[16] Although it is rare, they can be fatal,[16, 17] with death occurring six to sixty hours after a bite. Children and the elderly are most at risk.[15]

The principal local effects are pain (not invariably), oedema (sometimes within minutes but nearly always within two hours and occasionally massive), bruising and tissue tenderness, increasing during the first one to three days, then slowly subsiding.

Systemic Effects

Hypotension, the most important sign of systemic envenomation, usually develops within 2 hours but may be delayed for 12–24 hours. The victim may feel faint or drowsy and become semi-conscious. Nausea and vomiting are common, and diarrhoea may occur. Other systemic symptoms include abdominal colic; incontinence of urine and faeces; sweating; vasoconstriction; tachycardia; oedema of the face, lips, gums, tongue or throat; urticaria; and bronchospasm. Cardiotoxic components in the venom can cause T-wave inversion, myocardial damage and second-degree heart block. A blood sample may show neutrophil leucocytosis, thrombocytopenia and sometimes late anaemia.

BOX 4.2: TREATMENT OF SNAKE BITES

- Reassure the patient.
- Give paracetamol for pain.
- Remove jewellery or constricting clothing from the bitten limb as soon as possible.
- Immobilise the patient, especially the envenomed limb. Do not elevate.
- Transport urgently to hospital.
- Treat anaphylaxis with adrenaline.
- Avoid interference with the wound. Do not cut into or suck from the site.
- Do not apply tourniquets, ligatures or compression bandages.

Guidance for the first aid treatment of snakebites can be found in Box 4.2. Patients should be monitored closely in a hospital settling under specialist supervision for a minimum of 24 hours.[16]

Anti-Venom

Supplies of anti-venom, which reduces morbidity, prevents death and reduces convalescent time in moderate or severe cases, are maintained in emergency departments and should be administered if the patient has any of the following features:[18]

- Early anaphylaxis-like reactions to the venom
- Hypotension persisting for more than ten minutes, with or without features of shock

- Systemic features, including abdominal pain or diarrhoea/vomiting
- Definite leucocytosis (especially if over $20 \times 10^9/l$)
- ECG abnormalities (e.g. bradycardia or widespread ischaemia)
- Metabolic acidosis
- Elevated creatine kinase
- Severe local envenoming (even in the absence of systemic features) (i.e. swelling spreading beyond the next major joint)
- Any other evidence of systemic envenoming (e.g. spontaneous haemorrhage, pulmonary oedema)

CHEMICALS

Organophosphate Poisoning

Organophosphate insecticides inhibit acetyl cholinesterase and are used in agricultural pest control throughout the world. Due to concerns about their environmental effects and toxicity, their use is now tightly regulated in the UK.

Absorption is through skin, gut and bronchial mucosa. Accumulation of acetylcholine causes nausea, headache, vomiting, abdominal pain, diarrhoea, excessive salivation, miosis, blurred vision, sweating, sleep disturbance, anxiety, restlessness, muscle weakness and fasciculation.

Acute severe poisoning presents with widespread paralysis, respiratory failure, bronchospasm, pulmonary oedema, profuse respiratory secretions, convulsions and coma.[19]

Sheep Dipping

Organophosphate sheep dips were widely used in the past, usually without personal protective equipment (PPE), to control mites, blowflies, ticks and lice etc. Although now regulated, with a requirement for user training and PPE, regulations and guidelines are often impracticable and ignored. Since dipping is a long, hot, hard job, farm workers often have considerable skin contact with the sheep dip solution.

Acute poisoning is unusual in Europe but should be treated as in Box 4.3.

Chronic effects of low-grade exposure remain unclear. Several studies have detected no difference in symptomatology and CNS function between sheep dippers and controls, while other studies have shown that exposed sheep farmers are less able to sustain attention or process information, and they may have peripheral sensory loss.[20–22] Other studies suggest that sheep farmers are more vulnerable to psychiatric disorder than controls, but it is unclear how far this relates to organophosphates or to other economic and social factors.[21, 23] If chronic poisoning is suspected, discuss the patient with a specialist (in the UK, via the National Poisons Information Service), who may recommend a cholinesterase assay.

BOX 4.3: MANAGEMENT OF SUSPECTED ORGANOPHOSPHATE POISONING

- Wear protective clothing to avoid contamination.
- Provide basic life support as needed.
- Insert IV cannula.
- Measure blood cholinesterase level (EDTA tube on ice).
- Give diazepam to treat agitation and control convulsions.
- Treat bronchial secretions or bronchospasm with atropine IV (adult 2mg; child 0.02mg/kg), repeated every 5min, doubling the dose each time until the chest sounds clear, systolic BP >80mmHg and pulse >80. Some patients need >100mg of atropine.
- If atropine is required, also give pralidoxime (30mg/kg IV over 30min, followed by an IVI at 8mg/kg/hr).
- Improvement is usually apparent within 30 minutes.

INHALATIONAL DISEASES

Farmers are often exposed to dust, which may contain bacteria, fungi and their metabolites, endotoxins and mites. Over 60% of Irish farmers reported one or more chronic respiratory symptom, with high rates of non-smoking-related obstructive lung disease.[24]

Extrinsic allergic alveolitis or hypersensitivity pneumonitis (HP) and organic dust toxic syndrome (ODTS) represent parts of a spectrum of response to complex organic dusts rather than being distinct clinical entities.

Farmer's Lung

Farmer's lung is a hypersensitivity pneumonitis (extrinsic allergic alveolitis) recognised as an industrial disease, resulting from exposure to thermophilic actinomycetes spores from mouldy hay. The higher the rainfall, the more likely the hay is to be mouldy and the greater the prevalence of the disease. When disturbed, mouldy hay releases clouds of millions of spores.

Once common, incidence has fallen because of a change in farming practices away from hay production towards silage.

Symptoms: Fever, chills, malaise and flu-like symptoms, including cough and dyspnoea without wheezing begin four to eight hours after exposure.

Repeated exposure can cause irreversible lung damage.

Diagnosis: Serology for farmer's lung antibodies and lung CT scanning confirm the diagnosis. Pulmonary function tests show loss of vital capacity and exercise-induced hypoxaemia.

Treatment: Avoidance of hay and smoking cessation are imperative. Smoking reduces the ten-year survival rate from over 90% to 70%.[25]

A course of oral steroids in the acute phase improves both symptoms and pulmonary function. Long-term corticosteroid treatment is not beneficial. Without further antigen exposure, lung function usually recovers completely, although this may take several years. Chronic exposure results in irreversible lung fibrosis.

Other causes of hypersensitivity pneumonitis include mushroom worker's lung (*Micropolyspora faeni*), bird fancier's lung, paprika splitter's lung (*Mucor stolonifer*), doghouse disease (*Aspergillus versicolor*), cheese washer's lung (*Penicillium casii*) and sewage worker's lung (*Cephalosporium*). The principles of diagnosis and management are the same as farmer's lung.

Organic Dust Toxic Syndrome (ODTS)

ODTS is a febrile reaction to inhaled mould dust. Unlike hypersensitivity pneumonitis, which is associated with exposure over days or weeks,

ODTS is associated with extreme exposure on a single day. Symptoms, including malaise, myalgia, headache, dry cough, breathlessness, anorexia, nausea, vomiting and skin irritation, usually develop within hours. Most cases are mild and self-limiting, but some may progress to severe acute lung injury.[26]

Dust masks protect against dust inhalation and, therefore, ODTS.

ZOONOSES

Many zoonoses (infections passed to humans from animals) produce non-specific symptoms or sub-clinical illness in humans or remain undiagnosed. Others are diagnosed retrospectively by antibody tests.

Thomas et al. (1999) published baseline data on the prevalence and incidence of zoonoses in UK farmworkers.[27] Key messages were:

- Ringworm, orf, cowpox, *Coxiella, Chlamydia* and *Toxoplasma* were common.
- Leptospirosis was uncommon.
- *Coxiella* and *Toxoplasma* infections occurred more frequently in livestock farmers.
- Ringworm infection was associated with exposure to cattle.
- *Hantavirus* and cowpox infections were associated with exposure to rats.
- Orf was associated with sheep.
- *Coxiella* was associated with farm contact and exposure to cattle.
- *Chlamydia* was associated with sheep, specifically lambing.
- Antibodies to Q fever (27.3%), *Chlamydia* (79.6%) and *Toxoplasma* (50.2%) were common.
- Antibodies to leptospirosis (0.2%) and brucellosis (0.7%) were uncommon.
- Antibodies to *Toxoplasma, Chlamydia* and *Coxiella* were not matched by a history of relevant illness, indicating non-specific or sub-clinical illness.[27]

Anthrax (Notifiable Disease in the UK)

Anthrax is a potentially fatal disease caused by the bacterium *Bacillus anthracis*, a spore-forming organism.

> *Route of transmission*: Anthrax most commonly infects the skin through direct contact with infected animals or animal products but

can affect the gastrointestinal tract and respiratory system. Workers in wool and bone processing and tanning may be at risk. There have also been sporadic outbreaks in drug users injecting contaminated heroin.

Incubation period: Usually within 48 hours, may be up to seven days.

Incidence has declined since 1965 because of improved infection control. Between 1981 and 2015, only 30 cases were recorded in the UK.

Clinical: Presentation is usually a skin lesion with itching, followed by development of a papule which becomes vesicular, then a depressed black 'eschar' surrounded by oedema.

Inhalation anthrax presents with symptoms of a mild upper respiratory tract infection, followed by fever, shock and death within three to five days. Meningitis can develop.

Intestinal anthrax causes severe abdominal pain, fever and bloody diarrhoea.

Mortality: Untreated, anthrax of the skin has a mortality rate of 5–20%, but with antibiotic treatment, death is rare. Inhalation and intestinal anthrax have a high mortality.

Treatment: Antibiotics such as ciprofloxacin or vancomycin by a specialist infectious diseases team.[28]

Prevention: Vaccination is available but seldom recommended.

Brucellosis

Organism: *Brucella abortus* or *B. Mellitensis*.

Transmission: Handling infected animals or animal parts (through breaks in the skin), ingestion of unpasteurised milk from infected animals.

Incubation: 5–60 days.

Prevalence: Following its eradication from the cattle stock, brucellosis is no longer considered endemic in the UK. However, it remains a common disease worldwide, resulting in a small annual number of imported cases.

Diagnosis: Serology

Clinical: Non-specific with intermittent fever, headache, weakness, sweats, arthralgia, weight loss. Historically, 'chronic brucellosis' was used by many clinicians where a diagnosis of medically unexplained or functional symptoms might more properly be used now.

Echinococcus (Hydatid Disease, Tapeworm)

Organism: *Echinococcus granulosus* is a small tapeworm found in dogs.

Transmission occurs through hand-to-mouth transfer of eggs from dogs' faeces.

Incidence: Rare. There were 12 reported confirmed cases in Scotland between 2008 and 2017.[29]

Clinical: Cysts slowly enlarge in varying parts of the body, taking several years to develop and eventually mimicking tumours.

Diagnosis is by serology, with imaging evidence of cysts.

Prevention: Avoidance of animal viscera, regular worming of dogs and education about dog faeces.

Treatment. Antiparasitic drug treatment, usually albendazole, and either percutaneous or surgical excision of cysts or a 'watch and wait' approach.[30]

Erysipelas and Erysipeloid

Erysipelas is common, superficial skin cellulitis. Most cases are caused by *Group A beta-haemolytic streptococci*.

Erysipeloid is caused by *Erysipelothrix rhusiopathiae*. Erysipeloid manifests as a well-demarcated red or purplish, smooth and shiny urticarial plaque, usually on the hand. Blistering, lymphangitis, and regional lymphadenopathy can be seen. Low-grade fever and arthralgia are seen in 10% of cases. A rare diffuse cutaneous and a septicaemic form with endocarditis have been described.[31]

Transmission: Contact with infected animals (particularly pigs, fish, and birds) or decaying meat. Butchers, fishermen, farmers and cooks are at highest risk. Entry is via existing skin wounds or puncture wounds caused by splinters or fish bones.[32, 33]

Incubation period: One to seven days.

Diagnosis: Diagnosis is normally made clinically, with tissue culture if necessary.

Treatment: Most cases resolve within two to four weeks without treatment. If antibiotic treatment is required, penicillin is recommended with erythromycin or a cephalosporin as alternatives.

Infectious Diarrhoea

'Food poisoning' and 'infectious bloody diarrhoea' are notifiable diseases in the UK.

Campylobacteriosis

Organisms: *Campylobacter jejuni* and *Campylobacter coli* are the most commonly isolated gastrointestinal pathogen in the UK.[29] They are present in the gastrointestinal tract of many animals, particularly poultry and cattle, but also cats and dogs, pigs, sheep and rodents.

Transmission: Outbreaks are often associated with undercooked chicken, unpasteurised milk and non-chlorinated water supplies.

Incubation: 2 to 5 days (range 1–11 days).

Clinical: Diarrhoea, sometimes severe, with abdominal pain and fever. Many infections are asymptomatic.

Diagnosis: Isolation of the organism from faeces.

Treatment: Most cases are self-limiting and antibiotic treatment unnecessary. However, high fever, bloody or high output diarrhoea or immunocompromise should prompt consideration of antibiotic treatment, usually with clarithromycin or ciprofloxacin. Antibiotic resistance is increasing.[34]

Cryptosporidiosis

Organism: Cryptosporidium parvum.

Transmission: The parasite, which is resistant to chlorine, can be found in humans, cattle and other domestic animals. Infection follows faecal contamination of water or food.

Incubation: Two to ten days (average seven days).

Clinical: Profuse, watery diarrhoea, abdominal pains and fever, normally settling spontaneously within one month. Immunocompromised people, e.g. those with AIDS, may be unable to overcome the infection, which may then contribute to death.

Diagnosis is by demonstrating oocysts in stool samples.

Treatment is supportive, with fluid and electrolyte replacement as necessary. Most cases are self-limiting with no intervention required. There is no specific licensed treatment in the UK.

Entero-Haemorrhagic *E. Coli* (0157)

Organism: *E. coli* are normal human gut flora. Some serotypes, verotoxic *E. coli*, (VTEC), particularly the 0157 strain, produce verocytotoxin, an enterotoxin.
Other strains of VTEC cause traveller's diarrhoea.

Transmission: Inadequately cooked beef, unpasteurised milk and infected water supplies. Small doses of infected material can cause disease. Person-to-person spread is common.

Incubation: Usually three to four days but up to eight days.

Clinical: *E. coli* 0157 causes diarrhoea, which ranges from mild to extremely severe, and sometimes major haemorrhage, especially in the elderly and children. Normally, there is no fever. Nearly one-third of confirmed cases are hospitalised.[35]

Infection carries two rare but serious potential complications:

- Haemolytic uraemic syndrome (HUS) (notifiable disease in the UK)
- Thrombotic thrombocytopenic purpura (TTP)

Diagnosis: Stool culture.

Treatment is supportive by fluid and electrolyte replacement. There is no effective antibiotic treatment.

Salmonella

Organism: Many strains of *Salmonella*, found in poultry, pigs, cattle, rodents, cats, dogs and human carriers.

Transmission: Usually contaminated food or non-chlorinated water supplies. The infective dose may be as little as 1,000 organisms. Person-to-person transmission is often seen. Epidemics are usually due to mishandling of food and poor temperature control.

Incubation period: Normally 12–72 hours. A small proportion of infected people become carriers, excreting the organism for over one year.

Clinical: Diarrhoea with stomach cramps, usually lasting four to seven days. Systemic effects: headache, nausea and vomiting and dehydration may be severe.[36]

Diagnosis: Culture of faeces. Serological tests are not useful.

Treatment: Supportive with fluid and electrolyte replacement. Most cases are self-limiting.

High fever, bloody or high output diarrhoea or immunocompromise should prompt consideration of antibiotic treatment, which, due to widespread resistance, should be guided by specialist advice.

Leptospirosis (Weil's Disease or Haemorrhagic Jaundice)

Organism: Bacterial spirochaetes, including *Leptospira icterohaem-orrhagica* from rats, *Leptospira hardjo* from cattle, *Leptospira heb-domidis* etc.

Transmission: Contact with infected urine or water contaminated by urine, particularly from rats and cattle. The organism may be ingested or enter through cuts and abrasions, mucous membranes including conjunctivae or aerosol inhalation. Leptospirosis is a recreational hazard for bathers, campers and sportspeople and an occupational hazard for water bailiffs, fish processors and sewerage workers etc.

Person-to-person transmission is rare.

Incubation period: Usually 7–14 days (range 2–30 days).

Incidence: Common worldwide, particularly in the tropics, leptospirosis is a rare diagnosis in the UK, with 91 recorded cases in 2019[37] and zero to five UK deaths per year.[38]

It is more common in men than in women at a ratio of 9.5:1. Around a quarter of cases are acquired by holidaymakers when abroad.[39]

Clinical: Most infections are asymptomatic or result in only mild illness and recovery within two to six weeks. Features are often non-specific and influenza-like with fever, myalgia (commonly calves and low back), arthralgia, anorexia, nausea and vomiting, conjunctival suffusion and headache.

However, infection can result in a serious illness, Weil's disease and death, with a case fatality rate of around 5% in the UK.[39] Features: jaundice, purpura, petechiae, epistaxis, haemoptysis, hepatomegaly, vasculitis, encephalitis and renal failure, liver failure, myocarditis, pulmonary haemorrhage and rhabdomyolysis.

Severe disease may be biphasic with mild early symptoms before a second phase (usually around day four to six) characterised by cytokine storm.[40]

Treatment: A 2012 Cochrane review concluded that there was insufficient evidence to make recommendations for or against the use of antibiotics.[41]

Guidance should be sought from a specialist infectious diseases service.

If antibiotics are used, doxycycline or azithromycin are usually first-line treatment, with amoxicillin or ampicillin as alternatives. Cefotaxime, ceftriaxone and penicillin G are used in severely ill patients.

Lyme Disease

Organism: Deer or sheep ticks *Ixodes ricinus* act as vectors for the spirochaete *Borrelia burgdorferi*, which causes the disease.

B. Burgdorferi has several sub-species, notably:

1 *B. burgdorferi sensu stricto*, associated with arthritis
2 *B. garinii*, associated with neurological manifestations
3 *B. afzelii*, associated with skin manifestations

Lifecycle: Having hatched from its egg, the tick's lifecycle (egg-larva-nymph-adult) requires it to feed on the blood of three separate vertebrate hosts, including deer, sheep, cattle, humans and dogs.[42]

The usual reservoirs of infection are small mammals and birds. In an environment dominated by cattle and sheep, with few reservoir-competent hosts, ticks tend to feed only on the cattle and sheep, reducing the risk of them carrying infection.[43]

Incidence: Lyme disease is the most common vector-borne human infection in the UK, with 2.7 recorded cases per 100,000 in 2017.[42] Many cases are diagnosed and treated without laboratory testing. The UK primary care Clinical Practice Research Datalink database, which includes both clinical diagnoses and those confirmed in the laboratory, estimated an annual incidence of 12.1 per 100,000 in 2019.

Route of transmission: Tick saliva is injected when it feeds on its host's blood. Spirochaetes reach the saliva from the tick's midgut 17 to 36 hours after feeding has started, resulting in a delay in transmission.[43] Thus, the risk of infection if an attached tick is removed before 17 hours is very small.

Incubation period:[44] The typical erythema migrans rash usually appears one to four weeks after the initial tick bite but can arise as soon as three days.

Clinical.[44]

Early localised disease: Erythema migrans is present in 70–89% of cases, with associated headache, malaise and fluctuating and migratory joint or muscle pains in 5% of cases. Fever and sweats also occur, but these are rare.

Early disseminated disease within three months of exposure. Features include erythema migrans rash in multiple sites, headache, malaise, fatigue, migratory joint or muscle pains, lymphadenopathy, fever and sweats and facial and other cranial nerve palsies. Also seen are meningitis (2% of cases), mononeuritis multiplex, motor and sensory radiculopathy, paraesthesia, pericarditis (1%), heart block (rare) and keratitis (rare).

Late disseminated disease, more than three months after exposure, can present in a variety of ways. A violet-coloured rash, particularly on the limbs, 'acrodermatitis chronica atrophicans', is seen in 1–3% of cases. Inflammatory arthritis affecting one or more joints occurs in 3–7%. Uveitis, encephalitis and neurocognitive dysfunction are also seen.

Diagnosis. Ask about tick bites! The primary erythema migrans rash should be diagnosed clinically and treated promptly, based on history and examination. NICE and other expert guidance[45, 46] recommend against the use of acute phase serological testing, which has a poor sensitivity and can result in delay in initiating treatment.

Lyme disease should be considered in patients presenting with:

- Non-specific symptoms: fever and sweats, swollen glands, malaise, fatigue, neck pain or stiffness, migratory joint or muscle pains or paraesthesia
- Focal neurological symptoms: facial or other cranial nerve palsies, meningitis, mononeuritis multiplex, radiculopathy, encephalitis, neuropsychiatric or unexplained white matter changes on MRI
- Inflammatory arthritis affecting one or more joints, particularly if fluctuating or migratory
- Pericarditis, heart block
- Uveitis, keratitis
- Acrodermatitis chronica atrophicans
- Lymphocytoma

Post-treatment symptoms or 'post-Lyme Borreliosis syndrome' include persistent fatigue, musculoskeletal pain or difficulties in concentration and memory reported by 11–15% of patients at six months post-treatment. Microbiological studies showed neither convincing evidence of ongoing borrelia infection nor that further or prolonged antibiotic treatment was beneficial.[43]

NICE recommends that, in patients with suspicious symptoms but no history of tick attachment, Lyme disease should not be ruled out.[45] Serological testing should be considered.

NICE guidance also recommends *against* making a diagnosis of Lyme disease in patients:

- Presenting with a history of tick bite but no symptoms
- With no clinical evidence or positive serology because of the risk of missing alternative diagnosis and/or providing inappropriate treatment

Investigations: A stepwise approach is recommended:[45]

- First an enzyme-linked immunosorbent assay (ELISA) test for IgM and IgG antibodies.
- If the ELISA test is positive, carry out an immunoblot test.
- If the ELISA test is negative, review symptoms and consider alternative diagnoses.
- If Lyme disease is still suspected in a patient who had a negative ELISA within four weeks of the onset of symptoms, repeat the ELISA test after four to six weeks.
- If Lyme disease is still suspected after a negative ELISA and symptoms for twelve weeks or more, carry out an immunoblot test.
- If testing is negative but suspicion of Lyme disease persists, consider specialist referral.

Treatment: Reference should be made to the most up-to-date local or national treatment guidelines. Current first-line treatment with doxycycline for 21 days is recommended in NICE and other expert guidelines,[43-45] amoxicillin as second line, doxycycline for carditis and ceftriaxone for central nervous system involvement.

Prevention and Removal of Ticks: See 'Arthropods: Ticks' earlier in this chapter.

Orf (Contagious Pustular Dermatitis or Ecthyma)

Listen to your patient; he is telling you the diagnosis.

(William Osler, 1849–1919[47])

Most patients know the diagnosis and come to the doctor for confirmation and management advice.

Organism: Parapoxvirus that normally affects lambs' lips but can affect cattle and goats. The virus is resistant and may survive in dust, on walls and on the wood of sheep pens.

Route of transmission: Through skin contact. Person-to-person transmission is uncommon.

Human orf is an occupational hazard for farmers and shepherds and those who handle sheep carcasses, including abattoir workers and vets.

Incubation period: Three to four days.

Clinical: The lesion is a single, macular then papular rash, usually on the hand or lower arm, evolving into a soft, solid lesion, usually up to 2cm in diameter. The mature lesion looks like a pustule, but incision (best avoided) shows only a solid, soft keratosis. The whole lesion disappears within one to six months. Several lesions can occur in the same patient. Generally, the patient remains well, but there may be associated fever, lymphadenopathy and lymphangitis.

Erythema multiforme and bullous pemphigoid are sometimes seen.[33]

Treatment: Usually, no treatment is necessary, and the patient can be assured of complete recovery. Immunity develops so that subsequent infections are less likely.

Q Fever

Organism: *Coxiella burnetii*, an obligate intracellular gram-negative coccobacillus. Difficult to detect and highly resistant to physical and chemical agents.[48]

Transmission: From sheep, cattle and goats, although it can also be found in pets and wildlife, including birds, reptiles, fish and ticks.[49]

Main route of transmission is through inhalation of infected dust from premises containing placental tissue, birth fluids or excreta of infected animals. Person-to-person transmission is rare.[48]

Incubation period: Usually two to three weeks.

Incidence and prevalence: Infection is asymptomatic or non-specific in more than 50%,[48, 50] with low numbers of reported cases but high prevalence of antibodies (29.2%) in serological studies.[27]

There are about 50 reported annual cases in the UK.[51]

Clinical: Acute Q fever presents as a non-specific influenza-like illness lasting about 10 days (range 5–57 days) with fever, retrobulbar headache, rigors, sweats, malaise, myalgia, arthralgia, anorexia and weight loss. Fever is not always present. There is an associated rash in 5–20% of cases. Pneumonia (50% of cases) is usually mild and often productive, with pleuritic chest pain. Other complications are hepatitis (hepatomegaly and abnormal liver function tests, rarely jaundice), myocarditis, pericarditis, meningitis and encephalitis. Rarer complications are erythema nodosum, Guillain-Barre syndrome, neuritis, myelitis and peripheral neuropathies.[48, 49, 52]

Post Q fever fatigue syndrome, characterised by chronic fatigue, night sweats, headaches, muscle and joint pain, mood changes and sleep disturbance occurs in up to 20% of patients.[53]

Chronic Q fever occurs in approximately 5% of cases, commonly presenting as endocarditis. Case mortality is negligible in treated cases but up to 2% if untreated.

Q fever infection or recrudescence of infection during pregnancy can result in miscarriage, premature deliveries and stillbirths.[54]

Diagnosis: Serology.

Treatment: Acute infection is self-limiting in most cases. Resolution is within two to three weeks with or without treatment.

Antibiotic treatment with doxycycline is recommended for the acute illness, including pneumonia.[48] Second-line antibiotics include moxifloxacin, clarithromycin, co-trimoxazole and rifampicin.[55]

Risk of progression to chronic disease may be lifelong. Past infection should be coded prominently in the primary care record and patients counselled to remind clinicians of their past infection should they develop non-specific symptoms in the future. Women of childbearing age should be counselled of the risk of recrudescence of the infection during pregnancy.

If chronic Q fever is suspected, specialist guidance should be sought.[55]

Prevention: Education of farming communities about sources of infection, hygiene measures and safe disposal of birth products.

Case reporting and surveillance to enable identification and containment of outbreaks.

There is currently no licensed vaccine in the UK.

Ringworm

Organism: *Trichophyton mentagrophytes* and *Trichophyton verrucosum*, which affect cattle and horses, and *Microsporum canis*, which affects dogs and cats. Microsporum fluoresces under Wood's lamp, but *Trichophyton* species do not.

Incubation period: 1–3 weeks.

Clinical: Starts as a small papule which slowly extends with central healing to become an enlarging ring with an active raised edge and normal central skin. Kerion, a more severe variant, causes a boggy, raised, suppurating lesion.

Diagnosis is confirmed by microscopy of skin scrapings.

Treatment is with a topical imidazole cream such as clotrimazole or miconazole. Improvement usually occurs within one week and cure within one month.

Widespread or refractory cases, kerion and those involving the scalp may require systemic antifungal treatment.

Secondary infection may occur, particularly in cases of kerion, and require systemic antibiotics.

Tetanus (Notifiable Disease in the UK)

Organism: *Clostridium tetani* grows anaerobically and produces a neurotoxin (tetanospasmin).

Transmission. Spores can survive for long periods and enter through wounds from contaminated soil, dust and animal (especially horse) or human faeces. Transmission can also occur during injecting drug misuse.

Incubation: Usually 3–31 days (range 1 day to several months).

Incidence: Although tetanus is preventable by immunisation, it causes an estimated 57,000 deaths annually worldwide.[56] Neonatal tetanus, caused by infection of the umbilical stump, remains an important disease in low- and middle-income countries, accounting for approximately half of cases worldwide. Tetanus is a much rarer disease in high-income countries, with fewer than ten cases per year in England and Wales. Adults, particularly over 65s who are most likely to be under-immunised, are most at risk.[57]

Clinical: Primarily a clinical diagnosis. Four forms are described.

Generalised tetanus (80% of cases) is an acute illness with at least two of:

- Trismus (painful muscular contractions, primarily of the masseter and neck muscles, leading to facial spasms)
- Painful muscular contractions of trunk muscles
- Generalised spasms with opisthotonos (backward arching of the head, neck and spine)[57]

Localised tetanus (uncommon) causes painful muscle spasms restricted to the site of injury. It may be self-limiting or progress to generalised tetanus.

Cephalic tetanus (uncommon). Following head injury or otitis media cranial nerve palsies are seen prior to progression to generalised tetanus if untreated.

Neonatal tetanus follows umbilical stump infection. Clinical features include rigidity with spasms, inability to suck, grimacing and irritability.

Diagnosis. Laboratory tests support a clinical diagnosis. Treatment should never be delayed while a test result is awaited.

Available investigations (in order of sensitivity) are PCR or culture detection of *C. tetani* in wound material, detection of toxin in serum and detection of IgG against tetanus toxoid in serum. Their sensitivity is relatively poor. A negative result should not be used to exclude a diagnosis of tetanus.[57]

Treatment involves the prevention of toxin uptake, control of muscle spasms and supportive care for autonomic instability. Intensive care unit admission is commonly required.

Because tetanus neurotoxin binds irreversibly to the neuromuscular junction, intravenous immunoglobulin (IVIG) treatment must be given without delay.

Wounds should be cleaned and debrided to remove organisms and promote an aerobic environment.

Antibiotic choice should be guided by a specialist microbiology service. Benzylpenicillin and metronidazole are commonly used.

Diazepam helps to relieve muscle spasms but, in more severe cases, the patient is paralysed and ventilated.

Prior infection does not confer ongoing immunity, so tetanus immunisation should also be carried out.[57]

Prevention: In the UK, all children should be immunised routinely in the first year of life. A primary course of three injections of tetanus vaccine at monthly intervals over three months is followed by two booster vaccines, one at five years after primary vaccination followed by a further dose after an interval of a further ten years. Full immunisation is considered to provide satisfactory long-term protection.

Wound management: Tetanus-prone and high-risk wounds should be cleaned thoroughly, with surgical debridement where indicated.

Immediate administration of a reinforcing dose of tetanus vaccine, prophylactic treatment with intramuscular tetanus immunoglobulin (IM-TIG) and prophylactic antibiotic treatment (for example, metronidazole, benzylpenicillin or co-amoxiclav) should be considered, guided by wound risk, vaccination status and time since last vaccination. Current UK guidance is summarised at https://cks.nice.org.uk/topics/lacerations/management/laceration-high-infection-risk/.

Tetanus-prone and high-risk wounds:[57]

- Puncture-type injuries acquired in a contaminated environment (e.g. gardening injuries)
- Wounds containing foreign bodies such as splinters
- Compound fractures
- Wounds or burns with systemic sepsis
- Bites and scratches from animals that have been rooting in soil or in an agricultural setting
- Heavy contamination with material likely to contain tetanus spores (for example, soil, manure)
- Wounds or burns with extensive devitalised tissue
- Wounds or burns with surgical intervention delayed for more than six hours, even if contamination was not heavy

This list is not exhaustive. Individual risk assessment is recommended.[57]

Toxoplasmosis

Organism: *Toxoplasma gondii*.

Transmission: Cats are the normal host for *Toxoplasma gondii*, but intermediate hosts include sheep, goats, rodents, swine, cattle and chickens. Infection may also be acquired from raw or undercooked meat, particularly pork and mutton containing toxoplasma cysts, or from food or water contaminated with cat faeces.[29] Oocytes remain viable for several months.

Occupational exposure includes infected sheep, particularly during lambing; workers in contact with cats or cat faeces; and those who work with other infected animals or their materials.[32]

There is no evidence of person-to-person transmission, except from pregnant mother to foetus. Antibodies persist for many years.

Incubation period: 5–23 days.

Incidence: There were 298 laboratory confirmed cases in England and Wales in 2017.[29]

Clinical: Infection may be asymptomatic. Like infectious mononucleosis, toxoplasmosis can present with lymphadenopathy, maculopapular rash, fever and lymphocytosis, persisting for days or weeks. As the illness subsides, cysts containing viable organisms may remain in the tissues, reactivating later if the immune system becomes compromised.

Rare but serious or potentially life-threatening consequences include retinochoroiditis, myocarditis and encephalitis (particularly resulting from reactivation of latent infection in patients with HIV/ AIDS).[58] Infection during pregnancy (particularly during the first trimester) can lead to stillbirth, miscarriage, visual impairment and brain damage.[32]

Diagnosis is by detection of blood antibodies.

Prevention and treatment: Washing fruit and vegetables, avoiding raw or undercooked meat and handwashing after gardening or handling cats, particularly important for pregnant women and the immunocompromised people, who should also avoid contact with sheep and lambs during the lambing season.[58]

Treatment is not usually necessary for a healthy person. For severe cases such as toxoplasma encephalitis, specialist referral should be made.[58]

DERMATOLOGICAL CONDITIONS

Irritant contact dermatitis results from exposure to irritants including cold, damp, friction, plants, chemical agents and animal waste.

Allergic contact dermatitis is caused by an immune response. Those more common rurally include pesticides, rubber accelerants (found in protective equipment such as gloves, face masks, ear defenders, work boots and agricultural fungicides and pesticides) pollens, and the plant group Compositae.

Phytophotodermatitis

A skin reaction to naturally occurring chemicals in the sap of wild flowers such as rue, hogweed, parsley, parsnips, celery and carrot, followed by exposure to UVA radiation in sunlight.

Twenty-four to forty-eight hours after exposure, irritation and erythema develop in exposed areas, classically the hands, arms and lower legs, often with blistering and sometimes with ulceration. Healing can take several weeks.

Persistent post-inflammatory hyperpigmentation can occur.

At-risk activities are diverse. They include strimming, with splattering of vegetation to the face, neck and other exposed skin, and children making peashooters from hollow stems, contaminating their lips.

Treatment is with cool compresses and topical steroids with analgesia, if required.

Prevention is through avoidance and the use of appropriate personal protective clothing.

If sap exposure is identified prior to UVA exposure, sunscreen with high UVA protection and skin protection with clothing may reduce the severity of the reaction.

REFERENCES

1. Sharma H, Meredith AD. A report of 18 blackthorn injuries of the upper limb. *Injury.* 2004;35(9):930–5.
2. Kelly JJ. Blackthorn inflammation. *J Bone Jt Surg.* 1966;48B(3):474–7.
3. Public Health Wales. Blue-Green Algae—Public Health Wales [Internet]. https://phw.nhs.wales/services-and-teams/environmental-public-health/blue-green-algae/ [Accessed 7 January 2022].
4. Leftley JW, Hannah F. A literature review of the potential health effects of marine microalgae and macroalgae. Bristol: Environment Agency, 2009, 79 p.
5. Imray C, Grieve A, Dhillon S. Cold damage to the extremities: Frostbite and non-freezing cold injuries. Postgrad Med J. 2009;85(1007):481.

6. Imray CHE, Richards P, Greeves J, Castellani JW. Nonfreezing cold-induced injuries. J R Army Med Corps. 2011;157(1):79–84.
7. Van Demark RE, Hofer KL, Tjarks BJ, Hayes M, Becker HA, Anderson MC. Accidental pig vaccine injection injury. J Hand Surg Glob Online. 2019;1(4):236–9.
8. O'Neill JK, Richards SW, Ricketts DM, Patterson MH. The effects of injection of bovine vaccine into a human digit: A case report. Environ Health. 2005;4(1):21.
9. National Institute for Clinical Excellence. Insect bites and stings—Treatment [Internet]. nhs.uk. 2019. www.nhs.uk/conditions/insect-bites-and-stings/treatment/ [Accessed 31 December 2021].
10. Resuscitation Council UK Guidance: Anaphylaxis [Internet]. Resuscitation Council UK. www.resus.org.uk/library/additional-guidance/guidance-anaphylaxis [Accessed 31 December 2021].
11. National Institute for Clinical Excellence. Anaphylaxis with or without angio-oedema Management Guidance [Internet]. https://cks.nice.org.uk/topics/angio-oedema-anaphylaxis/management/anaphylaxis-with-or-without-angio-oedema/ [Accessed 31 December 2021].
12. Krishna MT, Ewan PW, Diwakar L, Durham SR, Frew AJ, Leech SC, et al. Diagnosis and management of hymenoptera venom allergy: British Society for Allergy and Clinical Immunology (BSACI) guidelines: BSACI venom allergy guidelines. Clin Exp Allergy. 2011;41(9):1201–20.
13. Diaz JH. Chemical and plant-based insect repellents: Efficacy, safety, and toxicity. Wilderness Environ Med. 2016;27(1):153–63.
14. National Institute for Clinical Excellence. Insect bites and stings: Antimicrobial prescribing | Guidance | NICE [Internet]. NICE. www.nice.org.uk/guidance/ng182 [Accessed 31 December 2021].
15. Coulson JM, Cooper G, Krishna C, Thompson JP. Snakebite enquiries to the UK National Poisons Information Service: 2004–2010. Emerg Med J. 2013;30(11):932–4.
16. Warrell DA. Treatment of bites by adders and exotic venomous snakes. BMJ. 2005;331(7527):1244–7.
17. Reading CJ. Incidence, pathology, and treatment of adder (Vipera berus L.) bites in man. Emerg Med J. 1996;13(5):346–51.
18. Lamb T, Stewart D, Warrell DA, Lalloo DG, Jagpal P, Jones D, et al. Moderate-to-severe Vipera berus envenoming requiring ViperaTAb antivenom therapy in the UK. Clin Toxicol. 2021;59(11):992–1001.
19. Wyatt JP, Taylor RG, Wit K de, Hotton EJ, Illingworth RJ, Robertson CE. Toxicology [Internet]. Oxford Handbook of Emergency Medicine. Oxford: Oxford University Press. https://oxfordmedicine.com/view/10.1093/med/9780198784197.001.0001/med-9780198784197-chapter-4 [Accessed 30 November 2021].
20. Rosenstock L, Keifer M. Chronic central nervous system effects of acute organophosphate pesticide intoxication. Lancet. 1991;338(8761):223.

21. Stephens R, Spurgeon A, Calvert IA, Beach J, Levy LS, Harrington JM, et al. Neuropsychological effects of long-term exposure to organophosphates in sheep dip. Lancet. 1995;345(8958):1135–9.
22. Roldán-Tapia L, Parrón T, Sánchez-Santed F. Neuropsychological effects of long-term exposure to organophosphate pesticides. Neurotoxicol Teratol. 2005;27(2):259–66.
23. Mearns J, Dunn J, Lees-Haley PR. Psychological effects of organophosphate pesticides: A review and call for research by psychologists. J Clin Psychol. 1994;50(2):286–94.
24. Cushen B, Sulaiman I, Donoghue N, Langan D, Cahill T, Nic Dhonncha E, et al. High prevalence of obstructive lung disease in non-smoking farmers: The Irish farmers lung health study. Respir Med. 2016;115:13–9.
25. Ohtsuka Y, Munakata M, Tanimura K, Ukita H, Kusaka H, Masaki Y, et al. Smoking promotes insidious and chronic farmer's lung disease, and deteriorates the clinical outcome. Intern Med. 1995;34(10):966–71.
26. Seifert SA, Essen SV, Jacobitz K, Crouch R, Lintner CP. Organic dust toxic syndrome: A review. J Toxicol Clin Toxicol. 2003;41(2):185–93.
27. Thomas DR, Salmon RL, Coleman TJ, Morgan-Capner P, Sillis M, Caul EO, et al. Occupational exposure to animals and risk of zoonotic illness in a cohort of farmers, farmworkers, and their families in England. J Agric Saf Health. 1999;5(4):373–82.
28. National Institute for Clinical Excellence. BNF: British National Formulary— NICE [Internet]. NICE. https://bnf.nice.org.uk/treatment-summary/anthrax. html [Accessed 22 December 2021].
29. Public Health England. UK zoonoses report 2017 [Internet], 2017. https:// assets.publishing.service.gov.uk/government/uploads/system/uploads/ attachment_data/file/918089/UK_Zoonoses_report_2017.pdf [Accessed 16 December 2021].
30. Brunetti E, Kern P, Vuitton DA. Expert consensus for the diagnosis and treatment of cystic and alveolar echinococcosis in humans. Acta Trop. 2010;114(1):1–16.
31. Wang Q, Chang BJ, Riley TV. Erysipelothrix rhusiopathiae. Vet Microbiol. 2010;140(3):405–17.
32. UK Health and Safety Executive. Zoonoses—UK HSE guidance [Internet]. www.hse.gov.uk/agriculture/topics/zoonoses.htm [Accessed 28 December 2021].
33. White GM. Diseases of the skin: A colour atlas and text. 2nd ed. London: Mosby, 2005.
34. Nichols GL, Richardson JF, Sheppard SK, Lane C, Sarran C. Campylobacter epidemiology: A descriptive study reviewing 1 million cases in England and Wales between 1989 and 2011. BMJ Open. 2012;2(4):e001179.
35. Public Health England. Shiga toxin-producing Escherichia coli (STEC) data: 2018 [Internet]. Gov.UK. www.gov.uk/government/publications/escherichia- coli-e-coli-o157-annual-totals/shiga-toxin-producing-escherichia-coli-stec- data-2018 [Accessed 23 December 2021].

36. UK Health Security Agency. Salmonella: Guidance, data and analysis [Internet]. Gov.uk. www.gov.uk/government/collections/salmonella-guidance-data-and-analysis [Accessed 23 December 2021].

37. UK Health Security Agency. Common animal-associated infections (England and Wales): Third quarter 2021 [Internet].Gov.uk. www.gov.uk/government/publications/common-animal-associated-infections-2021 [Accessed 28 December 2021].

38. Office for National Statistics. Deaths registered in England and Wales—21st century mortality—Office for National Statistics [Internet]. www.ons.gov.uk/peoplepopulationandcommunity/birthsdeathsandmarriages/deaths/datasets/the21stcenturymortalityfilesdeathsdataset [Accessed 28 December 2021].

39. Forbes AE, Zochowski WJ, Dubrey SW, Sivaprakasam V. Leptospirosis and Weil's disease in the UK. QJM. 2012;105(12):1151–62.

40. Senavirathna I, Rathish D, Agampodi S. Cytokine response in human leptospirosis with different clinical outcomes: A systematic review. BMC Infect Dis. 2020;20(1):268.

41. Brett Major DM, Coldren R. Antibiotics for leptospirosis. Cochrane Database Syst Rev [Internet]. 2012;(2). www.cochranelibrary.com/cdsr/doi/10.1002/14651858.CD008264.pub2/full [Accessed 28 December 2021].

42. Public Health England. Lyme disease epidemiology and surveillance [Internet]. Gov.uk. www.gov.uk/government/publications/lyme-borreliosis-epidemiology [Accessed 1 January 2022].

43. Stanek G, Wormser GP, Gray J, Strle F. Lyme borreliosis. Lancet. 2012;379(9814):461–73.

44. Razai MS, Doerholt K, Galiza E, Oakeshott P. Tick bite. BMJ. 2020;370:m3029.

45. National Institute for Clinical Excellence. NICE Guidance—Lyme disease [Internet]. NICE. www.nice.org.uk/guidance/ng95/chapter/recommendations#clinical-assessment [Accessed 1 January 2022].

46. Halperin JJ. Lyme disease: An evidence-based approach. Second edition. Lyme disease : An evidence-based approach. Wallingford, Oxfordshire: CABI, 2018.

47. Gandhi JS. Re: William Osler: A life in medicine. 14 December 2021. www.bmj.com/content/321/7268/1087.2/rr/760724 [Accessed 28 December 2021].

48. Parker NR, Barralet JH, Bell AM. Q fever. Lancet. 2006;367(9511):679–88.

49. Cutler SJ, Bouzid M, Cutler RR. Q fever. J Infect. 2007;54(4):313–8.

50. Maurin M, Raoult D. Q fever. Clin Microbiol Rev. 1999;12(4):518–53.

51. Halsby KD, Kirkbride H, Walsh AL, Okereke E, Brooks T, Donati M, et al. The epidemiology of Q fever in England and Wales 2000–2015. Vet Sci. 2017;4(2):28.

52. Cutler SJ, Paiba GA, Howells J, Morgan KL. Q fever—a forgotten disease? Lancet Infect Dis. 2002;2(12):717–8.

53. Ledina D, Bradarić N, Milas I, Ivić I, Brnčić N, Kuzmicić N. Chronic fatigue syndrome after Q fever. Med Sci Monit. 2007;13(7):CS88–92.

54. Raoult D, Fenollar F, Stein A. Q fever during pregnancy: Diagnosis, treatment, and follow-up. Arch Intern Med 1960. 2002;162(6):701.

55. Kersh GJ. Antimicrobial therapies for Q fever. Expert Rev Anti Infect Ther. 2013;11(11):1207–14.
56. Yen LM, Thwaites CL. Tetanus. *Lancet.* 2019;393(10181):1657–68.
57. Public Health England. Tetanus: Guidance on the management of suspected tetanus cases and on the assessment and management of tetanus prone wounds [Internet]. Gov.uk. www.gov.uk/government/publications/tetanus-advice-for-health-professionals [Accessed 2022 Jan 7].
58. Furtado J, Smith J, Belfort R, Gattey D, Winthrop K. Toxoplasmosis: A global threat. J Glob Infect Dis. 2011;3(3):281.

CHAPTER 5

Rural Mental Health

....

Andrew Brittlebank

It is widely recognised that providing care for people who have problems with their mental health is a major part of the work of modern primary care. According to the Royal College of General Practitioners of the UK, this consists of several elements:

- The diagnosis, investigation and management of mental health conditions, including making appropriate referrals
- Communicating effectively, professionally and sensitively with patients, relatives and carers
- Assessing risk to make the patient's safety and the safety of others a priority
- Coordinating care with other organisations and professionals, including the appropriate use of mental health and capacity legislation
- Avoiding diagnostic overshadowing and offering advice and support for patients, relatives and carers regarding mental and physical multimorbidity

DIAGNOSIS OF MENTAL HEALTH CONDITIONS IN RURAL POPULATIONS

Although the core features and diagnostic criteria of the major mental disorders are not affected by rurality, there may be important differences in the way that people present with mental illness in a rural context. Variations in the prevalence of some disorders can lead to a lack of familiarity with

DOI: 10.1201/9781003302438-10

those conditions. Preconceptions about the prevalence of some problems or differences in the ways they present, particularly substance use, can cause them to be under-recognised.

Traditional models of psychiatric diagnosis and classification do not translate well to primary care settings,[1] and overlapping combinations of anxiety, depression, somatization and substance misuse present challenges for diagnostic decision making. Traditional psychiatric diagnostic classification systems emphasise the identification of positive psychotic phenomena such as hallucinations and delusions. In practice, however, many people with early psychosis present with non-specific symptoms such as mood change, social withdrawal and anxiety, often in the context of substance misuse. These issues are also encountered in rural primary care, but with nuances.

Epidemiological studies that have compared the prevalence of mental illness in urban and rural areas have generally been inconsistent in their findings.[2] This may be due to methodological issues, such as using mental health service utilisation as a proxy measure of morbidity or failure to control for confounding variables, such as employment or poverty.[3] Within this, one recurring finding has been that the prevalence of severe psychotic illnesses, especially schizophrenia, is lower in rural areas than in urban settings. This may be at least in part explained by the 'urban drift' hypothesis whereby, as a consequence of the disorder, persons with schizophrenia 'drift' towards more urban areas.[4] More recent findings have demonstrated that rurality may be associated with worse outcomes for people with schizophrenia.[5] It is currently unclear why this might be the case, but it is suggested that differences in treatment practice or aetiology may account for this variation. Notwithstanding, there is an indication that the prevalence of other mental health challenges, including depression, anxiety and substance misuse problems, is probably no less in rural areas. The prevalence of learning disability is probably higher in rural communities.[6]

While wider society may be becoming more accepting of mental illness, the experience of many people who live with mental illness is that attitudes encountered in the rural population may be stigmatising and judgemental.[3, 7]

These attitudes can affect the way that people who have more common mental illnesses present. In rural populations, symptoms such as anxiety and low mood are more likely to be attributed to social factors than to mental illness.[3] This increases the challenge to primary care workers to correctly identify the nature of a problem and help the patient make the most appropriate informed choices around treatment.

Attitudes of shame and stigmatisation about severe mental illnesses as well as their lower prevalence in rural areas may combine to make such diagnoses and their management more challenging for the primary care practitioner.

There may be a misconception that substance misuse problems are confined to deprived urban areas; a survey of urban and rural Scottish youth found there to be no difference.[8]

Tips for the Rural Practitioner

- Have a low threshold for enquiry about psycho-social aspects.
- Be alert to clues about substance misuse, not just alcohol, and be aware that there are drug problems in rural areas.
- Be alert to the possibility of psychosis in a young person who presents with behavioural and mood changes.
- Often, this person will be returning to the family home: for example, a student returning early from college or university because of mental health issues.

ASSESSING RISK

It is often suggested that suicide rates in rural populations are higher than elsewhere, but it is unclear whether this is actually the case for the rural population overall. What is clear is that risk is higher for some groups, particularly males in certain rural occupations such as farming.[2] The more ready access to violent means such as firearms, agricultural chemicals, machinery and rope for making ligatures, together with the tendency for farmers to not seek help for psychological problems,[9] means that the risk of completed suicide is increased. There is increasing recognition that being perceived as 'different' in a rural community, for example by being gay, can also increase a person's risk.[7]

Despite being on the 'front line' of suicide prevention, primary care staff often have limited training in this area.[1] Health professional education can reduce shame and stigma associated with disclosing suicidal thoughts and feelings,[10] and it is of value to tailor such training to reflect the needs of rural primary care.

Charitable organisations such as the National Suicide Prevention Alliance in England and the Scottish Association for Mental Health, alongside local government and NHS bodies, advocate community-based public health approaches that link clinical teams with community resources such as 'suicide safer' communities—partnerships of organisations, including statutory agencies, third sector and faith groups—and, in rural settings, the National Farmers' Union (NFU). The close-knit nature of some rural communities may facilitate this, but support cannot be taken for granted. Success of such projects may require the disproportionate input of a very limited number of individuals when compared to similar projects in larger communities. Public Health Scotland has produced a helpful suite of tools to help prevent suicide in rural areas by emphasising a whole-system approach to developing a local strategy to reduce suicide in a rural community.[11]

COORDINATING CARE

Rurality is frequently associated with remoteness from metropolitan areas where most specialised mental health services are located, resulting in reduced access to support and services. People in rural areas are less likely to use specialised mental health services, but this is only partly explained by rural differences in morbidity.[3]

A survey of people living with mental health challenges in rural Scotland found that while perception of remoteness may not always coincide with geographical measures of remoteness, the lack of access to transport was seen by many as a major impediment to their managing their mental health.[12] Most worryingly, the impediment was greatest among people who reported having suicidal thoughts or engaged in self-harming behaviours.

The relational and support implications of living in small communities can also create issues, especially if members of the primary care team live in the same community. The experience of people living with mental health challenges in rural communities is mixed.[12, 13] There is no doubt that there are benefits in terms of social connection to living in small, close-knit communities. But this can have drawbacks, especially if a person experiences their community to be judgemental about mental illness.

Tips for the Rural Practitioner

- Be particularly alert to sensitivities about privacy and boundary issues.
- Be sensitive to the needs of those who may feel they are 'different' in a rural community, particularly those who identify as LGBT+.
- Take opportunities to work with the primary care team and wider community to address stigma through education.
- Hosting mental health clinics in practice premises helps patients in rural areas gain access to specialist expertise and promote joint working, but thought must be given to how the patient's privacy can be protected.

- Prominent displays of information about mental health issues and strong links to community well-being groups can go some way to overcoming stigma and shame.

Challenging behaviours associated with an exacerbation, for example of psychosis or hypomania, can be extremely public and have a long-lasting social impact, including isolation and estrangement in some circumstances. Recovery, particularly for those whose relationships have been damaged by their illness, can be disproportionately challenging in rural communities, where the pool of people with whom new connections can be made is smaller and more spread out.

DIAGNOSTIC OVERSHADOWING

There is growing recognition that people living with mental illness have poorer general health than other people. They are likely to have more physical illness, and the presence of mental ill health worsens the outcome of physical illnesses. Life expectancy for people with the more severe forms of mental disorder is reduced by 10–25 years.[14, 15]

Much of this 'mortality gap' is explained by the increased incidence of preventable physical illness, such as heart disease and chronic lung disease, the experience of which is not significantly affected by location. The continuity and longitudinal relationship-building advantages of care delivered by the smaller primary care teams seen in rural locations may be used as an opportunity to achieve better outcomes for this vulnerable group of patients.

Recommendations for Further Reading

Gask L, Kendrick T, Peveler R, Chew-Graham C. *Primary care mental health.* 2nd ed. Cambridge: Cambridge University Press, 2018.[1]

REFERENCES

1. Gask L, Kendrick T, Peveler R, Chew-Graham C. *Primary care mental health* 2nd ed. Cambridge: Cambridge University Press, 2018.
2. Gregoire A. The mental health of farmers. *Occup Med (Oxford).* 2002;52(8):471–6.
3. Nicholson LA. Rural mental health. Advances in psychiatric treatment. *Royal Col Psychiat J Cont Prof Devel.* 2008;14(4):302–11.
4. Goldberg EM, Morrison SL. Schizophrenia and social class. *Br J Psych.* 1963;109(463):785–802.

5. Wimberley T, Pedersen CB, MacCabe JH, Støvring H, Astrup A, Sørensen HJ, et al. Inverse association between urbanicity and treatment resistance in schizophrenia. *Schizophrenia Res.* 2016;174(1–3):150–5.
6. Wellesley DG, Hockey KA, Montgomery PD, Stanley FJ. Prevalence of intellectual handicap in Western Australia: A community study. *Med J Aus.* 1992;156(2):94–102.
7. Cohn TJ, Hastings SL. Resilience among rural lesbian youth. *J Les Stud.* 2010;14(1):71–9.
8. Forsyth AJM, Barnard M. Contrasting levels of adolescent drug use between adjacent urban and rural communities in Scotland. *Addiction (Abingdon, England).* 1999;94(11):1707–18.
9. Booth N, Briscoe M, Powell R. Suicide in the farming community: Methods used and contact with health services. *Occupat Environ Med (London, England).* 2000;57(9):642–4.
10. Mann JJ, Apter A, Bertolote J, Beautrais A, Currier D, Haas A, et al. Suicide prevention strategies: A systematic review. *JAMA.* 2005;294(16):2064–74.
11. National Guide on Suicide Prevention in Rural Areas [Internet]. www. healthscotland.com/documents/21002.aspx [Accessed 2 April 2022].
12. Skerratt S, Meador J, Spencer M. National rural mental health survey Scotland: Report of key findings [Internet], 2017. https://ruralwellbeing.org/ [Accessed 28 March 2022].
13. Aisbett DL, Boyd CP, Francis KJ, Newnham K, Newnham K. Understanding barriers to mental health service utilization for adolescents in rural Australia. *Rur Remote Heal.* 2007;7(1):624.
14. Holt RI, Hind D, Gossage-Worrall R, Bradburn MJ, Saxon D, McCrone P, et al. Structured lifestyle education to support weight loss for people with schizophrenia, schizoaffective disorder and first episode psychosis: The STEPWISE RCT. *Health Technol Assess.* 2018;22(65):1–160.
15. Fiorillo A, Sartorius N. Mortality gap and physical comorbidity of people with severe mental disorders: The public health scandal. *Ann Gen Psychiatry.* 2021;20(1):1–5.

CHAPTER 6

Animal Diseases

....

Neil Frame

INTRODUCTION

An understanding of patients' occupations helps health workers not only appreciate health needs but also 'speak the same language'. There is considerable overlap between veterinary medicine and human medicine. This chapter describes animal husbandry and some common diseases and lay terms commonly used by patients in GPs' consulting rooms.

Some diseases, e.g. zoonoses, may have a direct effect on patients' health. Others, e.g. foot and mouth disease (FMD) in 2001 and tuberculosis (TB) in cattle, affect patients' mental well-being through compulsory slaughter policies, the loss of genetically irreplaceable stock and dire financial consequences.

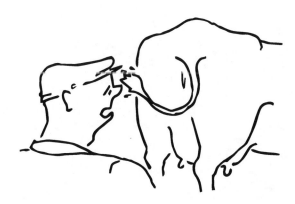

DOI: 10.1201/9781003302438-11

In the UK in 2020, there were approximately 9.5 million cattle, 15 million sheep and 4.5 million pigs. There were 300,000 farmers and farm workers, a number that has nearly halved in the last 30 years due to intensification, lower animal numbers and difficulty enticing young workers into a career with a reputation for long hours and low financial reward.

Farmers are under pressure as never before: ensuring succession on the farm (the average age of the UK farm owner in 2020 was 59 years), trying to plan ahead without knowing post-Brexit what subsidies will be paid, the pressure from supermarkets to drive down prices leading to further intensification and lowering of welfare standards and environmental pressures towards 're-wilding'.

Most animal diseases are predisposed by poor knowledge, poor management and intensive farming methods. Early identification and diagnosis and owner co-operation are crucial to success.

SHEEP

Sheep are reared mainly for their fleece (wool) and meat (mutton and lamb), although there are increasing numbers of milking flocks where, like dairy cattle, the production of offspring is a means to milk production.

Sheep farms are categorised according to their height above sea level into lowland, upland or hill farms. Sheep are bred to suit the terrain and altitude at which they are kept. Hill breeds such as Scottish Blackface, Swaledale and Herdwick are extremely hardy, and their ewes are attentive mothers. Ewes may be crossed with lowland tups such as Cheviot or Border Leicester to produce more fertile and productive offspring. Young female lambs (gimmers) are sold to upland farms for breeding. Breeds such as Suffolk and Texel, which are less robust but which have good feed conversion, are kept on lowland farms.

Tups (male breeding sheep) are turned out with ewes and hoggs (females in their first breeding season) in the autumn when decreasing hours of daylight stimulate ewes to ovulate. The ewes are turned onto better grass to help stimulate ovulation. 'Sponging' the ewes (pre-tupping with progesterone vaginal implants) or running 'teasers' (vasectomised tups) with the ewes prior to tupping also stimulate ovulation and help ensure a tight lambing period. The majority of the ewes should conceive within six weeks (i.e. two oestrus cycles). Coloured 'raddle' dyes may be applied to the tups' briskets (chests) directly or by a harness to mark the ewes they have served. The dye colour is changed regularly so that the farmer can predict the lambing date.

The gestation period is five months. Twinning is desirable, except in hill flocks where there may be insufficient food to raise two lambs. Triplets require excellent husbandry and much labour to ensure their survival. They account for 15% of lambs but 45% of neonatal mortality in the UK.

Abortion ('throw') is endemic in many sheep flocks. The most common causes of enzootic abortion of ewes (EAE) are *Toxoplasma gondii* and *Chlamydia psittaci*. Both are dangerous to pregnant women. Amniotic fluid contains a heavy burden of contagious organisms, which readily vaporise from a drying fleece. Despite increasing awareness of the dangers to pregnant women of involvement with sheep around lambing time, it is still not unusual to find premature newborn lambs being warmed in the farm kitchen.

Both toxoplasma and chlamydia attack the placenta rather than the ewe or foetus. Lambs may be born alive but weak or premature. Vaccines against these organisms are available and effective. Listeria monocytogenes, *Salmonella* spp (particularly *typhimurium* and *dublin*) and *Campylobacter* spp may also cause ovine abortion.[1]

Lambing, a period of concentrated activity on the farm, may occur indoors or outdoors, depending on the time of year. Lowland farms may aim to lamb around Christmas while hill farms commonly lamb in April.

Caesarean section may be necessary because of foeto-maternal oversize or incomplete dilation of the cervix (ringwomb).

Unlike humans, domestic animals confer little immunity through the placenta, immunoglobulins being instead absorbed from the colostrum. The neonate lamb is most capable of such absorption during the first four hours of life; therefore, it is imperative to ensure that small, weak lambs receive adequate colostrum soon after birth. Newborn lambs are particularly susceptible to disease if colostral uptake is poor.

E. coli septicaemia in lambs under 72 hours of age becomes more prevalent at the end of the lambing season with increasing faecal contamination of the lambing shed or pasture. 'Watery-mouth', 'rattle-belly' and 'lamb scour' (diarrhoea) are all descriptive lay terms for the symptoms. Most shepherds are skilled at administering intraperitoneal glucose to hypoglycaemic ('starved') lambs and oral electrolyte therapy for diarrhoea.

Gram positive bacteria (especially *A. pyogenes*) can enter via the navel (navel-ill), causing infective arthritis (joint-ill). Joint cartilage is a predilection site for such bacteria.[2]

During late pregnancy, pregnant ewes may exhibit neurological symptoms caused by pregnancy toxaemia (twin-lamb disease). In lowland breeds, this is invariably complicated by fatty liver syndrome.

Other common neurological diseases include:

- Scrapie, the ovine equivalent of CJD in humans and BSE in cattle
- 'Staggers', a descriptive term for magnesium deficiency
- Listeria, a soil-borne organism ingested by sheep and cattle from big bale silage, which can cause abortion and meningitis (circling disease)
- 'Gid' or 'sturdy' and parasitic (coenurus) cyst in the brain
- Hypocalcaemia ('milk fever'), which results in progressive ataxia and recumbency[3]

Some dermatological conditions such as sheep scab, caused by the mite *psoroptes ovis*, cause such intense pruritus that they may be mistaken for a neurological condition.

Despite the availability of an excellent vaccine, orf, a *poxvirus*, is still prevalent in sheep and, therefore, in sheep farmers and their families.

PIGS

Most of Britain's pig rearing takes place indoors in intensive farming systems. However, recent much-needed welfare legislation and concerns about endemic diseases are leading many farmers to return to outdoor breeding. Outdoor arcs for hardier breeds of pigs (which 25 years ago had almost become obsolete), where a sow and her piglets stay in a loose family group until weaning, are becoming more common again.

Artificial insemination is not used to the same extent as it is in the dairy industry. Pig farmers determine whether a sow is in season by leaning on its back. If the sow will 'brim' or 'stand' for the farmer, she should do the same for the boar.

With a gestation period of three months, three weeks and three days, a sow can produce two litters each year. Thirteen to eighteen piglets are born at approximately five-minute intervals. Within seconds of birth, the newborn piglets stand and walk towards the sow's udder (or an artificial heat source).

Although parturition is usually an uncomplicated procedure, particularly in fitter outdoor breeds, birthing problems can include vaginal or uterine prolapse and metritis-mastitis-agalactiae syndrome or 'farrowing fever', a rapidly developing, life-threatening septicaemia. Treatment must be prompt to save the sow.

Diseases of the newborn, such as *E. coli* enteritis and septicaemia and streptococcal meningitis, are common in intensive systems.

Young pigs are intelligent, inquisitive creatures. Lack of environmental stimulation can lead to behavioural vices such as tail biting.

Problems such as enzootic pneumonia caused by *Mycoplasma hyopneumoniae* are difficult to eliminate. Sometimes it is necessary to cull all the sows and give a house a period of rest. However, even if replacement gilts (young sows) are obtained from so-called 'disease-free status' herds, infections such as enzootic pneumonia often return within a year or two.

Britain is currently free of classical swine fever, a serious pig disease prevalent in some European countries. It will have enormous welfare and economic significance if it finds its way into British herds.

CATTLE

Cattle in Britain are grass-grazed during the summer months and generally loose-housed in cubicles and fed silage in the winter, although there is a depressing trend to house dairy cows throughout the whole year (zero grazing) in ever-increasing group sizes to minimise management costs. This trend originates from supermarkets driving down their costs and consumers' blissful ignorance of the welfare of the animals whose produce they consume. Large amounts of concentrates are fed to dairy cows to boost milk production. Most dairy herds consist of modern Holstein cows, which, at peak yield, produce 50 litres of milk every day and over 10,000 litres during each ten-month lactation.

The bovine gestation period is nine months. In both dairy and beef herds, the farmer's aim is to attain a calving index of 365 days (i.e. a calf born by each cow every twelve months). To achieve this, a cow should conceive 90 days after calving, the optimum interval for maximum milk output and calf production without detriment to the cow. Like sheep and horses, cows ovulate and display oestrus behaviour approximately every 21 days. Rectal palpation or ultrasound 28–32 days post conception can confirm pregnancy. Poor ovulation and absent oestrus behaviour occur commonly when a cow is 'milking off its back' (i.e. its food intake is inadequate for its milk production).

The cow is 'dried off' (i.e. milking is stopped) two months prior to calving. The cow calves, and the cycle begins again. Obstetrical problems include malpresentation or uterine torsion, both of which may be corrected under epidural anaesthesia. Foeto-maternal oversize is managed by caesarean section using a flank approach, preferably under paravertebral anaesthesia with the mother standing.[4]

Introduction of heavily muscled continental bulls to the British beef herd has resulted in significant increases in caesarean sections due to foeto-maternal oversize. This is a welfare issue that is receiving increasing recognition by farmers and consumers.

Viral enteritis ('scour'), commonly caused by a rotavirus or coronavirus, is particularly prevalent in the first 14 days of life and can cause death if fluid and electrolyte therapy is not initiated rapidly.

Other causes of 'scour' include *Cryptosporidium* infection, which is increasingly common in suckler calves and may contaminate human water sources if contaminated slurry is spread on the land; *Salmonella*; and *E. coli* spp. They are also potential zoonoses.

In the autumn and winter, housed calves less than four months of age are particularly susceptible to pneumonia. In dairy calves, pneumonia is usually caused by respiratory syncytial virus (RSV) or para influenza virus (P.I.3). Vaccines against these viruses are used routinely, but the response is variable because of interference from maternal antibodies acquired from colostrum and the weak antigenicity of the vaccine.[5]

Pneumonia in beef calves may be viral but is often bacterial, caused by *Pasteurella haemolytica, Mycoplasma bovis or Haemophilus somnus*.

Copper deficiency during pregnancy causes locomotor problems in the newborn ('swayback') due to lack of myelination of nerve sheaths. Muscular weakness and paresis in calves and lambs may be caused by selenium deficiency ('white muscle disease'). Better understanding of nutrition has made these trace element deficiency diseases much less common.

Parasite diseases in young cattle (e.g. the respiratory disease 'husk' caused by *dictyocaulus viviparus*) have also become less common. However, acquired resistance to anthelmintic therapy is increasing, so this favourable situation may change.

Outbreaks of *trichophyton* ringworm, lice and mange (caused by sarcoptic or psoroptic mites) are usually associated with poor nutrition. 'Ringworm' (fungal skin infection) is not uncommon among farmers. Ticks (*Ixodes ricinus*) are common in parts of the country and may be vectors of disease such as 'louping ill' in sheep (caused by *Cytoecetes phagocytophilia*) and 'tick-borne fever' (caused by *Ehrlichia ovis*). Lyme disease (*Borrelia burgdorferi*) is often unrecognised in domestic animals, perhaps partly due to the lack of the classic skin rash seen in man.

Heifers calve for the first time between 24 and 30 months of age. Unlike sheep flocks, abortion epidemics in cattle are now rare, mainly because of compulsory eradication of *Brucella abortus* ('contagious abortion'). Many herds are routinely vaccinated against other abortogenic agents, e.g. *Leptospira hardjo*. Leptospirosis is a zoonosis passed via the splashing of infected cows' urine in milking parlours to workers.

Hypocalcaemia ('milk fever') in the periparturient period can quickly progress from ataxia through recumbency to death by respiratory failure. Hypomagnesaemia ('grass staggers') can cause cardiac arrest and death even more quickly.

Calving can cause birth tract damage and lead to peritonitis, as can undiagnosed retained foetal membranes. Toxaemic mastitis, usually caused by *E. coli*, can rapidly lead to death in the periparturient period. Treatment must be rapid and intense before the toxins cause lasting organ damage. It is not unusual to have to administer 60–80 litres of intravenous fluid during the first 12 hours of treatment.

Viral diseases can cause high morbidity and serious economic loss.[6] Farmers are familiar with the shortened descriptions of the viruses: for example, infectious bovine rhino-tracheitis (IBR) and bovine viral diarrhoea (BVD). Routine vaccination programmes help control these diseases.[7]

Primary acetonaemia, when milk outstrips energy intake, is known to all as 'slow fever'. Apart from the classic ketone breath, some truly bizarre neurological manifestations can arise which can include obsessional self-licking or roaring like a bull.

Cows and sheep have four stomachs. Conditions of the fourth stomach, the acid-producing abomasum, are inextricably linked to high levels of concentrate feeding and the shorter fibre length of silage compared to hay.[8] The abomasum may displace from its usual right flank position to become entrapped between the left flank and the rumen (first stomach). In the condition, known to farmers as 'twisted stomach', there is no entrapment of blood supply, unlike the less common 'right torsioned abomasum'. Here, the omental attachment of the abomasum tears, allowing rotation. Surgical intervention is corrective in both conditions. Many dairy farms experience several such operations each winter.

Cows eat some 40 kgs of silage plus up to 10 kgs of cereal-based ration ('straights') every day. Under poor management, they are in a constant state of metabolic acidosis and at risk of a variety of conditions ranging from abomasal stomach ulcers to laminitis (an inflammatory process involving the sensitive laminae of the feet).

Many other infectious feet problems (e.g. 'foul of the feet' and 'lure') are predisposed by poor horn growth following laminitis. Dairy cows spend most of their lives walking on concrete and in acidic slurry. Sole ulcers and a foot condition known as digital dermatitis (caused by *Treponema spp.*, found in the slurry) require significant amounts of veterinary intervention.

Many cows are slaughtered because they have chronic feet problems, infertility or recurrent mastitis. However, preventative veterinary medicine programmes have made enormous progress in minimising these chronic problems.

Large-scale epidemics such as bovine spongiform encephalopathy (BSE) in the 1990s and foot and mouth disease (FMD) at the beginning of the century had a devastating effect on farm economics and the farming community. Tuberculosis is a current large-scale problem in cattle. In 2018, 44,656 outwardly healthy cattle were slaughtered as 'reactors', and there were 4,395 new herd 'incidents'. There were 50% more cattle slaughtered in 2018 than in 2005. This may be partly due to more rigorous testing. TB can also be found in other domestic animals: e.g. camelids, sheep, goats, pigs, farm cats and deer. The problem is complex because of the unreliability of routine intra-dermal skin testing, previous reluctance to finance further research into cattle vaccine because of concerns about interference with skin test results, imperfect research behind badger culling and their dubious results and welfare implications and the lack of political will to vaccinate badgers. There was a huge surge in new outbreaks of TB in England after the FMD epidemic in 2001 due to cattle movement associated with restocking.

The lessons of biosecurity painfully learned after FMD seem to have been largely forgotten. Farmers are urged by veterinary surgeons to make more effort to disrupt access by wildlife to cattle feed stores. It is also conjectured that the stress of intensification and production demands as well as concomitant disease may make cattle less resistant to TB.

Jonathan Couch 1789–1870
Polperro, Cornwall

For 60 years, Jonathan Couch was the doctor in Polperro, a small fishing village on the south coast of Cornwall between Fowey and Looe. He became one of Britain's greatest naturalists.

An only child, he was apprenticed to two local doctors before continuing his medical education at Guy's and St Thomas's in London and returning to Polperro in 1810.

While practising medicine, he pursued interests as an apothecary, classicist, historian and illustrator, but more particularly as a natural historian. His major contribution was the study and description of fish. He trained local fishermen to assist him in his observations and recording.

His finest work was the four-volume *A History of the Fishes of the British Isles* (1860–65), with illustrations in colour from his own drawings. He maintained a correspondence with other naturalists and cooperated with Thomas Bewick, William Yarell and Thomas Edward, among others, contributing to publications by both Bewick and Yarell.

He also published numerous papers in scientific journals and wrote articles for more general publications on the habits of British animals, cetaceans and shellfish. His *Cornish Fauna* was completed by his son Richard Quiller Couch in 1844.

He was a local antiquary, recording local words, customs and historical artefacts in his *History of Polperro*, which was published after his death by another son, Thomas Quiller Couch.

Jonathan was a grandfather of the writer Sir Arthur Quiller Couch.

— Philip Evans

POULTRY

Some farms house more than a million birds, and 20 million are slaughtered in the UK every week. Welfare issues are rife, but great strides are being made as the consumer becomes more aware, and large companies respond; 50% of eggs sold are now free range, and 3% are organic.

FISH FARMING

Fish farming takes place predominantly on the west coast of Scotland. Salmon accounts for most of the stock, although trout and other species are increasing. While providing employment and making cheap salmon available to consumers, the industry has attracted much controversy. Numbers of up to 50,000 fish per cage in the early days caused, in some cases, 20% mortality. The industry has improved. but many fish are recorded with fin and tail damage and lens cataracts caused by stress. Sea lice have become a huge problem, and vast amounts of chemicals such as ivermectins can be released into the environment along with escaped fish, carrying disease to the diminishing wild population. Organic waste under the pens also provides an environmental problem.

HORSES

While cattle owners focus on veterinary problems of the feet, udder and genital tract, horse owners' attention is centred largely on wind and limb. This is because horses are largely kept for athletic pursuits, and anything, however slight, adversely affecting oxygen exchange or locomotion can result in poor performance.

Horses, particularly young horses kept in large groups, can be affected by viruses of the upper respiratory tract ('the cough'), but effective vaccines for equine flu virus and equine herpes virus have reduced the incidence greatly. Regular flu vaccination is compulsory for horses racing under Jockey Club rules.

Much attention is paid to the presence of an inspiratory noise ('roaring') while a horse is exercising. This hereditary dysfunction of the left recurrent laryngeal nerve, which leads to paralysis of the left arytenoid cartilage, is common in hunter types. 'Tie back' surgery, replacing the left crico-arytenoid muscle with a prosthetic ligament, is usually successful, although it may cause mild dysphagia.

As many as 10% of Britain's horses are sensitised to the fungal spore *Microsporum faenii* and other small particles such as pollen, leading to the respiratory condition incorrectly known as 'broken-winded'. The term is misleading because, unlike 'farmer's lung' in humans, there is practically no alveolar involvement. The symptoms of coughing and exercise intolerance are due to bronchospasm, goblet cell metaplasia and excess mucus production. The situation is totally reversible.

Most lameness is centred on the distal limb or foot, predisposed by poor foot care, shoeing and conformational problems. Young thoroughbreds are predisposed to osteochondritis dessicans (OCD) lesions, damage to the digital flexor tendons,[9] periostitis of the metacarpus ('bucked shins') and spontaneous fractures of the first and second phalanx ('split pastern') caused by excessive exercise of immature limbs.

Hunter types are predisposed by breed, weight and poor foot care to proliferative and degenerative osteo-arthritic conditions (e.g. 'heel pain syndrome'), a degenerative condition of the navicular (distal sesamoid) bone; 'spavin', a progressive arthritic condition of the inter-tarsal and tarso-metatarsal joints; and 'ringbone', an exuberant arthritis of the inter-phalangeal joints.[10]

As with many humans nowadays, many horses and ponies are over-fed and under-exercised.[11] Native ponies are predisposed by well-meaning over-feeding to laminitis, an extremely painful and life-threatening condition. Excessive carbohydrate intake leads to a rapid build-up of lactic acid in the large bowel, death of gut commensals and severe metabolic acidosis with endotoxaemia. This situation leads to serum exudation at the laminae or 'white line' of the foot. The ensuing pressure can cause permanent damage to the foot ('foundered') with rotation or downward displacement ('sinker') of the pedal bone.

Horses, which are monogastric with fermentation taking place in the large bowel, are prone to bouts of abdominal 'colic' predisposed by the anatomical arrangement of the gut, verminous aneurysms of the mesenteric arteries, poor dentition and feeding. As well as alleviating pain, the veterinarian's task is to quickly differentiate medical from surgical colic, (e.g. intussusception), for which urgent surgery is essential.

Some colics do not involve the bowel. Tears to the broad ligament in the parturient mare, bladder calculi and 'grass sickness', a disease of the autonomic nervous system, are the most common examples.

CONCLUSION

People associated with animals are familiar with birth, life, death, disease, hard work, long hours, invasive veterinary procedures such as caesareans and suffering. This affects the way they regard their own health and mortality and those of their families.

All this combines to help make such people phlegmatic and patient, tolerant and understanding.

A request for medical intervention on their own behalf by farmers, farm workers, farriers, vets and other agricultural workers will rarely be unnecessary or concern anything trivial.

Glossary

BROKEN-WINDED
Misnomer in horses. More correctly known as recurrent airway obstruction (RAO).

BUCKED SHINS
Periostitis of the metacarpal bones in young horses as they adjust to training.

CIRCLING DISEASE
Meningitis in ruminants, usually caused by *Listeria monocytogenes.*

CONTAGIOUS ABORTION
Abortion in cattle caused by brucella abortus. Currently eliminated in the UK.

DRYING OFF
Bringing an end to lactation, usually about two months prior to calving.

E. COLI MASTITIS
Mastitis causing acute endotoxaemia.

FLAT BAG
Sudden drop in milk yield often associated with *Leptospira hardjo.*

FOUL (LURE)
Inter-digital infection in cattle caused by *A. pyogenes.*

FOUNDERED
Anatomical changes in the horse's foot as a sequel to laminitis.

GID (STURDY)
Symptoms in sheep associated with a space-occupying lesion in the brain.

GIMgMER
Young female sheep who has yet to produce a lamb.

GRASS SICKNESS
Autonomic nervous disorder in horses of unknown aetiology, causing often fatal colic-like symptoms.

HEIFER
Female cow who has not yet produced a calf or recently calved her first calf and is lactating.

HOGG
A male or female sheep, older than a lamb but still in its first year.

HUSK
Respiratory disease in young grazing cattle associated with lung worm.

JOINT ILL
Bacterial infection of the joints in young animals.

LAMINITIS
Inflammation of the laminae of a horny foot (e.g. in cows or horses).

LOUPING ILL
A nervous disorder in animals caused by a tick-borne virus.

MILK DROP
Precipitous drop in milk yield, usually associated with *Leptospira hardjo* infection.

MILK FEVER
Nervous symptoms leading to recumbency and eventual death, usually in peri-parturient cows, associated with hypocalcaemia. Easily treated with i/venous calcium borogluconate.

NAVEL ILL
Ingress of bacteria at birth through the umbilicus. May lead to a generalised septicaemia.

NAVICULAR
Degeneration of the distal sesamoid bone in the horse's foot. Now known as 'heel pain syndrome'.

RATTLE-BELLY
Symptom of *E. coli* septicaemia in neo-natal lambs associated with functional pyloric stenosis.

RING-BONE
Proliferative osteo-arthritis involving distal phalangeal bones of horses.

RING-WOMB
Incomplete dilation of the cervix during second-stage labour.

ROARING
Inspiratory noise in horses caused by laryngeal hemiplegia.

SCOUR
Diarrhoea.

SINKER
Displacement of the distal phalynx caused by equine laminitis.

SLOW FEVER
Primary acetonaemia in lactating cows.

SPAVIN
A lay term for pathological change involving the equine tarsus.

SPLIT PASTERN
A fracture of the first or second phalangeal bone in the horse.

SPONGING
Using progesterone-impregnated vaginal implants in sheep to synchronise oestrus.

STAGGERS
Acute neurological signs associated with hypomagnesaemia in ruminants. Rapidly life threatening.

SWAY-BACK
Copper deficiency in ruminants.

TEASERS
Vasectomised male sheep used to help synchronise oestrus in ewes.

THE COUGH
Upper respiratory signs in horses of viral origin, usually influenza or herpes virus.

THROW
Abortion.

TIE-BACK
Corrective surgery for laryngeal hemiplegia.

TUBING
Insertion of intra-mammary drug or the passing of a stomach tube.

TUP
Male breeding sheep.

TWIN LAMB DISEASE
Pregnancy toxaemia in ewes.

TWISTED STOMACH
Displacement requiring correction of the abomasum in ruminants.

WATERY MOUTH
E. coli septicaemia in lambs.

WHITE LINE
Division between horn wall and sole of the foot.

WHITE MUSCLE DISEASE
Muscular dystrophy associated with vitamin E or selenium deficiency.

REFERENCES

1 Drost M, Thomas, GA. Infectious causes of infertility and abortion. In Smith BP (ed.) *Large Animal Internal Medicine*. St. Louis: CV Mosby, 1996, pp. 65–94.
2 Scott PR. *Sheep Medicine*. London: Mason Publishing Ltd, pp. 83–98.
3 Ibid, pp. 169–79.

4   Frame NW. Management of dystocia in cattle: Decision making and management. *In Practice.* 2006; 28: 470–6.

5   Baker JC. Bovine respiratory syncytial virus: Pathogenesis, clinical signs, diagnosis, treatment and prevention. *Compend Contin Educ Vet* 1986; 8: f31–8.

6   Moerman A, Straver PJ, de Jong MCM, Quak J, Baanvinger T, van Oirschot JT. Clinical consequences of a bovine virus diarrhoea virus infection in a dairy herd: A longitudinal study. *Vet Quart* 2011; 16(2): 115–9. https://doi.org/10.1080/01652176.1994.9694430

7   Boehringer Ingelheim Animal Health. National BVD survey 2021, 2021. www.bvdzero.co.uk/blog/bvd-survey-2021.

8   Guard C. Abomasal displacement and volvulus. In Smith BP (ed.) *Large Animal Internal Medicine.* St. Louis: CV Mosby, 1996, p. 792.

9   McIlwraith CW. Osteochondrosis. In Baxter GM (ed.) *Adams and Stashak's Lameness in Horses*, 6th ed. Hoboken, NJ: Wiley, 2011, p. 1155.

10 Baxter GM, ed. *Adams and Stashak's Lameness in Horses*, 6th ed. Hoboken, NJ: Wiley, 2011 pp. 475–535.

11 Furtado T, Christley R, Pinchbeck GL, Perkins L. Exploring horse owners' understanding of obese body condition and weight management in UK leisure horses. *Equine Vet J.* 2021; 53(4): 752–62. https://doi.org/10.1111/evj.13360.

CHAPTER 7

Teamwork

....

Martin Woodham

Teamwork is a common enough concept. Readers will have their own working definitions, along with examples of good and bad teamwork. For our purposes, we define teamwork as that set of values, capabilities and activities that delivers healthcare by multiple organisations and individuals, exactly as the patient would wish them, acting as one.

Almost all human enterprises, even those that seem solitary, require or benefit from some level of teamworking. A champion tennis player appears as a lone figure when on court but, in fact, has coaches for physical and psychological aspects, physiotherapists, training partners and an administrative team behind them, taking care of everything aside from the actual game.

A GP practice team is highly visible. Whether it is working well or not is highly visible too.

For even the most minimal patient interaction, a patient may speak to several people: a receptionist to make an appointment, a triage doctor on the phone, a second receptionist on arrival and (hopefully) the same doctor who triaged them for a consultation. Afterwards, they might deal with a dispenser for medication or a referrals clerk for a referral to an external service.

The benefits of teamwork are largely obvious—being able to achieve more, more quickly and with better efficiency. Michael West and Carol Borrill[1] have identified the following specific outcomes of effective teamwork in the healthcare sector:

DOI: 10.1201/9781003302438-12

- Reduced hospitalisation and costs
- Improved service provision
- Lower patient mortality
- Enhanced patient satisfaction
- Improved staff motivation and well-being.

Clearly, these are worthy goals for any healthcare system. To understand how they can be delivered, especially in a rural setting, we need to consider two complementary teams working in healthcare: the core community or locality team and the system team within which it sits.

There are two levels of teamworking in rural healthcare: the *community team* centred on the GP practice and the *system-level team* within which it sits. Although these two levels of teamworking share some traits, there are significant differences in how they are operationalised and optimised. Rurality places additional demands on both. The challenge lies in straddling our notions of 'community' and 'system-level' teams and making disparate organisations and individuals appear as a single entity at the point of delivery.

COMMUNITY TEAM

From the patient's point of view, the community team is distinct from any particular organisational structure. What the patient regards as their 'community team' is the core group of people primarily concerned with delivering healthcare to them within their community. This team usually consists of core members of a GP practice, including doctors, nurses, dispensers, pharmacists, paramedics and healthcare assistants. Other associated healthcare professionals, such as those in community nursing and midwifery, mental health, podiatry and dietetics, may also provide input.

The attributes of this team can be summarised as:

- Being onsite, identifiable to patients
- Being easily able to have face-to-face conversations within the team, immediately if necessary
- Sharing information rapidly and easily
- Knowing each other and being familiar with team members and their roles
- Working together constantly
- Having shared routines, values and beliefs
- Fitting within a clear leadership/governance structure (management, GP partners/other senior clinicians) that gives consistent direction

Patients rarely understand or care about organisational distinctions between diverse healthcare roles and services. In many cases, patients regard everyone as part of the GP practice, with the ultimate accolade to a high-achieving team being that they assume that all staff are employees of the practice.

Ideally, patients experience a single team that operates as one. Organisationally, however, team members have different employers with different lines of accountability requiring different approaches to their operation and management.

SYSTEM-LEVEL TEAM

The 'system level' team involves a wider group of healthcare service organisations that may or may not be involved in a patient's care. Regardless of the current organisational structure of the health service, it is likely that these will include diagnostic services such as imaging and blood tests, acute hospital(s) for procedures, admissions and specialist secondary and tertiary care, ambulance services, social care, community and hospital mental health specialists, voluntary agencies providing a range of services, commercial services and others. Patients' experience of healthcare is hugely influenced by how well their 'system-level' organisations and individuals are joined up. If they are not, the challenges of navigating a complex system easily cause a poor experience. A second level of teamwork is generally unseen but equally vital: the range of supporting services into which primary care is a conduit.

The characteristics of the system-level team are different to those of the community team:

- Rarely in one place
- May have never met
- Often based in towns
- Variable structures, accountability, governance and leadership
- No shared values other than the overarching remit to provide the best care to patients/clients
- No shared language (health staff say 'patient'; social care say 'service user' or 'client')
- Often poorly established lines of communication other than to request support from each speciality
- No rehearsed mechanisms for collaboration
- Rarely the same individuals involved due to capacity, area of operation or rotation
- Often ongoing organisational change on one or more specialities, which can shift structures, roles and individuals

- Roles and accountabilities may overlap or be unclear
- Differing agendas/priorities/budgets/operational areas per speciality

Because collaboration and networking cross organisational and geographic boundaries, coordination and leadership of this team are complex. Governance involves each stakeholder organisation, and leadership is either by consensus or (more usually/more efficiently) by one individual/specialism taking the lead.

Once engaged with the system-level team, the patient journey is often complex. Patients generally do not understand the various organisational structures involved, nor should they have to. The key issue from their point of view is how to navigate complex systems: Who is involved in their care; what is each person's/team's remit; how do different investigations and treatments dovetail; who should they contact; what happens next?

The solution to this complexity is having a single point of contact who can explain the patient's journey to them while facilitating progress.

While this role often defaults to a GP or practice nurse, new roles, such as care navigators and social prescribers, are being established to assist patients on their journeys.

KEY ATTRIBUTES OF GOOD TEAMWORK

J Richard Hackman identifies the following key attributes of good teamwork:[2]

- The team must be a real team, rather than in name only.
- It has compelling direction for its work.
- It has an enabling structure that facilitates teamwork.
- It operates within a supportive organisational context.
- It has expert teamwork coaching.

Healthcare teams should have an unambiguous 'compelling direction' in that the best interests of patients are sacrosanct. Clarity of the objective should therefore never be in question, although how best to achieve it may well be up for debate.

PATIENT EXPERIENCE

Patient experience, the quality of care perceived by users of healthcare systems, benefits greatly from a high-performing team. Where the team is an integral part of a rural community, experience can be very good indeed.

A good example is a holistic approach to appointment scheduling. Patients who need regular contact (e.g. for diabetic monitoring) frequently require multiple team contacts—a healthcare assistant takes blood samples, a nurse assesses peripheral blood flow and a doctor reviews medication. Other professionals may be involved, from mental health to podiatry to social prescribing.

An effective team works in concert so that appointments are conveniently scheduled for the same day at around the same time. Blood samples are taken, blood pressure measured and the vascular check performed on the same day that the podiatrist is available. The doctor's review is carried out once the blood results are available. Checks required to manage other conditions are done in the same appointment or at least on the same day so that the patient only needs to attend the practice once.

The impact of the unseen or indirect cost to the patient of multiple attendances can be significant, not to mention the better experience of getting everything sorted at once.

There is also an improvement in continuity of care with this mode of working. Because care is planned, it is possible to ensure that the same professionals are involved. This provides for a better patient experience due to everyone involved being fully cognisant of the patient's situation.

When staff recognise and check in a patient before they have even set foot in the building, when patients are recognised by voice on the phone, when staff understand the patient's family situation well enough to anticipate the consequences of a hospital admission and are able to offer support, when a patient's unspoken needs are known and can be sensitively dealt with, when staff have insight into the patient's home and social life, then patient care can transcend a simple visit to the doctor, and the resources of the whole team can be brought to bear on optimising the patient experience and outcomes.

REMOTE AND RURAL

It is perhaps no surprise that the highest-rated GP practices are rural, tight-knit teams. Five out of the top six GP practices (as rated by their patients) are rural or semi-rural, two of which are also rated 'Outstanding' by their regulator, the Care Quality Commission.[3]

The reasons for this are varied, but the key factors for patients are access to healthcare, trust in the professionals that they consult with and being listened to and supported. Rural practices tend to be deeply embedded in their communities, which is a strong motivator for high-quality delivery.

Staff in rural communities tend to be 'local', which brings advantages in knowing the population, getting to work easily (rural travel is easily affected by bad weather), willingness to support each other and their community, local knowledge and longevity of service. However there are also challenges:

- Staff are harder to recruit as the employment pool is small.
- Role clarity and progression can be tricky with a small team where everybody 'mucks in'.
- Part-time working is almost inevitable as staff tend to have several calls on their time, whether from friends and family or from the demands of the farming calendar.
- Rural practices generally have many patients who are related to staff members. Maintaining confidentiality requires discipline and integrity.

CASE STUDY 1

Multiple Practices Operating Together to Meet a Critical Need

In December 2020, GP practices in England were asked to set up and deliver centralised vaccination hubs to roll out COVID-19 vaccinations.

Vaccine handling requirements meant that these hubs would only be feasible for populations of at least 40–50,000; practices and community teams cooperated.

Keswick and Solway Primary Care Network (PCN), a group of seven GP practices operating in a large and sparsely populated area of north Cumbria, created a 'vaccination hub' based in the local community hospital.

Local practice provision was made to vaccinate patients unable to travel to the hub.

Rurality created the need, and an effective team made it work. Leadership was provided by the PCN clinical director and an operations manager who worked with the local community hospital and the Northern Fells Group, a proactive voluntary organisation, to rapidly design a new service incorporating infection risk assessments, building modifications, computer network improvements and volunteer recruitment.

The vaccination hub opened to the first patients two weeks after the practices were asked 'Can you do it?' Key elements of success were:

- Key representatives from every practice engaged immediately on behalf of their teams.

- Pre-existing, well-rehearsed communication channels, including group messaging and daily team calls, allowed rapid decision making and information sharing.
- A highly effective voluntary organisation provided 200 volunteers.
- Managers remained onsite until the service was stabilised, refining the process and identifying and removing bottlenecks in real time.
- Team members had complementary skills and knew and respected each other.
- 'Back at base' practice teams identified and called patients in priority order.
- Strong cooperation existed at all levels between the practice teams.
- A 'drop everything and get it done' attitude was maintained throughout.

Challenges of Rurality for the System-Level Team

Services may have different geographic boundaries and varying scopes of practice. ('Yes, the neighbouring team can do home intravenous antibiotics, but we can't'.) Communications may be complex, with time delays in contacting the right team member. Accountability and ownership can be blurred, leading to poor continuity of care and a lack of joined-up delivery. In cases of urgent need, these issues come to the fore.

Patient choice plays a part too: rural folk would often prefer to stay at home rather than be admitted to a remote hospital, requiring community delivery of services that, in an urban area, would more normally be found in an outpatient department.

Patient experience may be highly variable. This is not surprising, given that each team is constructed in an ad-hoc manner, with different individuals participating. In addition, the team is largely invisible to the patient; they neither know nor care that Community Trust nurses are working with a specialist palliative care team from the acute hospital. To them, it's just 'the health service'.

The interconnected web of services supporting patients can become incomprehensible, and the more complex the patient's situation, the more complex (and the more error prone) are the supporting services. Patient autonomy is hard to achieve since the patient often struggles to navigate the complex health system they are presented with. Treatment schedules aren't joined up in time or geography; medications interact; different departments give different messages about care; and the patient becomes disoriented and anxious.

Addressing these challenges requires leadership of the highest order. The coordination of the system-level team is critical to success, consisting of assembling the right team quickly enough and leading it into stable delivery of interlocking services that are then managed as an holistic super-service that appears as 'one service' to the patient.

This requires that the right person adopts the role of patient advocate and takes responsibility for orchestrating care delivery while helping the patient understand their own place in the process.

Team Organisation—How Services Are Typically Delivered

Primary healthcare evolves. As new demands, new diagnostic methods and new treatments have become available, and as rural populations age, the GP team has expanded to cope with the resultant workload. Work is handled by appropriate team members, with administrative roles such as dispensers and referrals secretaries complemented by other roles ranging from healthcare assistants to well-being coaches.

Primary care services are operating at high volume and potentially high levels of criticality. Criticality drives the need for early diagnosis (or, at least, a safe management plan) and a decision as to whether the situation can be handled by the core practice team, or it requires external, system-level skills.

Having decided on the appropriate team to respond, the operation of the team and the lead clinician needs to flex accordingly. How care is provided, what the team role is, and how that team is optimised are determined by the team model in use.

In the core GP team, the doctor's role is to diagnose and then coordinate the core team to manage the patient's condition(s). The team role is to leverage the doctor's knowledge by taking on tasks that do not require their expertise. Optimising this model depends on each team member operating at the top of their licence.

Within the system-level team, the doctor's role after diagnosis is to identify and engage the right system-level specialities for the patient, then either coordinate care personally or hand off coordination to whichever specialist is appropriate. The optimising principle is to maximise the effectiveness of the team.

In primary care, the core team has a clear leader: The GP is accountable for the patient's care and so is 'on point' to orchestrate the practice team to deliver for the patient.

At the system level, leadership is less clear cut. The team is not formalised, and the person who has the initial diagnostic contact with the patient (usually the GP) may not have the time or skillset to lead the system level team.

Enablers of the System-Level Team

Because it works as a single unit, with members known to each other and able to practise cooperation on a daily basis, the core practice team is generally straightforward to manage and direct.

The system-level team, however, is a construct that is assembled only when needed and hence, has highly variable membership, depending on the patient situation.

There are some key enablers that allow this model to work effectively, without the high level of personal connection enjoyed by the core practice team.

- Standardised operating procedures as far as possible, as a minimum
- A standard way to engage each specialism, such as a single point of contact
- A standard referral form and communications channel
- Ideally, a named individual in a liaison role
- A clear understanding of each service's capabilities that allows service identification and contact points/engagement methods for all
- Clear accountabilities and operational scope across all services
- Escalation paths to address any cross-specialism governance topics

Rurality affects all these enablers to some degree; physical separation always makes synchronisation of services difficult to achieve, and communications need constant exercise to maintain quality and a good patient experience across service providers.

A case study from a rather different context helps highlight the extent to which standardisation enables rapid deployment and coherent operation.

CASE STUDY 2

Rigorous Standardisation Enables High-Quality Delivery

McDonalds operates in 120 countries and serves around 68 million customers a day. Started in 1940, the company has grown to almost 40,000 restaurants worldwide, with 200,000+ employees. Key to its growth is the consistent quality of its products that, aside from some regional localisations due to local customs, are identical all over the world.

This standardisation has been recognised by *The Economist*'s Big Mac Index, which provides a comparison between the purchasing power of world currencies by comparing the local price of a Big Mac as an alternative to foreign exchange rates.

Quality and consistency are achieved by rigorous standardisation of every aspect of food production. From control of (and, in some areas, ownership of) raw material supply through handling and storage requirements, food preparation and cooking to packaging and delivery to the customer.

All processes and systems in every restaurant and its inbound supply chain are absolutely identical, with the result that a Big Mac is identical whether it's served in London, Hong Kong or in McDonalds's birthplace, San Bernardino, California.

CONCLUSION

Primary healthcare teams operate at two distinct levels:

- *The community team*: A co-located, single organisation under the operational control of a locality-based clinical management team
- *A system team*: Constructed in response to a specific patient's set of needs

These teams share some characteristics but also differ widely.

The community team optimises clinicians' patient-facing time by taking on workload that does not require their skills, optimising the use of everyone's skills and, hence, patient care. Having every clinician working at the top of their licence optimises these scarce skills and focuses on patient need.

The system-level team is brought into being with the right mix of expertise and service capability to provide integrated services which the community team cannot deliver in isolation. The focus here is on joining up care for the patient so that diagnosis and treatment are seamless.

Rurality places additional burdens on both models. For the community team, this is centred around a widely spread population and the challenges of having enough of the right staff. For the system team, different organisations that are physically separate have different priorities, and good communication is hard to achieve.

These two models, operating simultaneously, require judgement as to which is required and a different leadership style for each: more collaborative yet directive for the community team, more facilitative and enabling for the system team. A clinician, usually but not necessarily the GP, is well placed to take the leadership role in both models.

The community team has the highest level of patient insight, the best contextual knowledge around the patient and the best knowledge of local factors that will impact care.

The key challenge in providing the best patient experience and outcome lies in operating these two teams simultaneously and in such a way that the patient can't detect the difference. An understanding of how teamwork differs across the two teams and a focus on integrating delivery from a patient's perspective will enable the seamless delivery and patient outcomes that all healthcare teamwork should aspire to.

FURTHER READING

Haas M, Mortensen M. The secrets of great teamwork. *Harvard Business Review.* 2016; 94(6): 70–6. https://hbr.org/2016/06/the-secrets-of-great-teamwork.

Hackman R. *Leading teams: Setting the stage for great performances.* Cambridge, MA: Harvard Business School Press, 2002. https://hbswk.hbs.edu/archive/leading-teams-setting-the-stage-for-great-performances-the-five-keys-to-successful-teams.

Maister DH. *Managing the professional service firm.* London: Simon & Schuster, 2003.

Robertson A, Abbey G. *Managing talented people: Getting on with—and getting the best from—your high performers.* London: Momentum, 2003.

REFERENCES

1 West M, Borrill C. The influence of teamworking. In Cox J, King J, Hutchinson A, McAvoy P (eds) *Understanding Doctors' Performance.* Oxford: Radcliffe, 2006.

2 Hackman JR. What makes for a great team? *Amer Psychol Assoc Sci Briefs.* 2004; 18. www.apa.org/science/about/psa/2004/06/hackman.

3 Ipsos Mori. GP patient survey 2021. www.ipsos.com/ipsos-mori/en-uk/2021-gp-patient-survey-results-released.

CHAPTER 8

Remote Healthcare

....

Sean Hudson, Kate King and Natalie Taylor

Healthcare in the UK is predominantly structured around population centres; however, there are locations in the UK and around the world where there is a significant distance, in either time or geography, between the patient and organised health systems. Remote medicine covers healthcare delivery on the mainland, islands, offshore, diving, altitude and anywhere inaccessible to traditional healthcare facilities.

The huge range of healthcare environments covered by remote medicine means that there is no single consensus statement on the definition. Themes of high-risk environments, physiological extremes, resource limitation, professional isolation and lack of communication are all favoured by different authors.[1-3] Wakerman offers the most encompassing definition, stating that remote healthcare is

> characterised by geographical, professional and, often social isolation of practitioners: a strong multidisciplinary approach; overlapping and changing roles of team members; a relatively high degree of GP substitution; and practitioners requiring public health, emergency, obstetric, anaesthetic and extended clinical skills.[4]

This can be extrapolated to demonstrate some of the issues with remote healthcare:

DOI: 10.1201/9781003302438-13

- Geographically remote. Healthcare is delivered at a distance from the main health system, either as a fixed remote provision or intermittent delivery through outreach. Effective planning is required.
- Professional isolation. Does the clinician have sufficient training or experience to provide for the health needs of the population? How do they access ongoing professional support or development to prevent normalisation of deviance?
- Communications.
- Limited resources.

This chapter aims to explore some of the considerations for remote primary healthcare in both UK fixed and mobile expeditionary teams.

MEDICAL PLANNING

An understanding of healthcare needs, the environmental considerations and management of risk underpins all remote healthcare delivery. For example, it is not practical or economically viable to provide a high-level trauma team in support of a single-person expedition to the Antarctic. Planning helps define the need and risks involved and identify unlikely but potentially catastrophic events. Adequate planning reduces risks to patient safety and increases the ability of clinicians to function effectively.

A detailed plan highlighting evacuation timelines; local political, environmental and geographical threats; and communication options is essential for expeditionary and mobile medical teams especially.

Knowledge of the local medical infrastructure and standards helps in defining the medical plan. Agreement about the standards of care to be achieved needs to be reached.

Medical care in remote locations can be delivered in a variety of ways, depending on the requirements of the population at risk, access for providers to the location, safety and security. The more diverse and complementary the skills and capabilities of the multidisciplinary team, the more robust and effective the clinical interventions.

A comprehensive medical plan should identify knowledge and skills gaps and the training needed to address these. Some gaps may be mitigated with good quality reliable reach-back communications. Consideration needs to be given not only to the medical management in the prehospital environment but also to the urgency of specialist intervention and ongoing management over potentially prolonged periods before casualty evacuation can be arranged. Clinicians overwintering in Antarctica may be completely isolated for months and need a programme of training aimed at developing an autonomous practitioner with extensive subspecialist skills.

As far as is possible, it is essential to make detailed plans with individual potential patients with robust safety netting to cover all eventualities. As well as ensuring that patients have sufficient regular medication, it may be necessary to prescribe medication to be taken if their conditions change or worsen.

TRAINING

Although remote healthcare has been delivered for thousands of years by armed forces and on expeditions, the search for oil and gas catalysed its development as a distinct healthcare discipline. This is now underpinned by training courses and academic research focused solely on the different areas of remote medicine (Figure 8.1).

Most clinicians working in remote healthcare require additional training beyond standard training pathways. For example, military GPs train to the national licensing standard set by the Royal College of General Practitioners but also need to be able to deliver prehospital care and anaesthesia, manage dental conditions and be competent in obstetric and paediatric emergencies.

A range of organisations offer training courses in medical specialities and emergencies that may be encountered in remote healthcare, but training courses do not equate to competence, and a period of apprenticeship or supported working in the remote environment is recommended before operating independently.

Academic certification, which recognises the training, preparation and resources that are needed to ensure safe and effective remote care delivery, is available from various institutions including the University of Central Lancashire, the Royal College of Surgeons of Edinburgh and Imperial College London. NHS Education Scotland leads on a remote and rural framework for credentialing experience and training, and their Remote and Rural Healthcare Alliance is developing multi-practitioner advanced-level education programmes.[5]

COMMUNICATION, TELEMEDICINE AND REACH-BACK

Communication is a central requirement for almost all remote medicine delivery. It is vital to be able to reach back for clinical advice and support and also to call forward assistance such as transport for casualty evacuation ('casevac'). Communications hardware, infrastructure and procedures should be part of medical planning. Networks and infrastructure can be fragile, time limited or a target for disruption, and back-up methods should be encouraged.

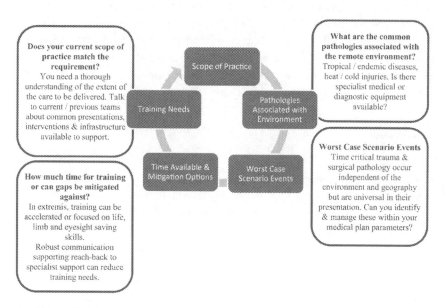

FIGURE 8.1 Training needs considerations.

New communication technologies have been embraced by patients and practitioners working in remote healthcare. They have allowed improved access and more advanced clinical care in traditionally hard-to-reach locations. Australia has led in the development of telecommunications-supported medicine, or 'telemedicine', to remote rural civilian communities. Militaries have used it to support the provision of specialist-level care in far-forward areas where it is not feasible to deploy the specialists themselves.

Reach-back uses telemedicine to supplement the clinical care available. It is used extensively for provision of care on oil rigs, remote expeditionary or exploration teams and to provide clinical support to conflict areas. At a basic level, asynchronous methods such as messaging can be used to obtain clinical advice, but in more advanced formats, synchronous physiological measurements can be shared from wearable devices and real-time video used to guide a forward clinician through a specialist practical intervention. There are increasing numbers of software applications and platforms designed to support secure, confidential medical reach-back.

Effective and robust reach-back can mitigate gaps in skills or experience of remote practitioners. In conflict areas, provision of reach-back can allow specialist care to be given from a supporting nation or non-governmental organisation when it is otherwise unsafe or impractical to send the specialist teams forward.

CLINICAL GOVERNANCE

Practice in a country requires registration with the country's medical council and insurance through a medical defence organisation (MDO). Remote practice and the provision of reach-back should be covered by your MDO, but check beforehand and keep them informed.

Medical record keeping should be no different to standard practice in a well-provided medical system. Environmental circumstances or security risks can temporarily limit documentation, but all interventions should be appropriately recorded as soon as the situation allows.

The planned use of audio devices, which enable real-time documentation, may be appropriate, as is now the case in major incident management. Some population groups in remote and hostile environments may be assigned numbers rather than names for security reasons.

CASE STUDY

Background

Nine hundred soldiers deploy to an Oman desert to conduct a military training exercise for eight weeks. There are no medical facilities for 50km and no metal roads for up to 30km. The nearest hospital is a minimum of a four-hour drive away from the edge of the training area or a 90-minute helicopter journey. The military have to plan what, if any, medical facilities they wish to deploy.

Considerations

Environment: The temperature is 12°C—40°C, light winds, occasional sand storms and risk of flash flooding. There are few trees to offer shade in the desert.

Common conditions (based on previous exercises in Oman) include exertional heat injury, dehydration, road traffic collisions (RTCs), musculo-skeletal injuries and skin rashes.

Host-nation medical facilities have been reviewed in the last year and deliver NHS-equivalent or higher care. There is a memorandum of understanding to ensure soldiers receive treatment locally if needed.

Setting up a Facility

The nature of the activity—fighting in armoured vehicles—meant that heat illness was a big concern alongside RTCs, so a prehospital facility with pre-hospital emergency care (PHEC) capability was deemed necessary.

The facility consisted of a Bulldog armoured personnel carrier with the ability to deliver 'tailgate' care. The Bulldog could drive the medical provider to the casualty to deliver care on the ground and in the back of the vehicle, allowing an injured person to be treated and transported quickly.

FURTHER READING

The following websites expand on resources discussed in this chapter:

Faculty of Remote, Rural and Humanitarian Healthcare—The Royal College of Surgeons of Edinburgh. www.rcsed.ac.uk/faculties/faculty-of-remote-rural-and-humanitarian-healthcare.

National Centre for Remote and Rural Medicine—University of Central Lancashire. www.uclan.ac.uk/schools/ncrrm.

National Centre for Rural Health and Care. www.ncrhc.org/.

Remote Medicine Intercalated BSc—Imperial College London. www.imperial.ac.uk/medicine/study/undergraduate/intercalated-bsc-programme/remote-medicine/.

The Remote and Rural Healthcare Education Alliance—NHS Education for Scotland. https://learn.nes.nhs.scot/786.

REFERENCES

1. Gumbley AE, Claydon MA, Blankenstein TN, Fell TH. Medical provision in forward locations in Afghanistan: The experiences of General Duties Medical Officers on Op Herrick 15. *J R Army Med Corps* 2013; 159: 68–72. DOI: 10.1136/jramc-2013–000036.
2. Hodgetts TJ, Findlay S. Putting role 1 first: The role 1 capability review. *J R Army Med Corps* 2012; 158: 162–170. DOI: 10.1136/jramc-158-03–04.
3. Martin-Bates AJ, Jefferys SE. General duties medical officer role 1 remote supervision in the era of army contingency operations. *J R Army Med Corps* 2016; 162: 239–241. DOI: 10.1136/jramc-2015–000478.
4. Wakerman J. Defining remote health. *Aus J Rur Heal* 2004; 12(5): 210–214. DOI: 10.1111/j.1440-1854.2004.00607.x.
5. The Remote and Rural Healthcare Education Alliance—NHS Education for Scotland. https://learn.nes.nhs.scot/786.

CHAPTER 9

Emergencies

....

Nick Wright

AMBULANCE SERVICES

Fourteen ambulance trusts in the UK and the National Ambulance Service in Ireland form the backbone of prehospital care coordination and response.

To improve both mortality and morbidity, the UK has adopted strategies to try to ensure that certain time-critical conditions, including major trauma, myocardial infarction and cerebrovascular accidents, receive specialist treatment in major trauma centres, primary percutaneous coronary intervention (PPCI) centres and hyperacute stroke units, as soon as possible.

DOI: 10.1201/9781003302438-14

With some exceptions—for example, in Scotland (see Chapter 2: What Is Rurality?)—this means that ambulance crews bypass their local emergency departments and transport time-critical patients directly to larger specialist centres.

The role of the ambulance service is therefore to:

- Identify patients meeting triage criteria
- Provide immediate interventions to allow safe transport
- Provide rapid transport to the relevant centre

In rural Britain, the implementation of such systems is challenging. Compared to the past, ambulance crews now care for critically unwell patients for significantly longer periods of time.

In response to this, paramedics have become more skilled. Training requirements have changed dramatically, with pre-registration training now at degree level. To facilitate treatment and transport to an appropriate facility, advanced clinicians and critical care teams have been added to the skill mix, and more specialist equipment and medications are available.

RURAL TRAUMA

With an outward migration of younger people and the inward migration of older people, rural populations in the UK are aging. As older people are more likely to have health and social needs, there is an increasing demand on local healthcare services. Only 55% of rural households compared to 97% of urban households in England live within 8km of a hospital, adding to the challenge faced by the ambulance service and other prehospital care providers. A tendency for older people to present to health services in moments of crisis further compounds the challenge as a more emergent, intensive and, at times, complex response is likely to be needed.[1]

Trauma occurring in rural populations is proportionally much lower than within an urban setting. The majority of patients sustaining injury in rural settings do not require trauma centre care. Agricultural injury accounted for 41 deaths in Great Britain in 2020–21, although the Health and Safety Executive (HSE) believe that serious injuries in farming, fishing and forestry are grossly underreported.[2] Each year, an estimated 12,000 people sustain agricultural accidents, including being struck by moving objects and vehicles, falls from height, contact with machinery and being injured by animals, a figure that is statistically significantly higher than for workers across other industries.[3]

PREHOSPITAL CARE TRAINING

Ambulance service emergency medical technicians and emergency care assistants are generally trained in house by ambulance trusts. They are likely to have access to a limited drug formulary which includes basic life-saving medications such as oxygen, glucagon and aspirin. They normally work alongside paramedics, who are autonomous, registered healthcare professionals who meet the regulatory standards set by the Health and Care Professions Council. The threshold entry level is a bachelor's degree with honours. Senior, advanced and critical care paramedics undergo additional vocational and academic training to expand their scope of practice and access to therapies and medications. Examples include ketamine sedation, surgical airways and surgical thoracotomy.

Paramedics are now included in many primary care, emergency department and offshore sector teams.

For doctors, prehospital emergency medicine (PHEM) is now a recognised subspecialty with training programmes open to those with base specialty training in anaesthesia, emergency medicine, intensive care medicine or acute medicine. PHEM clinicians work within critical care services including emergency helicopter services and physician response units.

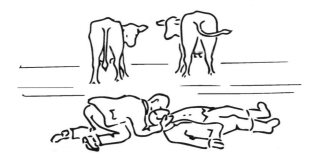

For those not wishing to complete a full training programme in PHEM, clinicians may consider short courses to give them some basic prehospital knowledge and skillset. Local British Association for Immediate Care (BASICS) schemes may run open training events too. The Diploma in Immediate Medical Care, awarded by the Royal College of Surgeons of Edinburgh, is a nationally recognised qualification for paramedics, doctors and nurses, including rural practitioners, working in prehospital emergency care. (See further reading at the end of this chapter.)

EQUIPMENT

Most equipment used in the prehospital setting is of single-use design to reduce infection and contamination risks. PHEM teams carry equipment to provide and perform prehospital emergency anaesthesia, road-side surgery and blood product infusions. Rural practitioners may choose to carry equipment appropriate to their scope of practice in the eventuality of being summoned to the scene of an accident. Those who do so must ensure that relevant clinical governance and insurances are in place.

Communications

The emergency services currently utilise Airwave technology. This secure radio system enables interoperability between emergency services, including Mountain Rescue. It uses similar technology to the mobile phone network and, in remote settings, has similar limitations. The emergency services will soon move to a new communication system: the Emergency Services Network (ESN), which will use 4G telecommunications networks to transmit voice, video and other data. Communications on the ESN will take priority over all other network traffic.

MASS CASUALTY AND EXTREME WEATHER EVENTS

Both man-made and naturally-occurring major incidents can be considered to have four stages:

- Initial response—the scalable response from those agencies responding to the incident.
- Consolidation period—other agencies with specific expertise may be requested, including the drawing of resources outside the local area.

- Recovery phase—the process of restoring, rehabilitating and rebuilding the community. Emergency services normally hand over to the local authorities.
- Restoration of normality—return to business as usual.

Rural areas have been the scene of many major incidents, including the Stonehaven train derailment, the Grayrigg train derailment, the Keswick coach crash, the West Cumbria shootings and the Ynyswen stabbings. Limited resources available in rural areas means that even an incident with a few casualties can easily overwhelm an initial response. Early identification and declaration of a major incident and the use of clinical triage tools may be required.

Safe access to and egress from scenes may require specialist input. This is led by the fire and rescue service, which may call on the additional skills of voluntary organisations such as mountain and lowland search and rescue teams.

Longer transfer times from rural areas to healthcare facilities can cause extended delays for evacuation from casualty clearing stations. Greater on-scene stabilisation and treatment capacity and capability may be required.

A number of major national emergency and disaster reviews have identified a need for improvements to coordination of emergency service activity, command and control procedures, deployment of resources and risk assessment. Outcomes regarding lessons relating to interoperability were published in the Pollock Report.[4] This resulted in development of the Joint Emergency Services Interoperability Principles (JESIP). The aim of JESIP is 'to help our emergency services save more lives when we experience major and complex incidents by working better—together'. The five principles to help achieve this aim are:

- Co-locate
- Communicate
- Coordinate
- Jointly understand risk
- Shared situational awareness

EMERGENCY PLANNING AND RESILIENCE

Significant weather events, flooding and heavy snowfall can paralyse remote communities, cutting off critical infrastructure and placing additional burdens on emergency services.

The Civil Contingencies Act 2004 and Contingency Planning (Scotland) Regulations 2005 place a statutory responsibility on local authorities to plan for emergencies. Specific details and terminology vary across the devolved administrations; however, the principles are similar, with local groupings of key stakeholders working together to create strategic plans. During a major incident, these key stakeholders come together to support a coordinated response.

Key stakeholders include emergency services, the Environment Agency, utility companies, local hospital trusts, mountain rescue teams and other voluntary organisations such as British Red Cross and St John's ambulance.

COLLABORATIVE WORKING

Successful collaborative working improves patient outcomes, but achieving this requires a good understanding of the capability and remit of each agency.

Most ambulance services in the UK use the Joint Royal Colleges Ambulance Liaison Committee (JRCALC) guidelines[5] to inform practice. These provides some uniformity between ambulance trusts.

Helicopter emergency medical services (HEMS), now more commonly referred to as PHEM services, have much more to offer a patient than air transport alone. Teams, normally consisting of a physician capable of rapid sequence induction (RSI) anaesthesia and a critical-care paramedic, are highly trained to deal with critically unwell trauma and medical patients. As well as RSI, their scope of practice includes sedation, surgical skills and diverse pharmacology, including blood products.

If, because of mechanical reasons, poor weather or darkness, a helicopter is unavailable, PHEM teams often respond in a rapid response vehicle.

The British Association of Immediate Care (BASICS) is a voluntary organisation whose members include a range of healthcare professionals, including rural GPs who work or volunteer in the prehospital setting. BASICS schemes are sanctioned and called out by local ambulance trusts. They often respond to road traffic collisions and are an important resource in the rural setting, offering an emergency or sometimes critical care service.

Voluntary mountain and lowland search and rescue teams cover most areas of the UK. As well as providing personnel and 4x4 vehicles for long or difficult evacuations, many team members are specifically trained and qualified to assess and treat trauma and medical casualties and to prescribe, dispense and administer medications from an agreed national formulary. Mountain rescue teams are unique in that non–healthcare professionals can administer drugs such as morphine and fentanyl lozenges to manage pain in remote areas.

FURTHER READING

British Association for Immediate Care. www.basics.org.uk/.
Diploma in Immediate Medical Care—The Royal College of Surgeons of Edinburgh. https://fphc.rcsed.ac.uk/examinations/diploma-in-immediate-medical-care.
Mountain Rescue England and Wales. www.mountain.rescue.org.uk/.

REFERENCES

1 Hart J. *Older People in Rural Areas: Vulnerability Due to Poor Health.* Craven Arms: Rural England, 2016. https://ruralengland.org/wp-content/uploads/2015/12/Final-report-Poor-Health.pdf.
2 Health and Safety Executive. *Fatal Injuries in Agriculture, Forestry and Fishing in Great Britain 2020/21.*Health and Safety Executive, 2021. www.hse.gov.uk/agriculture/pdf/agriculture-fatal-injuries-2021.pdf.
3 Health and Safety Executive. *Agriculture, Forestry and Fishing Statistics in Great Britain.* Health and Safety Executive, 2021. www.hse.gov.uk/statistics/industry/agriculture.pdf.
4 Pollock K. *Review of Persistent Lessons Identified Relating to Interoperability from Emergencies and Major Incidents Since 1986.* Emergency Planning College, 2013. www.jesip.org.uk/uploads/media/pdf/Pollock_Review_Oct_2013.pdf.
5 Joint Royal Colleges Ambulance Liaison Committee (JRCALC) guidelines. www.jrcalc.org.uk/guidelines/.

CHAPTER 10

Rural Pharmacy and Dispensing

....

Christopher E. Clark, Rosina Cross
and Sinéad T J McDonagh

INTRODUCTION

Most patients in the United Kingdom (UK) live closer to and enjoy easier access to a community pharmacy than a doctor's surgery.[1] This is not the case in rural areas, where general practices can hold contractual rights to dispense medications to patients. In England, Wales and Scotland, these rights generally apply where patients live more than one mile (1.6 km) from the nearest registered pharmacy. (Such an area is termed a *controlled locality*.) Where exceptional difficulties in access or communication can be demonstrated, patients who live nearer to a pharmacy also have a right to receive medication from their surgery.[2] In Northern Ireland, dispensing is permitted for patients who live more than five kilometres from a community pharmacy if their practice is more than one kilometre from a community pharmacy.[3] In the Republic of Ireland, although numbers are falling, GPs are permitted to dispense if they have only one practice centre, and it is three miles or more from the nearest retail pharmacist.[4]

There are over 1,100 dispensing practices in England in 2022, representing approximately 13% of general practices. They supply medication to approximately 3.5 million NHS patients (approximately 5% of the English population).[5]

Dispensing by UK doctors has been subject to regulation since the First World War. Modern regulations were introduced in 1983, when practices with existing dispensing were awarded historic rights.[6] Since then, patients registering with a practice must meet current dispensing regulations, so

DOI: 10.1201/9781003302438-15

historic rights are gradually becoming redundant. The Dispensing Doctors' Association maintains an accessible and informative website and regularly publishes updated guidance on current legislation.[7]

Dispensing practices are predominantly rural, overcoming geographical barriers to alternative pharmacy services.[8] Dispensing services are valued by practices and their patients. Comparisons with community pharmacy services, which serve most people in the UK, generally examine relative costs and safety with less emphasis on convenience, ease of access or other potential benefits for patients.

In this chapter, we explore the risks, benefits and impacts of dispensing from both patient and practice perspectives and conclude with thoughts on the future of practice dispensing and rural pharmacy.

BENEFITS OF DISPENSING

Dispensing can benefit patients, practice staff and practices as organisations.

PATIENT BENEFITS

The average minimum travel time for patients to access their GP surgery is 23 minutes using public transport or 42 minutes walking. These times are more than doubled in rural practices, and community pharmacies will be even further away.[9] Survey data from Scotland suggests that patient satisfaction is higher for rural practices than for urban ones.[10] Patients' convenience and access to medicines are the most commonly cited reasons for doctors to want to dispense.[11] The phenomenon of distance decay (whereby use of services declines with increasing distance) means that rural and remote healthcare services are highly valued and used by their communities because they are more accessible than urban-based pharmacies, minor injury units and secondary care services.[12] For many patients, rural practices are the natural setting for medication provision. In some areas, branch surgeries offer additional points of access.

Unravelling the relationship between dispensing status and clinical outcomes is problematic. Studies have shown that remoteness from urban centres, which relates to dispensing status, is not correlated with quality of care.[13] Distance decay seems important, but studies identify both positive (distance decay) and inverse (distance bias) relationships: for example, between survival rates for some cancers.[12] Such comparisons may be confounded by factors that are not easily adjusted for, including environmental and socio-economic factors, lifestyle, life expectancy and age. (A higher proportion of older people live in rural areas.)[14, 15] Established measures also fail to adequately categorise rural deprivation. (See Chapter 16: Rural Social Exclusion).[16] Other potential confounders include differences between practices and the variety of methods used to measure access to care.[12, 17] For all these reasons, high-quality evidence of the relationship between dispensing status and clinical outcomes is lacking.

Nevertheless, there is a link between dispensing status and medication adherence, an essential element of chronic disease management. Medication possession does not guarantee medication adherence, but adherence is not possible if the medication is not collected. In the UK, between 11% and 19% of prescriptions are never actually dispensed to the patient. This occurs more rarely in dispensing practices because of the temporal and geographical continuity of the prescribing and dispensing processes.[18] Easy access to provision of medication at the point of prescribing improves medication uptake and adherence because logistical barriers, such as travel costs and loss of work time, discourage patients from presenting their prescriptions elsewhere.[19-21] Blood pressure control is better in dispensing than in non-dispensing practices, although this is probably also due to other factors besides dispensing, such as greater uptake of ambulatory blood pressure monitoring in rural practices.[22, 23] This is supported by recent findings from interviews with multidisciplinary staff members in rural dispensing practices across England, where staff reported that they are more confident that patients will collect their medication and be compliant if medication is dispensed onsite, as opposed to travelling to a community pharmacy.[24] Staff members also emphasised the importance and value of dispensing for both patients and health professionals in improving access to and continuity of medication provision and enhanced quality of care. Improved adherence to medication and achievement of incentive targets have been associated with improved mortality outcomes.[25, 26]

Drivers of medication adherence are complex but include patients' beliefs and concerns regarding the effectiveness and safety of medication.[27-30] The patient-clinician relationship is a key contributor to achieving positive beliefs about treatment and medication adherence.[31,32] Dispensing doctors are well placed to reinforce this by incorporating the act of dispensing into their encounters with their patients. They can also tailor their information to patients' needs by taking a holistic approach to prescribing issues that may affect adherence, such as limited health literacy.[33, 34] Continuity of care, although in decline, is also relevant in maintaining the doctor-patient relationship that supports good medication adherence.[35] This could be one factor contributing to the association of continuity of care with reductions in mortality rates. (See Chapter 3: Role of the Generalist).[36]

STAFF BENEFITS

Dispensing adds significantly to the workload of a practice. A practice dispensing to a high proportion of its patients may allocate 40% to 50% of its costs to dispensing activity.[5] Benefits for staff may not be obvious but include job satisfaction and opportunities for training, qualifications and career development over and above the usual duties of non-clinical staff. Such opportunities are valued by staff and represent positive drivers to staff recruitment and retention. (See Chapter 7: Teamwork).[24]

Evidence from interviews with staff in rural dispensing practices suggests that dispensing services positively impact patient care because the service offers convenience for patients and an opportunity to build rapport with administrative and dispensing staff. Staff report that this combination of patient satisfaction, good clinical care and building of relationships between patient and staff results in in a high level of job satisfaction that staff members believe to be unique to rural dispensing primary care.[24]

These drivers may coincide with reports of low staff turnover, particularly in clinical roles, and emphasise the importance of teamwork, collaboration and compromise within multidisciplinary rural primary care teams, keeping practices running smoothly. Running a dispensary within a general practice relies on teamwork, which itself is emerging as an important contributor to staff well-being, satisfaction and retention.[37, 38]

PRACTICE BENEFITS

Financial gain from dispensing services has been reported to attract GP partners who see it as a potentially successful business opportunity as well as a means of paying higher wages for both clinical and non-clinical roles, thus supporting staff recruitment and retention. Dispensing can be a significant contributor to financial stability. Having a well-run and viable practice is attributed, to an extent, to the financial gains from dispensing. The proportion of total practice income attributable to dispensing rises according to the proportion of practice patients dispensed to, reaching above 50% of practice income for some fully dispensing practices.[5] Income is directly generated by remuneration for the dispensing of medications, according to regulations subject to periodic change, and from adherence to quality assurance schemes such as the Dispensary Services Quality Scheme.[39, 40] The potential for dispensing to improve medication adherence also contributes to practice target achievement (and further remuneration) for clinical indicators such as blood pressure and lipid levels.[23] Such income substantially underwrites running and recruitment costs and the viability of dispensing practices, particularly at satellite sites and branch surgeries which play a vital role in offering job opportunities and accessible healthcare to small communities, mitigating some socio-economic challenges to healthcare access.[41] Despite the significant workload and outlay related to dispensing, some practices would not be financially viable without the income it generates. Data suggest that, without dispensing income, many practices would be able to employ fewer staff, and some practice sites would become unviable, leading to mergers, loss of services and negative impacts on patient access and experiences, particularly in already deprived communities.[5, 42]

DISADVANTAGES OF DISPENSING

Higher Costs

The costs of rural healthcare delivery are higher than those in urban settings.[43] Dispensing costs contribute to this disparity and are cited as evidence of the 'perverse incentive' for dispensing doctors to prescribe more costly medications to maximise their profits. Historically, the system of remuneration has encouraged this. Dispensing practice was associated with less generic prescribing and higher drug unit costs than non-dispensing practice.[11, 44-46] However this perception is outdated. Since 2006–07, perverse incentives have been removed by NHS 'excessive or inappropriate prescribing guidance', which requires prescribers to choose the most cost-effective medication for patients, and replacement of remuneration on a percentage basis by fixed dispensing fees.[47]

Although a recent analysis of data for England found no evidence of higher rates of prescribing in dispensing practices,[23] community pharmacy costs per episode for managing minor ailments are lower than those of general practice.[8] Nevertheless, as previously discussed, barriers to access (including travel and time costs) make rural primary care the first and often the only accessible point of care for many patients. This also directly increases dispensing activity and costs, in comparison to pharmacy dispensing, because dispensing practices cannot sell over-the-counter remedies, and general practitioners have a contractual obligation to prescribe drugs as needed for their patients,[48] so over-the-counter medicines are provided by prescription.[11, 43]

Looking at NHS costs alone fails to take account of the indirect costs to patients of accessing healthcare and medication, which would increase if medications could not be provided locally.[43] When assessing service costs, a full health-economic assessment is required in order to avoid potentially misleading conclusions.[44, 49]

Pharmacy Expertise

Practice dispensing is the responsibility of the doctor as prescriber, whose employed dispensing staff are usually not trained pharmacists. In contrast, community pharmacy staff are contractually and professionally independent.

Dispensers can train to a level 2 NVQ qualification within practice but require the direct supervision of a pharmacist to reach level 3 dispensing technician status. This is harder to achieve in a dispensing practice than in a community pharmacy. As discussed next, this does not appear to carry safety implications but may represent a ceiling to career progression within the practice that is not found in community pharmacies.

Safety

Although it has been suggested that dispensing by doctors as opposed to pharmacists can compromise safety,[50] in 2016, an NHS England Short Life Working Group on Medicines Optimisation in Rural Practices, whose membership included the author, found no clear evidence that dispensing errors were more or less likely to occur in dispensing practices than in rural pharmacies; no actions for change or further work needed were identified. Anecdotally, the Care Quality Commission reported in the same year that dispensing practices seem to gain more outstanding ratings and fewer inadequate ratings than non-dispensing practices.[51] Assessment of dispensing arrangements is part of CQC inspections. A Department of Health and Social Care consultation on revised legislation to improve dispensing safety in pharmacies, published in 2022, specifically excluded dispensing doctors, citing the different contractual arrangements.[52] This omission appears to be an example of failure to rural-proof policies and planning.[53]

In summary, there is no convincing evidence for and anecdotal evidence against there being significant safety concerns for dispensing in practices as opposed to pharmacies.

Recruitment and Retention

One of the most significant challenges reported by rural practice staff is recruitment of dispensers, with dispensing posts going unfilled for months at a time. It is rare to employ a ready-trained dispenser, so in-house training is the norm. Salaries for dispensers are generally low relative to the training required and responsibilities of the job. Many find the prospect unappealing in comparison to more remunerative roles in larger towns. This also threatens retention where urban pharmacies may attract trained dispensers away from rural dispensing practices.[24]

Integration

Nevertheless, the question remains: if the training, skills and experience of pharmacists add value in hospitals and community pharmacies, why not enable rural dispensing practice patients to benefit too? Although its pilot studies did not include rural or dispensing practices, the NHS is facilitating integration of pharmacists into primary care teams, both dispensing and non-dispensing, through networks in England, with pharmacists potentially sharing expertise across several practices or through direct practice employment.[54] This welcome development supports greater teamwork and shared care approaches to chronic disease[55] and should ultimately render pharmacist-versus-doctor comparisons meaningless in the context of dispensing. Future patient-safety studies should be inclusive and address both dispensing and pharmacy provision for all patients.

DISPENSING AND RURAL PHARMACY IN THE FUTURE

Although there is a paucity of data on cost effectiveness,[56] integration of pharmacists into multidisciplinary primary care teams is a commonly stated ambition of practices.[57] Such integration benefits patients by, for example, improving control of high blood pressure through medicines optimisation—the adoption of a patient-focused approach to medicine use in order to get the best for patients from their prescriptions.[22, 58]

Health improvements achieved in primary care are often cost saving for secondary care: for example, by reducing referrals or adverse outcomes. Consequently, careful holistic assessment of cost effectiveness is needed.

Under current 'controlled location legislation', the co-location of a new community pharmacy in a rural area can have significant impact on general practice viability due to enforced loss of dispensing income. Dispensing practices fill the gaps where small rural pharmacies struggle to be financially viable. However, electronic prescribing, on-line ordering and delivery of prescriptions from pharmacies challenge the viability of some rural dispensing practices. Alternative models such as co-location of pharmacies in general practices in a shared business model may ameliorate the risk and benefit patients.

In summary, dispensing practices provide access to medication in rural areas where community pharmacies are relatively inaccessible. It is increasingly likely that rural and remote patients will be able to benefit from multidisciplinary primary care teams including both pharmacists and doctors through integration and co-location of their services and expertise, but the best models of care and their cost effectiveness are yet to be established.

REFERENCES

1. Todd A, Copeland A, Husband A, Kasim A, Bambra C. Access all areas? An area-level analysis of accessibility to general practice and community pharmacy services in England by urbanity and social deprivation. *BMJ Open.* 2015;5(5):e007328.
2. UK Statutory Instruments. *The National Health Service (Pharmaceutical and Local Pharmaceutical Services) Regulations 2013.* London: UK Government, 2013.
3. Northern Ireland Statistics and Research Agency. General pharmaceutical services: Annual statistics 2020/21: BSO family practitioner services information unit. https://hscbusiness.hscni.net/pdf/Annual%2020-21%20General%20Pharmaceutical%20Services%20Report.pdf.
4. Citizens Information. Prescribed drugs and medicines 2022. www.citizensinformation.ie/en/health/drugs_and_medicines/prescribed_drugs_and_medicines.html.
5. PricewaterhouseCoopers LLP. *Cost of service inquiry for dispensing practices.* London: Department of Health, 2010. https://assets.publishing.service.gov.uk/government/uploads/system/uploads/attachment_data/file/215502/dh_128817.pdf [Accessed 21 December 2021].
6. Department of Health—Medicines and Pharmacy. Guidance on the NHS (Pharmaceutical Services) Regulations 2012-dispensing doctors. In: Market entry by PNAs—Information for PCTs [Internet], 2012. https://assets.

publishing.service.gov.uk/government/uploads/system/uploads/attachment_data/file/212872/Chapter-15-dispensing-doctors-services.pdf [Accessed 10 May 2022].

7. Dispensing Doctors' Association Ltd. DDA Dispensing guidance 2019: Quality in practice—Guidance for dispensing practices in England, Scotland and Wales. In: Dispensing Doctors' Association Ltd, editor, 2019. https://www.dispensingdoctor.org/wp-content/uploads/2018/10/DDA-Guidance-Booklet_2019_WEB.pdf [Accessed 10 May 2022].

8. Watson MC, Ferguson J, Barton GR, Maskrey V, Blyth A, Paudyal V, et al. A cohort study of influences, health outcomes and costs of patients' health-seeking behaviour for minor ailments from primary and emergency care settings. *BMJ Open*. 2015;5(2).

9. Department for Environment Food & Rural Affairs. Statistical digest of rural England, 2022. https://assets.publishing.service.gov.uk/government/uploads/system/uploads/attachment_data/file/1100182/06_Statistical_Digest_of_Rural_England_2022_July_edition.pdf [Accessed 10 May 2022].

10. Iqbal I, Thompson L, Wilson P. Patient satisfaction with general practice in urban and rural areas of Scotland. *Rur Remote Heal*. 2021;21(4):6634.

11. Lim D, Emery J, Lewis J, Sunderland VB. A systematic review of the literature comparing the practices of dispensing and non-dispensing doctors. *Heal Policy*. 2009;92(1):1–9.

12. Kelly C, Hulme C, Farragher T, Clarke G. Are differences in travel time or distance to healthcare for adults in global north countries associated with an impact on health outcomes? A systematic review. *BMJ Open*. 2016;6(11):e013059.

13. McLean G, Guthrie B, Sutton M. Differences in the quality of primary medical care services by remoteness from urban settlements. *Qual Saf Heal Care*. 2007;16(6):446–9.

14. Department for Environment Food & Rural Affairs. *Statistical digest of rural England*. London: Government Statistical Service, 2017.

15. Lowe P, Speakman L. *The ageing countryside: The growing older population of rural England*. London: Age Concern, 2006.

16. Barnett S, Roderick P, Martin D, Diamond I. A multilevel analysis of the effects of rurality and social deprivation on premature limiting long term illness. *J Epidemiol Comm Heal*. 2001;55(1):44–51.

17. Kelly E, Stoye G. Does GP practice size matter? GP practice size and the quality of primary care. IFS Report, 2014. https://ifs.org.uk/sites/default/files/output_url_files/R101.pdf [Accessed 7 December 2022].

18. Gadkari AS, McHorney CA. Medication nonfulfillment rates and reasons: Narrative systematic review. *Curr Med Res Opinion*. 2010;26(3):683–705.

19. Dent LA, Stratton TP, Cochran GA. Establishing an on-site pharmacy in a community health center to help indigent patients access medications and to improve care. *J Amer Pharm Assoc (1996)*. 2002;42(3):497–507.

20. Wright WA, Gorman JM, Odorzynski M, Peterson MJ, Clayton C. Integrated pharmacies at community mental health centers: Medication adherence and outcomes. *J Manag Care Spec Pharm*. 2016;22(11):1330–6.

21. Syed ST, Gerber BS, Sharp LK. Traveling towards disease: Transportation barriers to health care access. *J Commun Heal*. 2013;38(5):976–93.

22. Mejzner N, Clark CE, Smith LF, Campbell JL. Trends in the diagnosis and management of hypertension: Repeated primary care survey in South West England. *Br J Gen Pract.* 2017;67(658):e306–e13.

23. Gomez-Cano M, Wiering B, Abel G, Campbell J, Clark C. Medication adherence and clinical outcomes in dispensing and non-dispensing practices: A cross-sectional analysis. *Br J Gen Pract.* 2021;71(702):e55–e61.

24. Cross R, McDonagh STJ, Cockroft E, Turner M, Isom M, Lambourn R, et al. *Recruitment and retention of staff in rural dispensing practice.* Preston: Society for Academic Primary Care Annual Scientific Meeting, 2022.

25. Ryan AM, Krinsky S, Kontopantelis E, Doran T. Long-term evidence for the effect of pay-for-performance in primary care on mortality in the UK: A population study. *Lancet.* 2016;388(10041):268–74.

26. Minchin M, Roland M, Richardson J, Rowark S, Guthrie B. Quality of care in the United Kingdom after removal of financial incentives. *N Eng J Med.* 2018;379(10):948–57.

27. Khdour MR, Hawwa AF, Kidney JC, Smyth BM, McElnay JC. Potential risk factors for medication non-adherence in patients with chronic obstructive pulmonary disease (COPD). *Eur J Clin Pharmacol.* 2012;68(10):1365–73.

28. Horne R, Weinman J. Patients' beliefs about prescribed medicines and their role in adherence to treatment in chronic physical illness. *J Psych Res.* 1999;47(6):555–67.

29. Mann DM, Ponieman D, Leventhal H, Halm EA. Predictors of adherence to diabetes medications: The role of disease and medication beliefs. *J Behav Med.* 2009;32(3):278–84.

30. Menckeberg TT, Bouvy ML, Bracke M, Kaptein AA, Leufkens HG, Raaijmakers JA, et al. Beliefs about medicines predict refill adherence to inhaled corticosteroids. *J Psych Res.* 2008;64(1):47–54.

31. Bultman DC, Svarstad BL. Effects of physician communication style on client medication beliefs and adherence with antidepressant treatment. *Patient Educ Couns.* 2000;40(2):173–85.

32. Arbuthnott A, Sharpe D. The effect of physician–patient collaboration on patient adherence in non-psychiatric medicine. *Patient Educ Couns.* 2009;77(1):60–7.

33. Ngoh LN. Health literacy: A barrier to pharmacist–patient communication and medication adherence. *J Amer Pharm Assoc.* 2009;49(5):e132–e49.

34. Schillinger D, Piette J, Grumbach K, Wang F, Wilson C, Daher C, et al. Closing the loop: Physician communication with diabetic patients who have low health literacy. *Arch Int Med.* 2003;163(1):83–90.

35. Tammes P, Morris RW, Murphy M, Salisbury C. Is continuity of primary care declining in England? Practice-level longitudinal study from 2012 to 2017. *Br J Gen Pract.* 2021;71(707):e432–e40.

36. Pereira Gray DJ, Sidaway-Lee K, White E, Thorne A, Evans PH. Continuity of care with doctors—a matter of life and death? A systematic review of continuity of care and mortality. *BMJ Open.* 2018;8(6):e021161.

37. Helfrich CD, Dolan ED, Simonetti J, Reid RJ, Joos S, Wakefield BJ, et al. Elements of team-based care in a patient-centered medical home are associated with lower burnout among VA primary care employees. *J Gen Intern Med.* 2014;29(Suppl 2):S659–66.

38. Lemieux-Charles L, McGuire WL. What do we know about health care team effectiveness? A review of the literature. *Med Care Res Rev.* 2006;63(3):263–300.

39. British Medical Association, NHS Employers. Dispensary services quality scheme: Supplementary guidance for revisions to the GMS contract 2006/07. https://dispensingdoctor.org/wp-content/uploads/2014/10/ciii8-GMSDispensary.pdf.

40. National Health Service Act 2006. www.legislation.gov.uk/ukpga/2006/41/pdfs/ukpga_20060041_en.pdf.

41. Ford JA, Turley R, Porter T, Shakespeare T, Wong G, Jones AP, et al. Access to primary care for socio-economically disadvantaged older people in rural areas: A qualitative study. *PLoS ONE.* 2018;13(3):e0193952.

42. Jordan H, Roderick P, Martin D, Barnett S. Distance, rurality and the need for care: Access to health services in South West England. *Int J Heal Geogr.* 2004;3(1):21.

43. Palmer B, Appleby J, Spencer J. *Rural health care: A rapid review of the impact of rurality on the costs of delivering health care.* London: National Centre for Rural Health and Care, 2019.

44. Goldacre B, Reynolds C, Powell-Smith A, Walker AJ, Yates TA, Croker R, et al. Do doctors in dispensing practices with a financial conflict of interest prescribe more expensive drugs? A cross-sectional analysis of English primary care prescribing data. *BMJ Open.* 2019;9(2):e026886.

45. Baines DL, Tolley KH, Whynes DK. The costs of prescribing in dispensing practices. *J Clin Pharm Therap.* 1996;21(5):343–8.

46. Wilcock M. Dispensing doctors and non-dispensing doctors—a comparison of their prescribing costs. *Int J Pharm Pract.* 2001;9(3):197–202.

47. Association BM, Employers N. Revisions to the GMS contract 2006/07 — Annex 8 Excessive or inappropriate prescribing guidance 2008. www.essexlmc.org.uk/wp-content/uploads/2014/04/Revisions_to_-GMS_-contract-_-full.pdf [Accessed 5 July 2022].

48. NHS England, NHS Improvement. *Standard general medical services contract.* London: NHS England, 2020. www.england.nhs.uk/publication/standard-general-medical-services-contract/ [Accessed 19 April 2022].

49. Baines D. Dispensing doctors. *BMJ Open.* 2019; 9(2). https://bmjopen.bmj.com/content/9/2/e026886.responses#dispensing-doctors.

50. Ryan M, Bond C. Dispensing physicians and prescribing pharmacists. *Pharm Econom.* 1994;5(1):8–17.

51. Billington S. *CQC matters: Regulating the safe and effective use of medicines.* Dispensing Doctors' Association annual conference. Birmingham: Best Practice, 2016.

52. Department of Health & Social Care. Rebalancing medicines legislation and pharmacy regulation programme: Consultation outcome 2022. www.gov.uk/government/consultations/pharmacy-legislation-on-dispensing-errors-and-organisational-governance/outcome/rebalancing-medicines-legislation-and-pharmacy-regulation-programme-consultation-outcome [Accessed 28 April 2022].

53. Annibal I, Sellick J, Turner JR, Haseldine J, Morris AM, Parish R. *APPG Rural Health & Care: Parliamentary inquiry.* Lincoln, NE: National Centre for Rural Health and Care, 2022.

54. Snow-Miller R. *Clinical pharmacists in general practice pilot.* London: NHS England, 2015.
55. Clark CE, Sims L. Hypertension care: Sharing the burden with pharmacists. *Br J Gen Pract.* 2018;68(675):458–459.
56. Hasan Ibrahim AS, Barry HE, Hughes CM. A systematic review of general practice-based pharmacists' services to optimize medicines management in older people with multimorbidity and polypharmacy. *Fam Pract.* 2021;38(4):509–523.
57. Stone MC, Williams HC. Clinical pharmacists in general practice: Value for patients and the practice of a new role. *Br J Gen Pract.* 2015;65(634):262–3.
58. Albasri A, Clark CE, Omboni S, McDonagh STJ, McManus RJ, Sheppard JP. Effective detection and management of hypertension through community pharmacy in England. *Pharm J* 2020; 304(7935).

CHAPTER 11

Rural Maternity Care and Family Support

....

Jaki Lambert and Helen Cheyne

INTRODUCTION

Maternity care in the UK has undergone repeated reorganisation over many years, with a consistent trend of centralisation and closure of rural services, based on the premise that maternity care in large urban centres is safer or 'better'. This is despite a lack of supporting evidence and government maternity policy that consistently recommends that women should have choice of place of birth and in contrast with many European countries where there is not the same drive to reduce variation in the size of obstetric units.[1] Workforce and education planning has increasingly focused on urban models of maternity care, making recruitment, retention and ongoing career development for staff in rural areas a challenge.[2]

Recent greater recognition in the UK of the need to respond to the voices of women and families, implement technology-enabled care and effective networks and encourage local access to reduce carbon footprint all appear to reflect a sea change in which maternity care is once again provided as locally as possible. Significant reviews of maternity services, however, highlight the importance of a systems approach to maternity care provision with effective leadership to ensure that, wherever care takes place, the workforce is supported by multidisciplinary care pathways and skills training so that identification, escalation, transfer and response are timely and ensure the best outcomes for women and newborns.[3]

This chapter focuses on how rural maternity care may be achieved in ways that provides forward-looking, safe, effective, evidence-based woman- and family-centred care.

DOI: 10.1201/9781003302438-16

CONTEXT OF RURAL MATERNITY CARE IN THE UK

In recent decades, the UK maternity landscape has changed considerably, with fewer obstetric units, reconfiguration of rural maternity units and rationalisation of neonatal units. There are currently only around 60 free-standing midwifery units in England, 22 in Scotland, 13 in Wales and 2 in Northern Ireland.[4]

The provision of maternity care in rural areas has long been subject to concerns about the development and maintenance of skills of staff and the safety of birth in rural areas versus the disruption of travel to more distant urban centres. It is widely acknowledged, both nationally and internationally, that a woman who is pregnant and lives in a rural area should have local access to maternity care and the option to give birth within her own community if she remains healthy, and her pregnancy is uncomplicated. In part, this is an issue of community resilience. Young families are less likely to settle in rural areas where no maternity care is available,[5,6] so removal of maternity services risks increasing the loss of young people, with an increasingly aging population and knock-on effects on the viability of rural schools etc. Current evidence indicates that, for healthy women with uncomplicated pregnancies, birth at home or in a midwifery-led unit is safe for mother and baby.[7,8,9] However, studies of maternity care in remote and rural settings highlight the importance of communication, understanding the local context, effective transfer options and respectful interdisciplinary working with knowledge and understanding of each other's roles. There is now increased recognition that culture, communication and context have as much impact on the safety of services as clinical skills.[10,11,12] There are, however, concerns that services are being removed rather than ensuring that all the systems are in place to provide safe, women-centred high-quality care locally. Co-production of care with the community supports resilience.

The rural workforce has also changed, with more advanced nursing roles and the welcome development of emergency medical retrieval teams[13] (critical care teams ready to respond by helicopter, plane or fast response vehicle) in some areas. New educational programs that recognise the challenges and training needs of rural practice have also been developed.

The COVID-19 pandemic has accelerated implementation of technology-enabled care (TEC), enabling more care to be brought around the family, with remote consulting and monitoring becoming the norm. For example, at the start of the pandemic, NHS Scotland rapidly rolled out a programme to support home blood pressure monitoring for pregnant women at higher risk of hypertension in pregnancy,[14] reducing the need for travel to the obstetric unit.

The use of TEC has revolutionised care provision, in some cases mitigating issues created by centralisation of services. Technology supports care that no longer relies on buildings and travel, building it around the woman and her family with coordination by the midwife.

Women and their families live within communities. For some women, pregnancy will trigger their first adult contact with health services. Others may have had input from several services pre-pregnancy. After discharge from maternity care, links with other services, including health visitors, continue.

Health visitors and midwives hold crucial roles in prevention and early intervention. Rural practice lends itself to true relationship-based care around the family, providing a seamless continuum from prebirth to school and beyond. Understanding of the impact of mental health and social and economic inequalities is key to future health and well-being, underpinning the need for effective family care and support in the early years.[15]

TEAMWORK OR A 'SPECIALIST' SERVICE?

The literature often describes 'stand-alone' midwifery units, but, in practice, maternity care in remote and rural settings is embedded in the local community and functions by linking it with the wider health and social care team. The composition of wider teams differs across the UK, but there are key aspects in common.

Rural areas require maternity care models that focus on relationships between professionals and service users that facilitate appropriate and informed care planning to safely meet the needs of women and families in or as close as possible to their homes and communities. This requires clear clinical pathways to tertiary care, access to the wider team when necessary and recognition of the role and value of generalists.

The challenge in rural areas is to balance equity of care provisions with increasing expectations and sustainability of services. Co-production of information for women on local service provision and realistic transfer times with input from local ambulance and paramedic services supports decision making.

Many rural services struggle to recruit and retain staff. This has been exacerbated by a trend towards a specialist model in which midwives and medics have specialist roles: for example, in perinatal mental health, diabetes or bereavement care. While this model may work well in urban areas with high population density, specialism can negatively impact available care provision and does not lend itself to sustainable or resilient services in dispersed communities with smaller workforces.

Rural maternity care relies, instead, on well-functioning generalist teams, but they are vulnerable because of overdependence on individuals to carry out specialist functions.

Members of generalist teams may still adopt special interests, acting as champions to keep the rest of the team updated and developing their careers. This model, the Buurtzorg international concept,[16] lends itself well to rural areas, supporting reflection and learning using a coaching model of supervision.[17]

To function effectively, teams require good communication, training together, mutual respect, understanding of local contexts and effective transport links.[18,19,20,21] The wider team will vary in different areas and between routine and emergency care. The key point is that rural practitioners need to know who their particular wider team is and undertake regular shared learning and scenario practice with them.[22] Table 11.1 describes the rural/remote rural care team for planned and unplanned care.

At the centre of care are the woman and her family within her community. Continuity of midwifery care is central to current UK maternity policy[23,24] and enshrined in Nursing and Midwifery Council Standards.[25] This means that all midwives work in models that enable a woman's primary midwife, supported by a team of midwives, to provide continuity of care through the maternity journey. There is robust evidence that continuity of care improves both clinical outcomes and women's experience of care.[26] However, as for any model, it requires effective workforce planning. There is also clear evidence from both midwifery and health visiting that care at

TABLE 11.1 Wider Teams for Planned and Unplanned Care

Wider Team Planned Care	Wider Team Unplanned/Emergency Care
Obstetric unit (referral centre)	Paramedic
Midwifery team including the primary midwife	Named/link obstetrician
Health visitor	Retrieval team
Maternity support workers	Emergency department
Sonography	Support staff
Mental health services	
Primary care	
Housing	
Social work	
Translation services	
Third sector	

home facilitates the woman feeling that her biopsychosocial needs are being met and supports prevention and early intervention.

EDUCATION AND TRAINING

There are two main questions to consider:

1   How can skills be maintained when exposure to some important aspects of clinical care and clinical emergencies is less frequent than in urban centres?
2   What specific skills are required to provide safe care in remote and rural settings?

There is now good evidence that simulation is an effective way to maintain competence in rarely used skills.[27,28,29] However, the ability to perform a skill in itself is not the only factor. Decision making and judgement are equally, if not more, important. Staff in remote and rural areas use the same clinical cues and make similar judgements as staff in urban centres, but decisions to take action or not vary widely.[30] Effective interdisciplinary working and communication are essential, including deciding when transfer and transport are required. Regardless of how effective simulation is, training must take into account human factors. Situational awareness of the context in which skills are applied should be integral to training.[31,32,33,34]

Evidence demonstrates that rural practitioners are able to identify situational risk factors just as well as their urban colleagues, but the barriers and challenges to effective care and confidence to practice are related to issues around transport, communication and the supportive relationship between teams.[35,36,37,38] Organisational culture, human factors and psychological safety all have an impact on quality.[39,40,41]

While simulation is effective in maintaining technical clinical skills, all team members who may be involved in managing an emergency should train together, whether in a maternity unit, emergency department or home situation, helping raise situational awareness and promote psychological safety. Linking community teams with larger units for training and updating improves relationships and helps all parties provide better care. Innovative ways of training have been accelerated during the COVID-19 pandemic through the use of technology.

What specific skills are required for remote and rural practice? Rural midwives need all the standard maternity skills plus additional skills and more frequent updating in:

- Advanced life support
- Risk assessment
- Triage
- Pre-transport care and transfer
- Communication with secondary care to prevent delays in recognition, transfer or action on arrival at the referral centre[42]

BENEFITS AND RISKS OF MODELS OF CARE

Remote and rural are not synonymous with isolation. The rural maternity care team should not be isolated from the wider services. Its model of care should be based around the community with strong networks to the wider team. Work on social capital clearly identifies that a well-functioning network is defined by the number and level of interactions and the ability of participants to contribute and influence. Conversely, in a poorly functioning network, information is transmitted one way only.[43]

In urban areas with dense populations, caseload size and acuity are key determinants for calculating midwifery workforce. Economies of scale are possible. Workforce planning for rural areas, where wide geographical areas with dispersed populations must be covered to provide a minimum safe service, is different. The ratio of midwives to births applied in urban areas does not apply. In order to provide safe 24/7 midwifery cover for birth and unscheduled care across a geographical locality or community, a team of between 5.2 and 5.8 WTE midwives is required, regardless of the number of births. Workforce planning also needs to take into account the requirement for additional time for training and education, reflecting the additional training required (see earlier in this chapter), travel time to courses and meetings and the need for placements in secondary referral units.[44] In practical terms, this means that 8 WTE midwives are required.

PATIENT EXPERIENCE IN DIFFERENT MODELS OF CARE

Policy and professional regulation prioritise person-centred care. Involving women and families in the design of care is important to ensure that the needs of individuals and the community are met. It is also important that the community understands the limitations of available services and that discussions regarding place of birth include a clear understanding of risk, including the services and skills available and the time required to transfer to an urban centre, if necessary.

This requires services to have access to their own data for audit, improvement and supporting decision making.

A number of studies from New Zealand, Canada, Australia and Scotland indicate that women want local birth and that travel for care can be distressing.[45,46,47,48,49] The way in which information is presented to women influences decision making. For example, only advising about risks or presenting options for care as recommendations does not facilitate true informed decision making. Lack of choice has increasingly resulted in women choosing 'freebirth', in which they give birth without NHS services.[50]

A survey undertaken biannually since 2014 in remote and rural Scotland has consistently indicated that women were happy to travel for care when it was essential but that routine travel for appointments, scans and consultations was costly and stressful. The lack of local provision results in the most vulnerable being at risk of not attending.

The voice of the community can be powerful in ensuring that local service provision can be maintained or a suitable model developed. However, challenges may arise when community expectations are not achievable. This can lead to a breakdown in communication and dissatisfaction with available care. Working with communities from the outset is therefore important to maintain relationships and to enable true co-production.

CONCLUSION

Maternity care in remote and rural areas is an essential part of a resilient community and has an important part to play in the future health of the population. The use of technology enables teams to move away from a focus on a centralised urban hub and to develop virtual teams and systems that enable oversight of care regardless of location. However, no matter how or where care is provided, the development of positive, respectful relationships across the whole maternity care team must be a priority.

REFERENCES

1   Sandall J. *Place of birth in Europe.* WHO, 2015. www.euro.who.int/__data/ assets/pdf_file/0010/277741/Place-of-birth-in-Europe.pdf   [Accessed   3 February, 2022].

2   Barclay L, Kornelsen J, Longman J, Robin S, Kruske S, Kildea S, Pilcher J, Martin T, Grzybowski S, Donoghue D. Rolfe M, Morgan G. Reconceptualising risk: Perceptions of risk in rural and remote maternity service planning. *Midwifery.* 2016; 38: 63–70. https://doi.org/10.1016/j.midw.2016.04.007.

3   Ockenden D. *Findings, conclusions and essential actions from the independent review of maternity services at The Shrewsbury and Telford Hospital NHS Trust.* London: HMSO, 2022. www.ockendenmaternityreview.org.uk/ wp-content/uploads/2022/03/FINAL_INDEPENDENT_MATERNITY_ REVIEW_OF_MATERNITY_SERVICES_REPORT.pdf [Accessed 19 May, 2022].

4   Coxon K. *Freestanding Midwifery Units: Local, High Quality Maternity Care.* Royal College of Midwives, 2012. www.rcm.org.uk/media/2353/ freestanding-midwifery-units-busting-the-myths.pdf [Accessed 6 April 2022].

5   Wishner J, Solleveld P, Rudowitz R, Paradise J, Antonisse L. *A Look at Rural Hospital Closures and Implications for Access to Care: Three Case Studies.* Kaiser Family Foundation, 2016. www.kff.org/medicaid/issue-brief/a-look-at-rural-hospital-closures-and-implications-for-access-to-care/ [Accessed 6 April, 2022].

6   Barclay L, Kornelsen J, Longman J, Robin S, Kruske S, Kildea S, Pilcher J, Martin T, Grzybowski S, Donoghue D, Rolfe M, Morgan G. Reconceptualising risk: Perceptions of risk in rural and remote maternity service planning. *Midwifery.* 2016; 38: 63–70. https://doi.org/10.1016/j.midw.2016.04.007.

7   Birthplace in England Collaborative Group. Perinatal and maternal outcomes by planned place of birth for healthy women with low risk pregnancies: The Birthplace in England national prospective cohort study. *BMJ.* 2011; 343: d7400. https://doi.org/10.1136/bmj.d7400.

8   Scarf VL, Rossiter C, Vedam S, Dahlen HG, Ellwood D, Forster D, et al. Maternal and perinatal outcomes by planned place of birth among women with low-risk pregnancies in high-income countries: A systematic review and meta-analysis. *Midwifery.* 2018; 62: 240–55. https://doi.org/10.1016/j. midw.2018.03.024.

9   Hutton EK, Reitsma A, Simioni J, Brunton G, Kaufman K. Perinatal or neonatal mortality among women who intend at the onset of labour to give birth at home compared to women of low obstetrical risk who intend to give birth in hospital: A systematic review and meta-analyses. *EClinicalMedicine.* 2019; 14: 59–70. https://doi.org/10.1016/j.eclinm.2019.07.005.

10 Kirkup B. *The report of the Morecambe Bay investigation,* 2015. https://assets. publishing.service.gov.uk/government/uploads/system/uploads/attachment_ data/file/408480/47487_MBI_Accessible_v0.1.pdf [Accessed 6 April, 2022].

11 RCOG Introduction to human factors in maternity I eLearning (rcog.org.uk).

12 Ockenden D. *Findings, conclusions and essential actions from the independent review of maternity services at The Shrewsbury and Telford Hospital NHS Trust.* London: HMSO, 2022. www.ockendenmaternityreview.org.uk/

wp-content/uploads/2022/03/FINAL_INDEPENDENT_MATERNITY_
REVIEW_OF_MATERNITY_SERVICES_REPORT.pdf [Accessed 19 May, 2022].

13 NHS Scotland. *Emergency medical retrieval service.* www.emrsscotland.org/ [Accessed 6 April, 2022].

14 Scottish Perinatal Network. *Home blood pressure and urine monitoring.* www.perinatalnetwork.scot/maternity/home-monitoring/home-bp-and-urine-monitoring/ [Accessed 6 April, 2022].

15 MBRRACE-UK. Saving lives improving mothers care, 2021. www.birthcompanions.org.uk/resources/244-mbrrace-uk-saving-lives-improving-mothers-care-2020 [Accessed 6 April, 2022].

16 Buurtzorg International. The Buurtzorg model. www.buurtzorg.com/about-us/buurtzorgmodel/ [Accessed 6 April, 2022].

17 Francis A. *Neighbourhood Midwives: The Model That Boosted Continuity of Care by 500%*, 2021. https://q.health.org.uk/event/neighbourhood-midwives-the-model-that-boosted-continuity-of-care-by-500-annie-francis/ [Accessed 6 April 2022].

18 Cheyne H, et al. Risk assessment and decision making about in-labour transfer from rural maternity care: A social judgment and signal detection analysis. *BMC Med Inf Dec Making.* 2012; 12: 122. www.biomedcentral.com/1472-6947/12/122.

19 Crowther S, Smythe E. Open, trusting relationships underpin safety in rural maternity a hermeneutic phenomenology study. *BMC Preg Childbirth.* 2016; 16: 370.

20 Gilkison A, Rankin J, Kensington M, Daellenbach R, Davies L, Deery R, Crowther S. A woman's hand and a lion's heart: Skills and attributes for rural midwifery practice in New Zealand and Scotland. *Midwifery.* 2018; 58: 109–16. https://doi.org/10.1016/j.midw.2017.12.009.

21 Harris FM, Van Teijlingen E, Hundley V, Farmer J, Bryers H, Caldow J, Ireland J, Kiger A, Tucker J. The buck stops here: Midwives and maternity care in rural Scotland. *Midwifery.* 2011; 27(3): 301–7. https://doi.org/10.1016/j.midw.2010.10.007.

22 Liberati EG, Tarrant C, Willars J, Draycott T, Winter C, Kuberska K, Paton A, Marjanovic S, Leach B, Lichten C, Hocking L, Ball S, Dixon-Woods M. Seven features of safety in maternity units: A framework based on multisite ethnography and stakeholder consultation. *BMJ Qual Saf.* 2021; 30: 444–56. https://qualitysafety.bmj.com/content/early/2020/09/25/bmjqs-2020-010988.

23 NHS England. *National maternity review. Better births; improving outcomes of maternity services in England.* London: NHS England, 2016.

24 Scottish Government. *The best start: A five-year forward plan for maternity and neonatal care in Scotland.* Edinburgh: Scottish Government, 2017.

25 Nursing and Midwifery Council. *Standards of Proficiencies for Midwives.* London: NMC, 2019. www.nmc.org.uk/globalassets/sitedocuments/standards/standards-of-proficiency-for-midwives.pdf [Accessed 6 April, 2022].

26 Sandall J, Soltani H, Gates S, Shennan A, Devane D. Midwife-led continuity models versus other models of care for childbearing women. *Cochrane Database of Systematic Reviews*, 2016. www.cochranelibrary.com/cdsr/doi/10.1002/14651858.CD004667.pub5/full.

27 Bergh A-M, Baloyi S, Pattinson RC. What is the impact of multi-professional emergency obstetric and neonatal care training? *Best Pract Res Clin Obstet Gynaecol.* 2015; 29(8): 1028–43. https://doi.org/10.1016/j.bpobgyn.2015.03.017.

28 Munro S, Kornelsen J, Grzybowski S. Models of maternity care in rural environments: Barriers and attributes of interprofessional collaboration with midwives. *Midwifery.* 2013; 29(6): 646–52. https://doi.org/10.1016/j.midw.2012.06.004.

29 Siassakos D, Crofts JF, Winter C, Weiner CP, Draycott TJ. The active components of effective training in obstetric emergencies. *BJOG.* 2009; 116(8):1028–32. https://doi.org/10.1111/j.1471–0528.2009.02178.x.

30 Cheyne H, Dalgleish L, Tucker J, Kane F, Shetty A, McLeod S, Niven C. Risk assessment and decision making about in-labour transfer from rural maternity care: A social judgment and signal detection analysis. *BMC Med Inf Dec Making.* 2012; 12: 122. www.biomedcentral.com/1472-6947/12/122.

31 Tunçalp Ö, Were WM, MacLennan C, Oladapo OT, Gülmezoglu AM, Bahl R, Daelmans B, Mathai M, Say L, Kristensen F, Temmerman M, Bustreo F. Quality of care for pregnant women and newborns—the WHO vision. *BJOG.* 2015; 122: 1045–49. https://doi.org/10.1111/1471–0528.13451.

32 Renfrew MJ, McFadden A, Bastos MH, Campbell J, Channon AA, Fen Cheung N, Silva DRAD, Downe S, Kennedy HP, Malata A, McCormick F, Wick L, Declercq E. Midwifery and quality care: Findings from a new evidence-informed framework for maternal and newborn care. *Lancet.* 2014; 384: 1129–45. https://doi.org/10.1016/S0140–6736(14)60789–3.

33 Cheyne H, Dalgleish L, Tucker J, Kane F, Shetty A, McLeod S, Niven C. Risk assessment and decision making about in-labour transfer from rural maternity care: A social judgment and signal detection analysis. *BMC Med Inf Dec Making.* 2012; 12: 122. www.biomedcentral.com/1472-6947/12/122.

34 Liberati EG, Tarrant C, Willars J, Draycott T, Winter C, Kuberska K, Paton A, Marjanovic S, Leach B, Lichten C, Hocking L, Ball S, Dixon-Woods M. Seven features of safety in maternity units: A framework based on multisite ethnography and stakeholder consultation. *BMJ Qual Saf.* 2021; 30: 444–56. https://qualitysafety.bmj.com/content/early/2020/09/25/bmjqs-2020–010988.

35 Cheyne H, Dalgleish L, Tucker J, Kane F, Shetty A, McLeod S, Niven C. Risk assessment and decision making about in-labour transfer from rural maternity care: A social judgment and signal detection analysis. *BMC Med Inf Dec Making.* 2012; 12: 122. www.biomedcentral.com/1472-6947/12/122.

36 Harris FM, Van Teijlingen E, Hundley V, Farmer J, Bryers H, Caldow J, Ireland J, Kiger A, Tucker J. The buck stops here: Midwives and maternity care in rural Scotland. *Midwifery.* 2011; 27(3): 301–7. https://doi.org/10.1016/j.midw.2010.10.007.

37 Gilkison A, Rankin J, Kensington M, Daellenbach R, Davies L, Deery R, Crowther S. A woman's hand and a lion's heart: Skills and attributes for rural midwifery practice in New Zealand and Scotland. *Midwifery.* 2018; 58: 109–16. https://doi.org/10.1016/j.midw.2017.12.009.

38 de Jong T. Linking social capital to knowledge productivity: An explorative study on the relationship between social capital and learning in knowledge-productive

networks. University of Twente, 2010. https://research.utwente.nl/en/publications/linking-social-capital-to-knowledge-productivity-an-explorative-s.

39 Crowther S, Smythe E. Open, trusting relationships underpin safety in rural maternity a hermeneutic phenomenology study. *BMC Preg Childbirth*. 2016; 16: 370. https://bmcpregnancychildbirth.biomedcentral.com/articles/10.1186/s12884-016-1164-9.

40 Reeves S, Perrier L, Goldman J, Freeth D, Zwarenstein M. Interprofessional education: Effects on professional practice and healthcare outcomes. *Cochr Database Syst Rev*, 2013. www.cochranelibrary.com/cdsr/doi/10.1002/14651858.CD002213.pub3/full.

41 Liberati EG, Tarrant C, Willars J, Draycott T, Winter C, Kuberska K, Paton A, Marjanovic S, Leach B, Lichten C, Hocking L, Ball S, Dixon-Woods M. Seven features of safety in maternity units: A framework based on multisite ethnography and stakeholder consultation. *BMJ Qual Saf*. 2021; 30: 444–56. https://qualitysafety.bmj.com/content/early/2020/09/25/bmjqs-2020–010988.

42 Rowe R, Draper ES, Kenyon S, Bevan C, Dickens J, Forrester M, Scanlan R, Tuffnell D, Kurinczuk JJ. Intrapartum-related perinatal deaths in births planned in midwifery-led settings in Great Britain: Findings and recommendations from the ESMiE confidential enquiry. *BJOG*. 2020; 127(13): 1665–75. https://doi.org/10.1111/1471–0528.16327.

43 de Jong T. *Linking social capital to knowledge productivity: An explorative study on the relationship between social capital and learning in knowledge-productive networks*. University of Twente, 2010. https://research.utwente.nl/en/publications/linking-social-capital-to-knowledge-productivity-an-explorative-s.

44 Lambert J, Marshall H. Do remote and rural practitioners maintain competence in skills required but rarely used? Helene Marshall, Principal Educator (NMAHP), NHS Education for Scotland Jaki Lambert, Midwifery Adviser to Scottish Government conference-programme.pdf (scot.nhs.uk), 2021

45 Coxon K, Chisholm A, Malouf R, Rowe R, Hollowell J. What influences birth place preferences, choices and decision-making amongst healthy women with straightforward pregnancies in the UK? A qualitative evidence synthesis using a 'best fit' framework approach. *BMC Preg Childbirth*. 2017; 17: 103. https://doi.org/10.1186/s12884-017-1279-7.

46 Kornelsen J, Kotaska A, Waterfall P, Willie L, Wilson D. Alienation and resilience: The dynamics of birth outside their community for rural first nations women. *J Aboriginal Heal*. 2011; 7(1): 55–64. https://med-fom-crhr.sites.olt.ubc.ca/files/2012/02/alienationandresilience.pdf.

47 Crowther S, Smythe E. Open, trusting relationships underpin safety in rural maternity a hermeneutic phenomenology study. *BMC Preg Childbirth*. 2016; 16: 370. https://bmcpregnancychildbirth.biomedcentral.com/articles/10.1186/s12884-016-1164-9.

48 Pitchforth E, van Teijlingen E, Watson V, Tucker J, Kiger A, Ireland J, Farmer J, Rennie A-M, Gibb S, Thomson E, Ryan M. 'Choice' and place of delivery: A qualitative study of women in remote and rural Scotland. *Qual Saf Health Care*. 2009; 18(1): 42–8. https://doi.org/10.1136/qshc.2007.023572.

49 Patterson J, Foureur M, Skinner J. Remote rural women's choice of birthplace and transfer experiences in rural Otago and Southland New Zealand. *Midwifery*. 2017; 52: 49–56. https://doi.org/10.1016/j.midw.2017.05.014.

50 Royal College of Midwives. *RCM clinical Briefing sheet: 'Freebirth' or 'unassisted childbirth' during the COVID-19 pandemic*. RCM, 2020. www.rcm.org.uk/media/3923/freebirth_draft_30-april-v2.pdf [Accessed 6 April, 2022].

CHAPTER 12

Rural Nursing

....

Tim Sanders, Margaret Nelson and Ruth Blundell

Nursing in rural communities is full of opportunities to deliver high quality, continuity-based, holistic, patient-centred care, collaborating as a member of a close-knit but diverse multidisciplinary team. Rural populations are frequently stoical and hardy, often presenting late with more developed pathologies. Many prefer to be cared for in the community, either at the surgery or in the home. Families are commonly on hand, quietly providing support to their relatives.

These multidisciplinary teams are increasingly diverse, including professionals not traditionally involved in rural primary healthcare, such as paramedics, physiotherapists and pharmacists, the latter of whose numbers increased by 40% in England in 2018–19, supported by the Additional Roles Reimbursement Scheme.[1, 2] Many teams include psychology and well-being practitioners who support physical and emotional well-being and promote personal responsibility for health through coaching and social prescribing.

Although there was an overall 2.8% increase in the number of full-time equivalent (FTE) staff working in the NHS in 2018–19, the number of nurses rose more slowly at only 1.5% over the same period and 3% over five years. The smallest increases were in community and general practice nursing. This is reflected in the pressures seen in these areas of clinical practice.

In 2019–20 there were 44,000 NHS nurse vacancies (equivalent to 12% of the workforce), with a projected shortfall of up to 100,000 over the next ten years.[3] The UK government has committed to increasing the number of nurses in training.[4]

DOI: 10.1201/9781003302438-17

As discussed in Chapter 16: Rural Social Exclusion, to compensate for the shortfall, which disproportionately affects rural areas,[5] rural health-care employers have substituted more registered nurses with unregistered support staff such as healthcare assistants. Over the last ten years, the proportion of clinical support staff to nurses increased by 10%.[2]

NURSING ROLES

A variety of different roles sit within community and practice nursing teams. Within the UK NHS, these have been formalised[6] and are summarised here:

- **Community Nursing**

  - *Healthcare assistant (HCA)*: Does not require a nursing qualification. Not registered. Provides care under the close supervision and guidance of a qualified healthcare professional (usually a practice or community nurse). Level 2 and 3 qualifications in healthcare support are desirable but not a pre-requisite.
  - *Nurse associate*: This is a new role that bridges the gap between an HCA and registered general nursing, strengthening a vocational

route into primary care nursing. Nurse associates have undertaken a level 5, two-year associate nursing foundation degree programme and are registered with the NMC. They can take responsibility for their own non-complex caseload and/or carry out duties under the direction of a registered nurse.

- *Assistant practitioner (AP)*: Like nurse associates, APs have undertaken a level 5, two-year foundation degree. For APs, this is in health or social care. AP training is broader based, encompassing a variety of disciplines including physiotherapy, occupational therapy, speech and language and lymphoedema, as well as general nursing. Like APs, they can take responsibility for their own non-complex caseload, but unlike APs, this role is not currently registered with any professional regulatory body.
- *Community staff nurse*: A registered general nurse. These practitioners have undertaken additional training modules relating to the community nursing role.
- *Community specialist practitioner (district nurse/team leader)*: A registered nurse holding an NMC specialist community practitioner qualification. This includes supplementary/non-medical prescribing. The team leader role includes management, governance, incident investigation, team leadership, promoting good practice and budgeting alongside clinical work.
- *Senior district nurse/team leader*: A district nurse with additional qualifications in mentorship or supplementary prescribing.
- *Advanced community nurse practitioner (ANP)*: A qualified nurse, registered with the NMC. ANPs have undergone additional training in clinical assessment and prescribing via a higher degree. ANPs carry out assessment and diagnosis and deliver care with a degree of autonomy beyond that of a practice nurse.

- **General Practice Nursing**

  - *Healthcare assistant (HCA)/nurse associate/assistant practitioner (AP)*: as per community nursing.
  - *General practice nurse*: Registered general nurse (RGN) with the Nursing and Midwifery Council (NMC).
  - *Senior general practice nurse*: A general practice nurse with additional qualifications in mentorship, prescribing and aspects of clinical practice.
  - *Advanced nurse practitioner (ANP)*: A qualified nurse, registered with the NMC. ANPs have undergone additional training via a

higher degree in clinical assessment and prescribing. ANPs carry out assessment, diagnosis and deliver care with a degree of autonomy beyond that of a practice nurse.

TRAINING

Since the late 1990s, nurse training has changed from predominantly vocational courses towards those with a more academic focus. Over that period, nursing has developed far greater professionalism and accountability, with a clear code of professional standards of practice set out by its regulatory body, the Nursing and Midwifery Council (NMC).[7] Nursing roles, too, have expanded, with a blurring of the boundaries between traditionally 'medical' and 'nursing' tasks. Nurses now delegate tasks to less qualified members of their teams rather than having tasks delegated to them by others. Better-defined training pathways and opportunities for higher training have enabled career progression and an increase in advanced practice nurse numbers from 17% in 2015 to 22% in 2019–20.[2]

COMMUNITY NURSING

Knowledge and Skills

Whether in rural or urban settings, community nurses' caseloads are very varied, requiring teams to include a wide skill mix. Additional training—for example, in palliative care, leg ulcer management, intravenous and central catheter care, syringe driver management and urinary catheter care—enables community nurses to fulfil the various aspects of their role. District nursing teams often nominate 'champion' roles in areas such as tissue viability or diabetes. Champions provide clinical opinions and knowledge to their teams.

Due to the smaller size of the teams they work in, rural community nurses have the opportunity to develop greater autonomy and a broader-based, more generalist skillset. Although opportunities to develop special interests exist (indeed, specialist expertise is highly valued within teams), there remains a strong need to be a 'Jack or Jill of all trades'. Support, where it is available, tends to come from a distance away, meaning that sound clinical knowledge, resourcefulness, resilience and an ability to think creatively help fulfil the need to be able to 'stand on your own two feet' to provide care while waiting for help to arrive.

Geography and Transport

Home visits tend to be spread out across a wide area. Good route planning is necessary to fit them all in efficiently, but clinical priorities and the need to coordinate with colleagues for visits that require more than one practitioner can complicate matters.

The aging rural population places additional pressure on rural community nursing services, which have greater-than-average per capita caseloads of frail, elderly and housebound patients, many of whom are unable to walk or take a short taxi or bus ride to the clinic. It is not unusual for farmhouses to be ten minutes or more away from the road along farm tracks that, while providing no obstacle to the intrepid nurse, some taxis are unwilling to cross. Suitable transport, where it is available, tends to be private, but additional time spent in transit is often exhausting for patients, leading to a need for more home visiting in rural areas.

Coupled with these transport challenges, economies of scale that are facilitated by grouping patients into dressings and catheter clinics in more densely populated areas are difficult to realise in the rural setting.

Seasonal variations resulting from tourism-related traffic on small rural roads and adverse weather events including heavy snow, flooding and fallen trees caused by storms can have a significant impact. During adverse weather events, communities tend to pull together, supporting the service, with colleagues being transported up to farms in tractors. The assistance of mountain rescue team volunteers who readily give up their time when it is needed can also be invaluable.

Working with the Wider Community Team

Extra distances take extra time, and considerable numbers of healthcare worker hours are lost to travel across a rural county. A proportion of this time is inevitably lost from patient care through shorter or less frequent visits.

It would be easy to view this negatively, but this additional pressure stimulates rural community teams to be innovative and work more efficiently. In some teams, focus is given to working collaboratively with other professionals in the skill mix. Allocation of a lead practitioner, who might be a nurse, occupational therapist, physiotherapist or HCA, for each patient helps reduce the number of practitioners visiting each patient's house. The lead practitioner provides continuity and aims to gather all necessary information for patient care, not limiting it to that required for their individual specialty. They aim to do as much as they can for their patients, calling on colleagues for advice or practical input when necessary.

Collaborative working between community and practice nursing teams enables skill-mix gaps to be filled when specialist skills, knowledge and experience are required: for example, in the management of patients with central lines, diabetes, COPD and asthma.

The small team–based nature of rural healthcare means that practitioners from all teams tend to work in closer proximity, with opportunities to meet both formally and informally throughout the working week. This makes it easier to take an overview of the needs of the patient so that the different teams can collaborate and avoid inefficient 'silo working'.

PRACTICE NURSING

Nurses are important members of GP practice teams, with a ratio of approximately one nurse to every two GPs.[2] In small rural practices, the practice nursing team may be very small with one whole-time equivalent RGN and one HCA for a practice population of 2,500 to 5,000 patients. This could lead to professional isolation, but locality nurse forums and protected learning time offer much-needed peer support and ease isolation. Increasingly, groups of practices are coming together to deliver more integrated care over a wider geography. This brings opportunities for a nominated lead nurse appointed to represent their profession and the community it serves.

GP nursing (GPN) teams have taken on increasing responsibility for chronic disease management, frail patients, preventative healthcare interventions, sexual health, coil fitting and cervical smears. Some of this activity is 'new', arising from the increased focus on long-term condition management seen in the UK over the last 20 years.[8] Shifting activity from general practitioners to nurses has freed up GP time, which, particularly in rural practices, allows them to focus better on caring for their proportionately higher aging populations with associated, complex comorbidities.

Within the older parts of rural communities, there remains a stoic, accepting population who present later and adopt a less questioning approach to their management. A more direct, 'straight-talking' approach can be necessary to meet the expectations of this group of patients.

Rural practice teams tend to be small, often with less attention paid to traditional professional hierarchies. Relationships are professional but commonly comfortably informal. Practice nursing teams benefit from the support and encouragement of more intimate teams so that they can find creative solutions to complex challenges. This leads to greater individual confidence and more rewarding, autonomous practice. It also contributes positively to managing practice workload and streamlining patient care.

Within the surgery, the complexity of care delivered has increased over time, with practice nurses seeing presenting problems and carrying out interventions that they would not have managed in the past. Protocols, guidelines and policies support the delivery of care, but in rural locations, flexibility, resourcefulness and the ability to act autonomously are valuable attributes. Rural experience during training helps those who are privileged to access it develop these attributes with greater confidence.

Patients expect accessible care and prefer not to have to travel to major centres for treatment. Frailer patients who can travel short distances to visit the surgery might be exhausted by a two-hour round trip to the local hospital. Rural practice nurses, therefore, need broad knowledge and a wide set of skills to offer care that, elsewhere, would be delivered by specialist services. Care delivered this way is supported by good liaison and shared care arrangements with specialist colleagues: for example, vascular and tissue viability teams and specialist diabetology services.

ADVANCED NURSE PRACTITIONER (ANP)

What started in hospitals as an informal delegation and local shifts of responsibility has subsequently been formalised into advanced practitioner roles with MSc-level training in advanced clinical practice. Training includes prescribing, which allows ANPs to prescribe within their scope of clinical practice with minimal restrictions. ANPs are now commonplace in primary care, making a significant contribution to management of the workload and enhancing the scope of the team by bringing clinical approaches, philosophies and experiences born out of their professional journeys.

Rural primary care ANPs usually develop a broad-based generalist skillset. Like all clinical practitioners, they need and benefit from good support, with clear lines of referral and escalation of cases that sit outside their scope of practice. They are well placed to take on clinical leadership roles—for example, hypertension management—working with other nurses and a pharmacist.

Unlike their hospital equivalents, rural primary care ANPs' specialist interests tend to be service rather than clinical specialty focused: for example, same-day primary care, out-of-hours care or home visiting, as opposed to gastroenterology or cardiology.

ANPs in rural locations make an important and cost-effective contribution to the workforce through their autonomous ability to make clinical assessments and diagnoses and provide treatments. They also provide community nursing skills and experience. This is particularly valuable in areas where recruitment and retention of primary care doctors and nurses are either not possible or economically unviable.

REFERENCES

1. NHS England. Network contract directed enhanced service: Additional roles reimbursement scheme guidance. www.england.nhs.uk/publication/network-contract-directed-enhanced-service-additional-roles-reimbursement-scheme-guidance/ [Accessed 18 May 2022].
2. Buchan J, Gershlick B, Charlesworth A, Seccombe I. Falling short: The NHS workforce challenge. *Health Foundation*, 2019. www.health.org.uk/publications/reports/falling-short-the-nhs-workforce-challenge [Accessed 18 May 2022].
3. Closing the gap. *The King's Fund*, 2019. www.kingsfund.org.uk/publications/closing-gap-health-care-workforce [Accessed 18 May 2022].
4. NHS Long Term Plan. www.longtermplan.nhs.uk/ [Accessed 18 May 2022].
5. All-Party Parliamentary Group on Rural Services. *The implications of national funding formulae for rural health and education provision: Summary report.* London: Rural Services Network, 2010. www.rsnonline.org.uk/images/files/appgfunding-summary-260310.pdf [Accessed 2 June 2022].
6. NHS Health Careers. Types of nursing. www.healthcareers.nhs.uk/explore-roles/nursing/roles-nursing [Accessed 31 July 2022].
7. The Nursing and Midwifery Council. The Code: Professional standards of practice and behaviour for nurses, midwives and nursing associates. www.nmc.org.uk/standards/code/ [Accessed 3 April 2022].
8. The King's Fund. The management of long-term conditions. www.kingsfund.org.uk/projects/gp-inquiry/management-long-term-conditions [Accessed 1 June 2022].

CHAPTER 13

Safeguarding

....

Venetia Young

Safeguarding means protecting a citizen's health, well-being and human rights, enabling a person to live free from harm, abuse and neglect.

Local authorities in the UK have a statutory duty to safeguard children and adults from risk of harm, working alongside the police, who are responsible for public protection and criminality. Health and education services are expected to support them in these roles.

Effective safeguarding in primary care is about forming good working relationships between patients, families and practice staff and across statutory and voluntary services. It is about thinking preventatively and proactively, not passively and reactively. It is also about the humble realisation that there is a lot 'we don't know that we don't know' and appreciating that this may be an unsafe position to be in, for our patients and ourselves.

Safeguarding child and adult patients in rural primary care presents further challenges. With increased distances between patients, professionals and support agencies, good communication and working relationships with adult and child social care agencies, police, schools, and secondary care health systems assume a greater significance.

Primary healthcare professionals are familiar with uncertainty in diagnosis and the need for the 'biological safety netting' of medication and management to ensure that patients are safe if things do not go as expected. The same principles, which also apply to suicide risk and psychological safety in mental health, can be applied to worrying and unsafe social

DOI: 10.1201/9781003302438-18

situations. Safeguarding procedures are really the formalisation of 'social safety netting'.

There are many domains of safeguarding: physical, sexual, emotional, financial and institutional.

Using case studies around family violence throughout the life cycle, this chapter aims to make safeguarding feel interesting, satisfying and worthwhile. There is a female focus in the cases as this is the commonest form of violence. Professional curiosity is essential. If the professional and voluntary sector support systems are known around each of the presentations of family violence at different life cycle stages, then it is possible to have the necessary challenging conversations to keep children and families safe.

In rural areas, domestic abuse is as prevalent as in cities but reported 50% less often. It lasts 25% longer than in urban settings.[1]

CASE STUDY 1

An Immobile Infant and a Bruise

A six-week-old baby who had recently moved to the area was brought to the mother's postnatal check. Previous records had not arrived.

A bruise was noted on the left chest wall. The mother's explanation was that the cat landed heavily on the baby. A little later, she changed her story, blaming her rough toddler.

There is a saying: 'Babies who don't cruise don't bruise'. Serious case reviews of infant deaths have shown repeatedly that, even with only one bruise presented, there may only be one opportunity to protect the child. The next injury may be fatal. Case reviews of babies who die frequently show that there were multiple old fractures and other undiagnosed injuries.[2]

What should the health professional's first thoughts be? Is the baby ill? Is the baby safe? First, rule out illnesses such as leukaemia and clotting disorders and then record detailed observations about who is present and what is said. Symptoms, signs and decisions must be documented carefully, but it is for social care services and police to do the detective work of who did what and when and decide what should happen.

The role of general practitioners and their health colleagues is simply to make sure the child is safe and properly investigated in conjunction with social care and police when needed. Noting other risk factors may be important in the referral: history of domestic violence and abuse (DVA), mental health problems and alcohol and drug misuse—called the toxic trio in child protection (CP).

In this case, a changing narrative around a bruise is a significant finding in itself. An immobile infant with a bruise should always be referred to paediatrics. A referral to children's services and also to police may be needed at the same time. See your local authority safeguarding website for details of local referral processes. In terms of injury prevention, ICON produce evidence-based advice for parents about managing crying babies.[3,4]

CASE STUDY 2

A Toddler Injury

A little boy, aged two, was already on the practice's 'serious concern list'— a list of children on formal child protection plans and of concern. The child was first seen in a rural minor injuries unit, having fallen onto the top of his head (not the usual site of toddler falls) and vomited once. He was referred to an accident and emergency department 25 miles away, admitted to the children's ward and discharged back to his mother's care the next day.

An astute administrative person in the practice noticed that there was no evidence in any of these contacts that child protection concerns were asked about. On being informed, the health visitor assessed the situation and ensured that he was promptly removed to his grandmother's care and re-referred to social care services, and a child protection plan was put in place.

The case was discussed at the primary care monthly safeguarding meeting held in the practice and a family tree constructed. Although the baby's 17-year-old single-parent mother had attended the out-of-hours general practice service several times when intoxicated, it was not on their records that she had a child at home. The baby's father, who was a patient in a different practice, also had a drink problem but was less visible to services.

Family trees are a good way of making visible the violent man who may move around local families creating harm.[5] Health visitors may also have relevant local knowledge.

The whole practice team held a significant event case discussion, which highlighted the importance of safeguarding being everyone's concern. The learning engaged staff on an emotional level, changing future practice. Every member of staff understood the need to report concerns to the practice safeguarding lead or the duty doctor. They understood how individual professionals may only see one part of the jigsaw puzzle and the need to report apparently small concerns: e.g. pushing and shoving in the waiting room, over-ordering or erratic ordering of prescriptions, shouting on the phone, a feeling of oppression when a father is in the nurse's room with a step-child. The practice's child protection antennae were developing.

As a result of the case discussion, the out-of-hours GP and local paediatric services were made aware of the observations.

The paediatric service was shamefaced that the little boy had been admitted six months earlier with suspicious bruising, but they had not connected the two admissions. Junior staff were trained to routinely ask referring GPs if there were child protection concerns.

Child protection training, based on the case, was implemented for all out-of-hours service clinical staff and documentation improved to include the names of parents and adults accompanying children, identifying who had parental responsibility. Practices are now notified of children who are frequent out-of-hours attenders.

This resulted in a mother of a one-year-old arriving very angry in the surgery, saying, 'They say I'm attending with trivial things'. The encounter was nevertheless worthwhile because she had an undiagnosed late-onset postnatal depression and bipolar disorder. She became grateful for the intervention, which meant that her illness was picked up speedily before she became really ill and put her child at risk. This is preventative safeguarding.

Lessons may be best learned on active or near-miss cases. Systems of care can change significantly as a result.

CASE STUDY 3

A Pill Check

An 18-year-old teenager came for a pill check with a poorly disguised bruised eye. She admitted ruefully that her boyfriend hit her after he'd been out drinking with friends. She proudly said that he had apologised the next day and said he loved her.

Interpersonal violence is frequently repeated. Two-thirds of female victims of reported non-sexual assault and half the victims of sexual assault have experienced more than one incident in the previous year. Some have experienced many episodes.[6] Teenagers have not had time to acquire wisdom or understanding of what may happen in the long term and how cowed women can become.

This consultation was an excellent opportunity for education with a discussion including:

> *How likely is this to happen again?*
> *How many times would it have to happen for you to decide enough is enough?*
> *If everyone in your family knew about this, what would they say?*

She decided that she didn't want anyone to know about the abuse, and, as an adult with mental capacity, she was empowered to take charge of her life. She was given advice about available victim support on a card to take away with her.

CASE STUDY 4

The Whole Primary Care Team

A practice manager received a request for urgent health information from the Multi-Agency Risk Assessment Committee (MARAC) coordinator about a couple registered with the practice. MARAC, usually chaired by the police with members from relevant children's and adults' services, discusses serious, complex and concerning cases of DVA. It agrees a multi-agency plan of action and communication aimed at keeping people safe and enabling help and support.

The police had not obtained consent for information sharing from the couple. How does this fit with data protection and confidentiality? What is a proportionate response?

The practice manager saw that the man had consulted about his use of anabolic steroids (which may increase violence) and that the woman had complained of his alcohol misuse and had several attendances over the last year with minor injuries. There were no children.

Because no children were involved, there was no statutory requirement to release confidential information. Adults with mental capacity can make their own decisions, including unwise choices of partners. Nevertheless, if violence has been serious and involves a coercive relationship, there is an increased risk of homicide, and information held in the primary care records could influence decisions made by MARAC. The clinician's decision whether or not to comply with the request must be documented. Discussion with a defence organisation and the named doctor may be helpful. The GMC offer clear guidance on data sharing and consent.[7] It may be risky to seek consent without discussing this with the police first.

CASE STUDY 5

A Violent Offender

A receptionist in a small, remote rural practice, staffed by older female receptionists with more female than male GPs, was unsure about registering a patient who attended accompanied by two community psychiatric nurses (CPNs). Her adult safeguarding antennae were working well!

The man, in his 30s, had a history of unprovoked attacks on older women. His care plan showed that he was subject to a multi-agency public protection arrangement (MAPPA), having been in prison for a violent offence against his mother. He was only to be seen by mental health professionals in pairs and in a room with two doors.

MAPPA is the set of arrangements through which the police, probation and prison services work together with other agencies to manage the risks posed by violent and sexual offenders living in the community in order to protect the public.

The practice initially refused to accept the patient, stating a clear need to provide a safe work environment for its staff. They asked for a formal risk assessment, which showed that he was at 9 out of 10 on a scale of risky behaviour towards women. A practice designated to deal with violent offenders and complex cases was 30 miles distant, too far away to be useful.

The practice accepted the patient provided that he only had phone contact with the surgery or, if necessary, appointments with two CPNs and a male doctor present. Reception staff were provided with a photograph of him should he turn up unannounced.

He was very surprised at this reaction, but the challenge enabled the CPNs to work well with him on the consequences of his behaviour, and the risk gradually decreased.

CASE STUDY 6

Coercive Control

A 55-year-old woman came with her husband for an annual review of her severe mental illness. She seemed to be sedated by quetiapine for her psychotic symptoms. Her husband answered for her, as he did whenever she was reviewed by the community mental health team where he had reported increasing symptoms, and they had prescribed increasing doses of antipsychotics.

When she was seen alone, she began to tell a story of domestic abuse and psychological coercive control. She was enabled to leave him safely and to come off medication altogether. Although separation should make things better, it can escalate the risks of harm.

Like victims of coercive control, health professionals can also be groomed to accept the stories they are told. Patients must be seen alone.

Coercive control became an offence in England in the Serious Crime Act 2015. Devolved nations and Ireland added similar legislation in the following years. Coercive control in a relationship makes femicide more likely. There may have been no history of physical violence.

CASE STUDY 7

Elderly Woman and a Diabetes Review

An elderly woman in her mid-70s with unstable insulin-dependent diabetes, hypertension and angina presented to the practice nurse for review. She and her husband lived in an isolated house along a long lane. She relied on her husband for driving.

She admitted to being frightened of her drug-addicted son, who had pushed and shoved her and broken things in her house. She now locked herself in her bedroom when he came home. She said that her 'bossy husband' wound their son up and never acted to protect her and that the police were 'useless . . . They just see him as a druggie and treat me as invisible'. She was worried because her son was about to be made homeless and to come to live with them.

'You won't tell anyone, will you?' she said to the nurse.

How worried should the nurse be about her safety? Is the patient safe to go home? Who should the nurse talk to? Who is available for advice?

Firstly, the nurse should talk with the practice safeguarding lead to see if there is any other relevant information. They should consider an urgent referral to the local adult safeguarding team for advice and management. She is an adult at risk of harm, unable to defend herself and run away. It is good practice to gain her consent to a referral, but it's not essential.

In UK legislation, an adult at risk is 'any person who is aged 18 years or over and at risk of abuse or neglect because of their needs for care and support'.

Adult safeguarding procedures should take a whole-family and whole-system view using the principles of the Care Act 2014[8]:

- Empowerment
- Proportionality
- Protection
- Partnership
- Prevention
- Accountability
- Transparency

For example, the local authority could arrange an emergency housing placement for the son. They should consider whether he, too, is a vulnerable adult with care and support needs. They can be clear with the husband about his need to protect his wife. The police can draw up a safety plan and develop a more productive relationship with the family.

CASE STUDY 8

Historical Abuse

One 45-year-old patient with fibromyalgia had been attending a pain clinic for ten years and taking prescribed opiates. She was shocked to be informed by her GP that her illness was likely to have had its roots in sexual abuse and violence during her childhood. Her body had responded by tensing and becoming hyper-vigilant. She was angry that the link hadn't been made earlier for her—she felt conned by the medical system. She commenced psychotherapy and, when she saw her abuser inviting a small girl into his house, reported her historical disclosure to the police, leading to his arrest for current probable abuse. She came off her opiates and learned to relax.

The term 'historical abuse' seems to distance the past from the present, when the effects of traumatic events may be repeating themselves with physical symptoms. Patients feel they have to bring their bodies to see doctors. These somatic experiences are easily medicalised and investigated. A veil is drawn over what has happened to the person. Bessel van der Kolk describes this well in his book *The Body Keeps the Score*.[9]

In 1998, Felliti et al. reported on their adverse childhood experiences (ACEs) study.[10] They found a highly significant correlation between ACEs and future mental health and addiction problems. They also found a markedly increased incidence of obesity, cardiovascular morbidity, chronic lung disease and diabetes mellitus. The mind and body cannot be considered separately.

There is now a considerable movement growing to relabel psychiatric diagnoses accurately by 'what has happened' to people rather than the symptom clusters of 'what is wrong'. For example, some personality disorders are more helpfully labelled as complex post-traumatic stress disorder caused by the trauma of historical abuse, meaning that successful trauma-focused treatment is more likely to be offered.

The Rural Landscape

In the National Rural Crime Network (NRCN) 2019 study of DVA in seven rural areas in England,[11] the structure of rural society was found to be patriarchal and controlling with many abusive men being prominent local figures: for example, in influential positions in local sports clubs and on rural committees. Women trying to report abuse were often not believed by their families or communities. They were shamed for speaking up, and many had to leave the area. Rural health professionals need to listen differently and respond carefully, knowing these nuances and the support networks. They are generally valued by rural abuse survivors as someone safe to talk to. GPs, however, may also be seen as part of the controlling network, particularly if they care for several generations of the same family. Allocating a different GP for husband and wife may be needed, putting this on a practice computer 'screen alert'.

The breadth of national safeguarding issues is alarmingly large and appears to be worsening, possibly partly because of increased reporting. Issues include modern slavery, people trafficking, female genital mutilation, county lines (drug marketing), forced marriage, child sexual exploitation, radicalisation, online bullying and financial fraud. All of these can be camouflaged by the 'rural idyll'.

BOX 13.1: KEY FINDINGS FROM THE NATIONAL RURAL CRIME NETWORK[12]

- Abuse lasts, on average, 25% longer in the most rural areas.
- The policing response is largely inadequate.
- The more rural the setting, the higher the risk of harm.
- Rurality and isolation are deliberately used as weapons by abusers.
- Close-knit rural communities facilitate abuse.
- Traditional, patriarchal communities control and subjugate women.
- Support services are scarce—less available, less visible and less effective.
- Retreating rural resources make help and escape harder.
- The short-term, often hand-to-mouth funding model has created competing and fragmented service provision.
- An endemic data bias against rural communities leads to serious gaps in response and support.

Health Safeguarding Support Systems

In England, a network of named doctors provide safeguarding support for groups of practices. Most practices have a safeguarding lead GP for adults and children (sometimes as separate roles).

Working to support these named doctors are designated nurses in child and adult safeguarding and designated doctors for child safeguarding, who are usually experienced paediatricians. There are also designated doctors for looked-after children (i.e. for children under the care of the local authority) and a few designated doctors for adult safeguarding.

In the devolved nations, there is a senior safeguarding GP lead working closely with all agencies. Practices are encouraged to have safeguarding lead GPs.

Training and Resources

Learning about safeguarding is a lifelong process and cannot simply be ticked off as done once and for all after a short course. Learning is best done on real cases in the practice as they come along. Near-miss cases (e.g. Case Study 2) are good for this, and whole-team discussions are effective.

Local authority adult and child safeguarding websites contain contact details for making referrals, reports on serious case reviews and lessons learned, up to date information on legislation, details of voluntary sector organisations. Time spent reading through the websites can count towards the training hours required for safeguarding.

The General Medical Council (GMC) sets standards in 'good medical practice'[13] and 'protecting children and young people',[14] including guidance on mental capacity, consent, information sharing and confidentiality. The GMC ethical hub shows how guidance can be applied: e.g. in relation to adult safeguarding.[15]

The Royal College of Nursing also publishes intercollegiate guidance on required skills for safeguarding children and young people[16] and adults.[17] These are helpful in detailing the required skills at each level, from receptionists to designated nurses and doctors.

The Royal College of General Practitioners (RCGP) publishes e-learning on safeguarding in remote/video consultations and toolkits for adult and child safeguarding on its website[18] with accessible information about differing legislation across the devolved nations of the UK, as does the NSPCC.[19]

IRISi[20] provides evidence-based training for primary care on domestic violence identification and referral using advocate educators. Following the NRCN report, they are now working in rural areas.

Can Reporting Safeguarding Concerns Make Things Worse?

This question reflects the concern about 'opening a can of worms'. Reporting safeguarding concerns to the local authority or to the police can involve challenging conversations with individuals, families and professionals. These may be highly emotional experiences which seem to mirror the experience of the child or vulnerable adult. Denial, minimisation, fear, denigration, blame, shame, coercion and isolation may stick themselves like barnacles to the process in subtle ways. It can be hard to get the voice of the vulnerable child or adult heard. The investigations for a serious case review can be harrowing for everyone involved and may take a long time to resolve. The press and social media may add to the pressure.

Education, training and working networks are essential for everyone's safety. Fear, which constricts the arteries to the frontal lobes, causes temporary executive dysfunction and freezes thinking. Nevertheless, fear is important because adults and children do die at the hands of others. In a rural community, a domestic homicide or child death has a ripple effect on many people, including practice staff.

Discussion with colleagues, particularly those more highly trained in safeguarding and with more experience, is invaluable in translating emotion into effective professional action. Case consultation gets the wide-angle view back.

Here are some guiding questions and ideas to anchor decision making:

- How safe are this person and their family right now?
- How can I (we) act as advocate(s) to ensure that the voice of a vulnerable child or adult is heard?
- Remember the principles of the Care Act: empowerment, proportionality, protection, prevention, partnership, accountability and transparency. Apply these to yourself first. Persistence and patience are important qualities. Escalation of concerns may be needed in the health safeguarding system but also in social care and the police.

The NHS,[21] GMC, RCN and other professional bodies are clear about the expectations of good safeguarding practice. Defence unions are clear that not reporting concerns is much more likely to lead to litigation than reporting concerns. All agree that documentation—who is present, what was said, clinical findings, how decisions were made etc.—is essential.

Patients want to be listened to by someone who knows what to do and is part of a team that will support them. They will be silenced by a dismissive response that minimises their worries. This may cause delay in reporting and further harm, especially in a rural area where they can't easily change GP practice. There is evidence that supporting a non-abusing parent improves outcomes for the children by empowering the parent.[22] This support may come from the primary care team. It is OK to admit ignorance and say, 'I don't know, but I will find out for you'.

What changes can you and your team make to ensure that vulnerable patients are protected?

Case studies have been altered to protect confidentiality.

REFERENCES

1 National Rural Crime Network. *Captive and Controlled: Domestic Abuse in Rural Areas.* National Rural Crime Network, 2019. www.ruralabuse.co.uk/wp-content/uploads/2019/07/Domestic-Abuse-in-Rural-Areas-National-Rural-Crime-Network.pdf [Accessed 20 April, 2022].

2 Royal College of Paediatrics and Child Health. *Child Protection Evidence; Systematic Review on Fractures.* London: RCPCH, 2020. www.rcpch.ac.uk/sites/default/files/2020-10/Chapter%20Fractures_Update_280920.pdf [Accessed 2 May, 2022].

3 ICON: I: Infant crying is normal; C: Comforting methods can help; O: It's OK to walk away; N: Never, ever shake a baby. https://iconcope.org.

4 Rattray J, Smith S, Jones K, et al. G83 Icon babies cry, you can cope: Pilot of abusive head trauma prevention campaign in general practice. *Arch Dis Childhood* 2019; 104: A34–5. https://adc.bmj.com/content/104/Suppl_2/A34.3.

5 Asen E, Tomson D, Young V, Tomson P. *Ten Minutes for the Family: Systemic Interventions in Primary Care.* London: Routledge, 2004.

6 Walby S, Allen J. *Domestic Violence, Sexual Assault and Stalking: Findings from the British Crime Survey.* Home Office Research Study 276. London: Home Office, 2004. https://openaccess.city.ac.uk/id/eprint/21697/1/Domestic violencefindings_2004_5BritishCrimeSurvey276.pdf.

7 General Medical Council. *Confidentiality: Good Practice in Handling Patient Information.* Manchester: GMC, 2017.

8 UK Parliament. Care Act 2014 c.23.

9 Van der Kolk B. *The Body Keeps the Score: Brain, Mind, and Body in the Transformation of Trauma.* New York: Penguin Books, 2015.

10 Felitti VJ, Andra RF, Nordenberg D, Williamson DF, Spitz AM, Edwards V, Koss MP, Marks JS. Relationship of childhood abuse and household dysfunction to many of the leading causes of death in adults. The Adverse Childhood Experiences (ACE) study. *Amer J Prev Med.* 1998; 14(4): 245–58. www.ajpmonline.org/article/S0749-3797(98)00017-8/fulltext [Accessed 31 July, 2022].

11 National Rural Crime Network. *Captive and Controlled: Domestic Abuse in Rural Areas.* National Rural Crime Network, 2019. www.

ruralabuse.co.uk/wp-content/uploads/2019/07/Domestic-Abuse-in-Rural-Areas-National-Rural-Crime-Network.pdf [Accessed 20 April, 2022].

12 National Rural Crime Network. *Captive and Controlled: Domestic Abuse in Rural Areas*. National Rural Crime Network, 2019. www.ruralabuse.co.uk/wp-content/uploads/2019/07/Domestic-Abuse-in-Rural-Areas-National-Rural-Crime-Network.pdf [Accessed 20 April, 2022].

13 General Medical Council. *Good Medical Practice*. Manchester: GMC, 2014.

14 General Medical Council. *Protecting Children and Young People: The Responsibilities of All Doctors*. Manchester: GMC, 2018.

15 General Medical Council. Adult safeguarding. www.gmc-uk.org/ethical-guidance/ethical-hub/adult-safeguarding [Accessed 20 April, 2022].

16 Royal College of Nursing. *Safeguarding Children and Young People—Every Nurse's Responsibility*. London: RCN, 2021.

17 Royal College of Nursing. *Adult Safeguarding: Roles and Competencies for Health Care Staff*. London: RCN, 2018.

18 Royal College of General Practitioners. Safeguarding. www.rcgp.org.uk/clinical-and-research/safeguarding.aspx [Accessed 20 April, 2022].

19 NSPCC Learning. Children and the law. https://learning.nspcc.org.uk/child-protection-system/children-the-law [Accessed 20 April, 2022].

20 IRISi Interventions. https://irisi.org [Accessed 7 May, 2022].

21 National Health Service. Safeguarding. www.myguideapps.com/projects/safeguarding/default/ [Accessed 20 April, 2022].

22 Centre of expertise on child sexual abuse. *Effectiveness of Services for Sexually Abused Children and Young People: Research Programme Briefing*. Ilford: Centre of Expertise on Child Sexual Abuse, 2019. www.csacentre.org.uk/documents/effectiveness-research-briefing/ [Accessed 2 May, 2022].

CHAPTER 14

Technology

....

Helen Atherton and Dan Lasserson

INTRODUCTION

Technology is increasingly a key element of healthcare delivery. Levels of implementation and use have accelerated since the onset of the COVID-19 pandemic.

Early versions of video consultation were used to navigate the distances involved in delivering care in rural countries such as Australia and New Zealand, where patients faced long journeys to receive specialist care.[1, 2] More recently, the availability of healthcare-related information on the internet and the widespread uptake of communications technologies and devices has expanded the ways in which healthcare is delivered[3] and how patients and providers engage more generally.

Technology offers access to healthcare that may not otherwise be possible, be that due to distance or a global pandemic. Challenges arise when the use of technology is scaled up, with technological access to healthcare delivered as a blanket offering rather than a necessary adjunct. This raises questions about who can access the technology and whether patients are excluded if they cannot. There is a tension between embracing the opportunities that technology can provide and managing implementation to ensure that everyone can access the care they need. This chapter covers the key forms of technology used in delivering healthcare at present and how they can work for rural patients and healthcare professionals.

DOI: 10.1201/9781003302438-19

DIGITAL INCLUSION AND RURALITY

Digital inclusion is about 'ensuring the benefits of the internet and digital technologies are available to everyone'.[4] It is determined by three key areas: digital skills, connectivity and accessibility.[5] A person or group may be digitally excluded based on one, two or all three of these categories.

- *Digital skills* include having the necessary skills to be able to use digital devices.
- *Connectivity* relates to access to the internet through broadband, Wi-Fi or mobile networks, with the necessary infrastructure to support ongoing use of services.
- *Accessibility* relates to making sure that digital services are designed with users' needs in mind.

Key barriers to digital inclusion include access, skills, confidence and motivation. In the UK, 90% of people have access to the internet, and 78% use a mobile device (phone or tablet) to connect. However, almost 5 million people do not go online at all, and just over 11 million lack the necessary digital skills.[5]

Being capable of using online services is not the same as having the confidence and motivation to do so. Some people are fearful of online crime. Others have concerns about who can see their data. This lack of confidence can extend to healthcare staff who may themselves lack confidence in using technology to deliver healthcare, particularly if using technology for healthcare purposes is new to them.

People living in rural areas are more likely to be digitally excluded. This is compounded by age, education, income, employment status and disability. Rural populations in the UK are on average older,[6] and older people are generally less likely to be technology users.[7] Socio-economically disadvantaged older people in rural areas already face multiple barriers to accessing primary healthcare.[8]

Rural areas are notoriously poorly served when it comes to internet access, with unstable broadband connections and inadequate download speeds. Without access, many technological options are unavailable to both patients and healthcare practitioners, regardless of their ability to use them. With the introduction of new channels of healthcare delivery that rely on internet-enabled technology comes the potential for patients living in rural areas to be excluded from using services that are delivered this way.

It is not necessarily the case that all patients must be able to access care online or utilise technology for their care; rather, they must be able to access the healthcare they require. Where technology supplements care but does not replace it, patients do not need to be excluded, but services must be carefully designed to ensure this.

Policy developed to digitise health services often assumes a 'one size fits all' model across location and patient populations. The experiences of rural populations in accessing healthcare differ from those of people living in towns and cities, and these patients face unique challenges. One key approach to ensuring inclusive services is to involve patients and the public in their development. This is known as co-production and is designed to ensure meaningful patient representation in how services are designed and delivered, particularly those who are vulnerable or marginalised.[9] It involves working with patients as partners and is increasingly used to ensure that new technologies work in practice and meet the needs of patients.[10] However, there are challenges in realising co-production. Some are practical—for example, the time and effort required—and some cultural: for example, challenging the existing frameworks of service development.[11]

PATIENT-FACING TECHNOLOGIES

Patient-facing technologies include a range of tools for delivering healthcare directly to patients. These include video consultation, tools for monitoring patient physical health status and tools that allow patients to manage their own health, such as apps.

Telemedicine refers to the 'remote diagnosis and treatment of patients by means of telecommunications technology'.[12] Within telemedicine, there are different approaches. Real-time telemedicine allows for a two-way connection between a healthcare professional and a patient: for example, a video consultation. Remote patient monitoring involves the use of technology to monitor and capture healthcare information directly from patients outside the clinic setting via the use of devices. Examples of remote monitoring devices include blood pressure machines, pulse oximeters, thermometers and weighing scales to detect deteriorating heart failure. Information is transferred to healthcare professionals using the telephone or internet.

Healthcare services relied on telemedicine to navigate the COVID-19 pandemic, which necessitated the avoidance of face-to-face contact where possible. Prior to March 2020, when the pandemic began, telemedicine was used variably across healthcare settings. It rapidly became an important tool in routine care.

Remote Consultation

Patient care now relies on use of digital consultation approaches more than ever before. Across the world, the use of remote digital consultations (video, email, online web platforms) has increased since 2020. Levels of video consultation use with patients have always been higher in rural areas, with Scotland, a mostly rural country within the UK, having a well-organised video consultation system allowing patients to consult using a video link for the majority of specialities.[13] Although both doctors and patients report limited benefits of video over and above what telephone can offer, video provides visual cues that the telephone cannot.[14]

Patients benefit from digital consultations through increased convenience, not needing to travel to a healthcare setting and consulting in their own home rather than in an unfamiliar space.

Email has not been routinely adopted as a method of consultation in UK healthcare, despite patients finding it convenient, timing saving and a way to maintain a good ongoing relationship with their doctor.[15-17] Clinicians express concerns about the potential impact of email consultations on their workload and the potential for misuse.[15, 16] UK-based research demonstrated that, in most cases, email consultations are short and resolved quickly.[18] In Denmark, where email consultation has been a mandatory offering in general practice since 2009, email consultation provides patients with a way to self-manage their health[19] and to enter and navigate the health system,[20] although general practitioners have reported instances of inappropriate and excessive use by patients.[17] The written and asynchronous nature of an email can be of benefit to patients but, conversely, means that clinicians must ensure they are satisfied with their responses before sending them and must take steps to ensure patient safety by applying safety netting.[21] Despite email consultation being associated with many benefits for patients, implementation in the UK has been difficult, and its benefits are not yet realised.

Digital consultations work best for both healthcare professionals and patients in the context of an ongoing relationship and long-term condition management. They are less appropriate for addressing new conditions or where physical examination is necessary. Although a face-to-face consultation is consistently seen as the 'gold standard',[22] in rural locations, clinical suitability for a video consultation is often secondary in the decision to use it.[23]

Key challenges to delivering telemedicine using patient-facing technologies in rural settings include:

- Organisational capacity
- Health professional knowledge and skills
- Patient skills[24]

Where people in rural areas cannot realise the benefit of telemedicine due to poor internet infrastructure, smartphones offer a possible alternative, using mobile data rather than broadband internet. However, mobile phone connectivity is also limited in many areas. This also introduces risk when healthcare professionals rely on smartphones to access patient data during home visits.

Application of telemedicine requires not only equipment but also resources, including training for staff. Rural areas, particularly areas of deprivation, are often under-resourced and understaffed and struggle to recruit healthcare professionals, leaving less capacity for the changes necessary to introduce telemedicine services.

Patients may need to be advised on what good equipment looks like and guided to use it.

With support at policy and healthcare system level, it is likely that the challenges can be addressed and the benefits more freely realised. This route to increased use of patient-facing technologies has undoubtedly been expedited by the pandemic.

Remote Monitoring

Remote monitoring has played a key role during the COVID-19 pandemic in helping patients monitor their health status. In COVID-19 patients, pulse oximeters have been used as a way to monitor how severely unwell patients are and to allow them to be managed remotely at home at a time when hospitals were under pressure.[25] Oncology patients testing positive for COVID-19 reported that remote monitoring made them feel connected to their healthcare professional during their period of isolation and helped prevent emergency room visits.[26] Patients with existing conditions have also been able to benefit from remote monitoring during the pandemic. Patients with amyotrophic lateral sclerosis found that they could ensure the assessment and monitoring of their condition by reporting their forced vital capacity using a spirometer over a video consultation, avoiding unnecessary clinic visits and reducing the risk of contracting COVID-19. These patients reported their satisfaction with the approach and were happy to keep using it.[27]

Remote monitoring also plays a role in the management of long-term conditions by allowing patients to routinely self-monitor and actively participate in their care. The widespread availability of devices such as smartphones and smart watches has led to more patients having the equipment needed to monitor their health and to engage with their healthcare. Patients report improved self-management and opportunity for shared decision making with their clinicians, with patients able to recognise early signs of deterioration in their condition.[28] There are potential benefits for patients in rural areas, with research demonstrating a reduced need for hospitalisations where remote monitoring is used.[29] However, there are challenges. For clinicians, these include concerns about the quality and quantity of data available for clinical decision making, concerns about the motivation levels of the patient to utilise the equipment and the changes that the introduction of technology makes to the relationship between doctor and patient.[30] Patients also recognise the changes that remote monitoring makes to the doctor-patient relationship, with interpersonal contact lost. Patients who are less familiar with technology worry about reliability and interpretation of the data generated and the increased personal responsibility that comes with processing their health data.[28]

Ensuring that patients understand how to use remote monitoring equipment is crucial, but it is also crucial to ensure that patients understand what happens next if their condition deteriorates. Safety netting should be applied to their use and clear escalation plans be in place and coordinated among the care team.

NEAR-PATIENT TESTING

One of the major challenges of delivering acute care in rural and remote settings is the need to make an accurate diagnosis far away from a traditional acute hospital setting, where the majority of diagnostic testing facilities are based. Many acute medical conditions can be treated outside an acute hospital setting as long as treating clinicians have access to parenteral therapies as well as oxygen, but this relies on accurate diagnostic testing. Furthermore, retrieval pathways can be time consuming and expensive, and therefore, the need for transfer from a remote setting to a central acute hospital for definitive care for an emergency should be established as securely as possible. Fortunately, near-patient testing or 'point-of-care' (POC) testing technology for blood tests as well as ultrasound has been developed and is robust when used outside acute hospitals, but there are some issues which should be considered to ensure that they deliver reliable results.[31]

The most reliable clinical systems for POC blood testing use closed cartridge systems. The benefits of these are

- There's no need for laboratory analytical techniques such as mixing of reagents or use of a centrifuge.
- Cartridges can be stored in a standard fridge for longer term (e.g. at a small or basic health facility) and can be at room temperature for shorter periods (usually days), enabling use in the home or open air.
- Only small volumes of blood are needed and can be directly inserted into the cartridge.
- The analytical unit is usually a 'handheld' size and very portable for rural and remote settings.
- Cartridges can analyse multiple tests at the same time, allowing for rapid results (usually minutes) of core analytes. This ensures efficiency for clinicians when working in remote environments.
- POC systems can integrate results into an electronic health record through automated uploading to a laboratory information management system (LIMS), ensuring that a continuous digital health record can be maintained.

The limitations of POC blood testing in remote environments are

- The need to ensure stock control, so cartridges are available when clinicians go out from a local base to make acute assessments in remote environments.
- The combination of analytes in cartridges are fixed and may not include all the results that are required in a clinical situation.
- To address the need for completeness of blood tests, a combination of different POC closed cartridge systems (i.e. different handsets/cartridges made by different manufacturers) may be needed, increasing cost and requiring clinicians to proficiently operate several systems.
- Initial training in use of POC blood tests needs to be overseen by a diagnostic support service that can ensure that clinicians use the correct technique.
- Access to quality control tests needs to be maintained so that results are reliable, and any drift of the system can be detected and corrected.
- Some POC systems need to be maintained in a temperature range which may preclude outdoor use in extreme environments (e.g. arctic or desert conditions).

Point-of-care ultrasound (POCUS) offers the potential for imaging to be undertaken outside the traditional healthcare setting. There are a range of handheld probes which display images on a smartphone or tablet (or an integral screen), which means that the imaging technology is portable and does not need the large cart-based system which would normally be used in a radiology department.

The advantages of POCUS are

- Rapid diagnosis of key acute problems after trauma (e.g. pneumothorax, pericardial effusion, free fluid in the abdomen).
- Rapid diagnosis of key acute medical problems (e.g. pneumonia, pleural effusion, reduced left ventricular function, ascites, hydronephrosis, urinary retention, deep vein thrombosis).
- Obstetric ultrasound can determine foetal heartbeat and breech position etc.
- Most handheld systems have an image-sharing function, enabling expert support from radiologists or specialist clinicians (with appropriate connectivity) for the remote clinician in making a diagnosis or monitoring treatment.

Important issues to consider with use of POCUS are

- Initial training to competency in an appropriate range of imaging techniques
- Ongoing governance arrangements to ensure skills are maintained, with an appropriate volume of scanning
- Portable technology that may not yield images as detailed as hospital-based ultrasound machines
- Costs

Patient experience of point-of-care ultrasound is high as there is greater confidence in the clinical team[32] as well as improved understanding of their own clinical condition. POC blood tests undertaken in the home are very well accepted by patients,[33] but clinicians themselves can sometimes be a barrier to implementation due to unfamiliarity with the technology being implemented.[34]

ARTIFICIAL INTELLIGENCE

Artificial intelligence (AI) in healthcare settings can support diagnosis, treatment, patient engagement and adherence and administrative activities. Several types of AI are relevant, including:

- Machine learning
- Natural language processing
- Rule-based expert systems and robotics[35]

Each is in a different stage of development and implementation, and some are more relevant to use in the rural setting than others.

Machine learning is the use of computer systems that can adapt and learn using statistical models and algorithms, drawing inferences from patterns in data.

Some newer types of clinical decision support software (CDSS) utilise machine learning. Conventional CDSS uses rule-based systems, with human experts devising the rules that software follows to support clinicians. It has a known provenance and is familiar, for example, in the commonly encountered triage tools in electronic health records. Conversely, machine learning–based CDSS looks for patterns in data sources rather than the software being programmed to follow expert knowledge. It relies on the quantity and quality of data.[36] There are concerns that healthcare professionals may be reluctant to rely on recommendations because they lack understanding of the logic machine learning uses to make decisions.

At a population level, machine learning provides a tool for epidemiology and the monitoring of health professional behaviours. Collection of intelligence comparing how different geographical areas perform in healthcare delivery is useful in making a case for more resources or special circumstances in rural areas.

Closely linked to machine learning is *natural language processing*, with computer systems drawing inferences from large datasets comprising natural language data. Both machine learning and natural language processing have been used to understand patient experience of healthcare: for example, by collating written comments, both solicited and unsolicited, left by patients online.[37] The ability to mine data provided by patients allows for real-time, area-specific patient experience data to be gathered, allowing healthcare providers to focus on how patients in particular areas and with particular characteristics experience healthcare. This can be useful for rural areas where, for example, there are specific health needs linked to an occupation such as farming.

The use of *robotics* ranges from physical robots—for example, those used to conduct surgical operations—through to robotic process automation, in which administrative tasks are automated, being completed by computer servers. An example of their use in healthcare is for scheduling of appointments. A hospital in the North Midlands, UK, uses robotic process automation to schedule imaging appointments, assigning dates and times based on patient preference and the required investigation, building in information about what appointments are available to allocate.[38]

AI also enables devices and tools to support people in independent living and monitoring, particularly in higher risk, older and widely dispersed populations. For example, 'conversational AI' enables people to connect to the internet through a voice interface, enabling them to speak to a virtual assistant such as Siri or Alexa to answer questions, undertake or direct tasks and seek assistance. In-house monitoring has been shown to detect cognitive decline.[39]

Artificial intelligence has the potential to support patients and healthcare professionals in rural settings, but the implementation is likely to be more difficult, particularly where there are challenges with resourcing, deprivation and access to the internet. A shift would be required before it is a realistic proposition.

TECHNOLOGIES FOR HEALTH PROFESSIONALS

The future of support for healthcare professionals is likely to include increasing amounts of AI alongside the technology that is already supporting the work of health professionals.

As well as its patient-facing role, telemedicine allows the communication of patient-specific information between health professionals.

Store and forward telemedicine allows a healthcare professional to share images and patient-related information with other healthcare professionals, e.g. between primary care and specialists. This is an 'asynchronous' system (i.e. not in 'real time' or synchronous, like a telephone or video consultation) that has long been utilised in rural areas where there are great distances between primary care and specialist care.

Traditionally, telephone consultation services between healthcare professionals and patients were used to support communication, but in recent years, online platforms have emerged to enable this communication. eConsult, developed in Canada, allows primary care providers to consult online with specialists. It is utilised across rural Canada and has been shown to avoid unnecessary referrals and journeys to specialists and to reduce waiting times for patients seeing specialists.[40] Despite the evidence supporting their use, such tools are still not universally available.

Multidisciplinary team (MDT) meetings bring together healthcare professionals, allied health professionals and other personnel involved in delivering care to patients, allowing different disciplines to interact and enabling teamwork. Traditionally, these were in-person meetings with a structured agenda. Arranging such meetings was difficult in rural settings where there are geographical and time restrictions, and they have often been held using telephone conferencing. The COVID-19 pandemic necessitated the use of a 'virtual' MDT meeting across all healthcare settings which, evidence suggests, provide more integrated, efficient, accessible and higher-quality care, overcoming geographical and timing barriers.[41]

As well as formal meetings, there has been a growth in the use of informal communications tools by healthcare professionals. The popular messaging tool WhatsApp provides end-to-end encrypted messaging, which is attractive to healthcare professionals who wish to share information about their work in confidence. However, it is associated with regulatory concerns and is not an approved method of sharing patient data.[42] Smartphone apps exist that support communications between healthcare professionals and have a role in rural healthcare: for example, where someone might be visiting patients alone and require contact with colleagues for advice and reassurance. It is anticipated that this area of communication is likely to grow as healthcare professionals become accustomed to using their smartphones for work purposes.

Tele-education has been used for many years to deliver distance learning to rural healthcare professionals.[43] Utilising online platforms, it enables continuing professional development. As with telemedicine, it can be synchronous or asynchronous and can take different forms, delivered using text, video and/or audio. Rural healthcare professionals may otherwise face a long journey to obtain educational opportunities, which takes time and incurs cost. Access to expertise, particularly in specialist areas of healthcare, is more difficult where distance is involved. Tele-education is valuable in providing rural areas with expertise that is not available locally. For example, in Ontario, Canada, multidisciplinary providers received case-based learning and video conferencing on chronic pain management from specialists whose expertise was not available in their underserved rural area,[44] improving their knowledge and skills.

Tele-education can also take the form of hands-on skills training, particularly helpful for procedure-based specialities. In surgery, this includes the use of interactive sessions via video call, where basic surgical techniques can be taught and monitored remotely.[45] The use of tele-education is low cost and high fidelity and offers the opportunity to build relationships and obtain mentoring, even when there is distance.[46]

Those working in rural areas have expertise of their own that they can share using tele-education from their own setting. Tele-education can also be used to train staff in the use of telemedicine, allowing them to further utilise the advantages provided by technology.

CONCLUSION

Technology brings numerous benefits to the delivery of rural healthcare, many of these facilitated by access to the internet. But these positive developments are tempered by poor rural broadband connections and mobile phone coverage. Such issues are not exclusive to health but apply to rural society as a whole.

The expansion of digital technology demonstrates the need to be alert to the unintended consequences of changes and the potential for exacerbating health inequalities. With careful implementation, imagination, support and consideration of the needs of both healthcare professionals and their patients, technology and digital inclusion have the potential to benefit everyone.

Bibliography

We outline some key texts that will enhance your thinking on technology and rural healthcare.

Digital Inclusion

www.goodthingsfoundation.org/the-digital-divide/health-and-wellbeing/.

Co-Production

www.involve.org.uk/resources/methods/co-production.

Remote Consulting

Bakhai,M.(2019). "Usingonlineconsultationsinprimarycare:Implementationtoolkit." www.england.nhs.uk/publication/using-online-consultations-in-primary-care-implementation-toolkit/.

Bakhai, M. and H. Atherton (2021). "How to conduct written online consultations with patients in primary care." *BMJ* 372: n264.

Telehealth

www.ruralhealthinfo.org/toolkits/telehealth.

REFERENCES

1. Day K, Kerr P. The potential of telehealth for 'business as usual' in outpatient clinics. *J Telemed Telecare*. 2012;18(3):138–41.
2. Do Campo J, Hannan T, Pava C. 'Skype me doc' (Telehealth consultations). *Intern Med J*. 2013;43:40.
3. Ferguson T. Digital doctoring—opportunities and challenges in electronic patient-physician communication. *JAMA*. 1998;280(15):1361–2.
4. Citizen Online. Digital inclusion 2022. www.citizensonline.org.uk/digital-inclusion/.
5. NHS Digital. What we mean by digital inclusion 2022. https://digital.nhs.uk/about-nhs-digital/our-work/digital-inclusion/what-digital-inclusion-is.
6. Department for Environment, Food and Rural Affairs. Statistical digest of Rural England Population, 2021. https://assets.publishing.service.gov.uk/government/uploads/system/uploads/attachment_data/file/1028819/Rural_population__Oct_2021.pdf.
7. Office for National Statistics. Internet users, UK, 2020. www.ons.gov.uk/businessindustryandtrade/itandinternetindustry/bulletins/internetusers/2020#:~:text=1.,aged%2075%20years%20and%20over.
8. Ford JA, Turley R, Porter T, Shakespeare T, Wong G, Jones AP, et al. Access to primary care for socio-economically disadvantaged older people in rural areas: A qualitative study. *PLoS One*. 2018;13(3):e0193952.
9. Park S. Beyond patient-centred care: A conceptual framework of co-production mechanisms with vulnerable groups in health and social service settings. *Public Manag Rev*. 2020;22(3):452–74.
10. Dobson J. Co-production helps ensure that new technology succeeds. *BMJ*. 2019;366:l4833.
11. Rycroft-Malone J, Burton CR, Bucknall T, Graham ID, Hutchinson AM, Stacey D. Collaboration and co-production of knowledge in healthcare: Opportunities and challenges. *Int J Health Policy Manag*. 2016;5(4):221–3.

12. NEJM Catalyst. What is telehealth? *NEJM Catalyst*, 2018. https://catalyst. nejm.org/doi/full/10.1056/CAT.18.0268.

13. Wherton J, Greenhalgh T, Shaw SE. Expanding video consultation services at pace and scale in Scotland during the COVID-19 pandemic: A national mixed-method case study. *J Med Internet Res.* 2021;23(10):e31374.

14. Donaghy E, Atherton H, Hammersley V, McNeilly H, Bikker A, Robbins L, et al. Acceptability, benefits, and challenges of video consulting: A qualitative study in primary care. *Br J Gen Pract.* 2019;69(686):e586–94.

15. Atherton H, Pappas Y, Heneghan C, Murray E. Experiences of using email for general practice consultations: A qualitative study. *Br J Gen Pract.* 2013;63(616):e760–7.

16. Atherton H, Brant H, Ziebland S, Bikker A, Campbell J, Gibson A, et al. Alternatives to the face-to-face consultation in general practice: Focused ethnographic case study. *Br J Gen Pract.* 2018;68(669):e293–300.

17. Grønning A, Assing Hvidt E, Nisbeth Brøgger M, Fage-Butler A. How do patients and general practitioners in Denmark perceive the communicative advantages and disadvantages of access via email consultations? A media-theoretical qualitative study. *BMJ Open.* 2020;10(10):e039442.

18. Atherton H, Boylan A-M, Eccles A, Fleming J, Goyder CR, Morris RL. Email consultations between patients and doctors in primary care: Content analysis. *J Med Internet Res.* 2020;22(11):e18218.

19. Bavngaard MV, Grønning A. Older (65+) patients use of e-mail consultations: A Danish qualitative study using a Foucauldian framework. *Catalan J Commun Cult.* 2021;13(2):179–94.

20. Grønning A. Struggling with and mastering e-mail consultations: A study of access, interaction, and participation in a digital health care system. *Nord Rev.* 2021;42(s4):7–21.

21. Bakhai M, Atherton H. How to conduct written online consultations with patients in primary care. *BMJ.* 2021;372:n264.

22. Hammersley V, Donaghy E, Parker R, McNeilly H, Atherton H, Bikker A, et al. Comparing the content and quality of video, telephone, and face-to-face consultations: A non-randomised, quasi-experimental, exploratory study in UK primary care. *Br J Gen Pract.* 2019;69(686):e595–604.

23. Thiyagarajan A, Grant C, Griffiths F, Atherton H. Exploring patients and clinicans experiences of video consultations in primary care: A systematic scoping review. *BJGP Open.* 2020;4(1).

24. DeHart D, King LB, Iachini AL, Browne T, Reitmeier M. Benefits and challenges of implementing telehealth in rural settings: A mixed-methods study of behavioral medicine providers. *Health Soc Work.* 2022;47(1):7–18.

25. Greenhalgh T, Knight M, Inada-Kim M, Fulop NJ, Leach J, Vindrola-Padros C. Remote management of COVID-19 using home pulse oximetry and virtual ward support. *BMJ.* 2021;372:n677.

26. Daly B, Lauria TS, Holland JC, Garcia J, Majeed J, Walters CB, et al. Oncology patients' perspectives on remote patient monitoring for COVID-19. *JCO Oncology Practice.* 2021;17(9):e1278–85.

27. Tattersall R, Carty S, Meldrum D, Hardiman O, Murray D. The patient's perspective of remote respiratory assessments during the COVID-19 pandemic. *Amyotroph La Scl Fr.* 2022;23(1–2):76–80.

28. Walker RC, Tong A, Howard K, Palmer SC. Patient expectations and experiences of remote monitoring for chronic diseases: Systematic review and thematic synthesis of qualitative studies. *Int J Med Inform*. 2019;124:78–85.

29. Hicks LL, Fleming DA, Desaulnier A. The application of remote monitoring to improve health outcomes to a rural area. *Telemed J E-Health*. 2009;15(7):664–71.

30. Davis MM, Currey JM, Howk S, DeSordi MR, Boise L, Fagnan LJ, et al. A qualitative study of rural primary care clinician views on remote monitoring technologies. *J Rural Health*. 2014;30(1):69–78.

31. Verbakel JY, Richardson C, Elias T, Bowen J, Hassanzadeh R, Shine B, et al. Clinical reliability of point-of-care tests to support community based acute ambulatory care. *Acute Med*. 2020;19(1):4–14.

32. Andersen CA, Brodersen J, Rudbæk TR, Jensen MB. Patients' experiences of the use of point-of-care ultrasound in general practice—a cross-sectional study. *BMC Fam Pract*. 2021;22(1):116.

33. Hayward G, Dixon S, Garland S, Glogowska M, Hunt H, Lasserson D. Point-of-care blood tests during home visits by out-of-hours primary care clinicians; a mixed methods evaluation of a service improvement. *BMJ Open*. 2020;10(1):e033428.

34. Richards T. Can you do what I'm asking you to do? *BMJ*. 2021;375:n3014.

35. Davenport T, Kalakota R. The potential for artificial intelligence in healthcare. *Future Healthc J*. 2019;6(2):94–8.

36. Sutton RT, Pincock D, Baumgart DC, Sadowski DC, Fedorak RN, Kroeker KI. An overview of clinical decision support systems: Benefits, risks, and strategies for success. *NPJ Digit Med*. 2020;3(1):17.

37. Khanbhai M, Anyadi P, Symons J, Flott K, Darzi A, Mayer E. Applying natural language processing and machine learning techniques to patient experience feedback: A systematic review. *BMJ HCI*. 2021;28(1):e100262.

38. Digital Workforce. Robot to help patients book X-ray appointments, 2021. www.uhnm.nhs.uk/latest-uhnm-news/posts/2021/may/robot-to-help-patients-book-x-ray-appointments/#:~:text=The%20robotic%20process%20automation%20(RPA,and%20time%20for%20an%20appointment.

39. Nakaoku Y, Ogata S, Murata S, Nishimori M, Ihara M, Iihara K, et al. AI-assisted in-house power monitoring for the detection of cognitive impairment in older adults. *Sensors*. 2021;21(18).

40. Liddy C, Bello A, Cook J, Drimer N, Pilon MD, Farrell G, et al. Supporting the spread and scale-up of electronic consultation across Canada: Cross-sectional analysis. *BMJ Open*. 2019;9(5):e028888.

41. Sillero-Rejon C, McLeod H, Huntley A. COV.43: Virtual multidisciplinary team meetings for the older population, 2020. https://arc-w.nihr.ac.uk/research-and-implementation/covid-19-response/reports/virtual-multidisciplinary-team-meetings-for-the-older-population/.

42. Masoni M, Guelfi MR. WhatsApp and other messaging apps in medicine: Opportunities and risks. *Intern Emerg Med*. 2020;15(2):171–3.

43. Tele-education. *J Telemed Telecare*. 2006;12(2):57–63.

44. Furlan AD, Zhao J, Voth J, Hassan S, Dubin R, Stinson JN, et al. Evaluation of an innovative tele-education intervention in chronic pain management for primary care clinicians practicing in underserved areas. *J Telemed Telecare*. 2018;25(8):484–92.

45. Quaranto BR, Lamb M, Traversone J, Hu J, Lukan J, Cooper C, et al. Development of an interactive remote basic surgical skills mini-curriculum for medical students during the COVID-19 pandemic. *Surg Innov.* 2021;28(2):220–5.
46. Williams TP, Klimberg V, Perez A. Tele-education assisted mentorship in surgery (TEAMS). *J Surg Oncol.* 2021;124(2):250–4.

CHAPTER 15

Public Health

....

Stephen Singleton

There is an obvious, longstanding and knotty problem for all healthcare providers: 'While I can fill my time with the urgent and the constant demands of the person I have in front of me now, how do I understand and balance the needs of all my patients, including their future demands and necessary help that is not even being requested, and how do I do something about it?'

Both the World Health Organisation and UK professional bodies define public health as 'the science and art' of both preventing ill health and promoting better health through 'organised efforts'.[1] Some of the science is well known—from vaccinations to brief interventions in smoking—and much of the art is about how great healthcare can be provided to all populations, some of whom are difficult to reach and engage. How do rural healthcare providers with their particular challenges become organised to think and act differently?

Thinking about a population as our patient, rather than just individuals, is the central tenet of all public health. A UK general practice has the huge advantage of a specified list of patients as 'their population', within which they can readily define groups of particular interest to focus on as 'their patients'. The rural healthcare practitioner has a further advantage in that the whole population they serve is likely to be smaller, more stable, better known and less diverse than that of their urban-based colleagues. Table 15.1 illustrates the various ways a population of interest could be defined.

DOI: 10.1201/9781003302438-20

TABLE 15.1 Rural Healthcare Populations of Interest

Population Group Characteristics	Examples for Action
Place	Especially remote
	Living in an institution
Condition	Diabetes, heart disease, previous stroke, cancer survival
	On particular medication requiring review, e.g. anticoagulants, disease-modifying antirheumatic drugs
	Dementia, frailty
	Past history of mental health problems
Health determinants	Low income, vulnerable housing, dangerous occupations, smoking etc.
Risk categories	Age, ethnicity, gender
Special needs	Learning disability, sensory and physical disabilities

Traditional public health strategies tend to consider and compare populations in particular places and over periods of time (for example, comparing life expectancies between different parts of the same town and setting long-term targets for change, such as reduced smoking rates or fewer deaths from particular causes). This makes little sense in a rural setting. Looking at simple averages, rural populations in the developed world tend to be more prosperous and healthier and live longer, having fewer long-term health problems than their urban compatriots. (It is a mixed picture; some very remote populations in Canada and Australia have lower life expectancy than the average. For a full review, see Smith 2008.[2]) But this general rural benefit disguises the relative disadvantages—financial, social, educational, health and life prospects—between close neighbours in many rural settings. There tends, therefore, to be no street, no town, no community to focus efforts on, and, in almost always smaller rural populations, merely counting outcomes (for example, how many of my patients have had a heart attack) will never guide action or prove results.

Nonetheless, in most rural areas, some particular diseases and risks are especially prevalent: suicide, some cancers (for example, cervical, melanoma and prostate), cardiovascular disease and obesity, road traffic accidents. The characteristics of groups and individuals at risk, therefore, create more meaningful populations of interest for the rural practitioner than place-based populations.

If the first challenge for effective public health practice in rural health-care is the definition of populations of interest (because simple place-based interventions will not work as well), the second challenge is to adapt the way we plan and deliver care. Even taking into account the different pay-ment systems and routes of access to healthcare in different national sys-tems, worldwide, most rural practitioners will start with a basic concept of fairness, based on giving the best possible healthcare to every patient. Unfortunately, inherent in giving everyone the same care—even if it is of the best conceivable standard—is the fact that outcomes will inevitably vary. The same social and economic drivers that cause variation in health needs change the patients' ability to access, understand and comply with healthcare interventions. This then compounds the general disadvantage of access to services for all rural populations, created by distance. For exam-ple, rural populations have lower levels of screening and more frequent, longer delayed diagnoses, which all contribute to adverse outcomes.[3]

Edward Jenner 1749–1823
Berkeley, Gloucestershire

Jenner, the pioneer of vaccination, is perhaps the most famous British country doctor.

Born in Berkeley, Gloucestershire, in 1749, he was apprenticed for seven years to Daniel Ludlow, a surgeon of Chipping Sodbury, before attending St George's Hospital, London, where one of his teachers was the surgeon John Hunter.

He returned to Berkeley, where he became a successful family doctor and sur-geon. In addition to his medical practice, he pursued both zoological and medical research. He was elected to the Fellowship of the Royal Society (FRS) for a paper in which he showed that that it is the fledgling cuckoo, not the adult, that pushes the host's eggs out of the nest.

In 1792, he was awarded a doctorate (MD) from St Andrews University for a study of angina pectoris and the role of coronary arteries.

In the 18th century, many lay and medical writers in Britain, Germany and France investigated and wrote about the scourge of smallpox and its possible prevention by inoculation with smallpox virus. This procedure, termed variolation, already in widespread use in Asia and Africa, was brought to Britain in 1721 by Lady Mary Montagu, who had observed it in Constantinople.

Noting the common observation that milkmaids did not usually succumb to smallpox, Jenner postulated that they were immunised by exposure to cowpox, a related but less virulent infection. In 1796, he scraped pus from a milkmaid's cow-pox blister and injected it into his gardener's eight-year-old son. The boy, James Phipps, developed a fever and was uneasy, but his reaction was mild and transient. When Jenner subsequently variolated the boy with smallpox, he developed no symptoms. Cowpox infection had protected him from smallpox.

Jenner repeated the experiment on 23 others, including his own 11-month-old son. His attempt to publish his findings in a paper submitted to the Royal Society in 1797 was rejected. Undeterred, he added more cases to his series and published his findings in a pamphlet in 1798.

Jenner may not have been the first person to suggest that cowpox infection led to immunity from smallpox or the first person to attempt immunisation using cowpox, but his work on vaccination (named after *vaccinia* or cowpox) gradually gained scientific acceptance and support.

By the early 1800s, his discovery had been implemented in much of Europe. Despite being at war with Britain, Napoleon had his French soldiers vaccinated and gave Jenner a medal.

His work contributed to the development and understanding of immunology and led, in 1980, to the worldwide eradication of smallpox.

— Philip Evans

To fully adopt a public health mindset is the second challenge. To desire equal outcomes automatically means we must vary the services we provide between patients (deliberately unequal inputs). Consider a simple example: an annual flu vaccination campaign. Planned, advertised, the staff organised, the vaccine procured: a good public health intervention? Certainly, for the people engaged and attending. But the necessary public health task is always to look at the population who didn't engage and attend. While it is clearly good practice to respect people's personal beliefs and wishes—and fully informed, competent individuals may decide to decline the immunisation offer—it is not sufficient merely to offer a service that hits a financial incentive target for vaccine coverage or 'do what we did last year'. Good practice also requires us to think about and anticipate why individuals may not attend. Clearly, this will include practical issues like distance and transport, mobility and other medical conditions, work and caring commitments, educational and competence issues, misinformation and peer pressure. Our plan has to meet the requirements of all individuals within our population. The offer of a clinic-based service and telephone access to appointments may work for the majority but is less likely to meet the needs of the most disadvantaged populations. Sometimes, our own actions add to the disadvantage of already vulnerable and disadvantaged groups, and we must plan to counter it.

CASE HISTORY 1

Rose is a general practitioner in a UK rural practice serving over 4,000 people in an area of nearly 300 sq km. Thinking about vaccinating housebound patients for COVID-19 protection, she first had to identify the group of patients:

> We used a three-list triangulation system. First, we find those who are coded as housebound (surprisingly few). Second, those who self-identified as housebound when they were offered the vaccination at our local hub, and finally, those our staff happen to know about.

Planning included

> considering consent. Many patients can consent for themselves, and others can't but might have a lasting power of attorney specifying who can do so on their behalf. The decision to vaccinate the final group is made under the best interests principles of the Mental Capacity Act, in discussion with next of kin if possible. . . . I check patients' records for any cautions or contraindications . . .
>
> We have two vials totaling 22 doses, meaning our lists have to make exactly 11 each, with reserves in case of drop-outs . . . and offer possible vaccination to some spouses and carers without making promises. It's a delicate balancing act.

Concerning delivery:

> My route begins with the patients closest to the surgery, then sweeps out east and south in a wide arc before heading back north to vaccinate the patients closest to the hub, allowing me to return my kit before the hub closes. . . . It snowed last night, but we're determined not to let that stop us, and I'm grateful to my pick-up truck (more accustomed to moving dogs, sheep and hay) for being an ideal mobile vaccination unit, resilient to whatever the weather throws at us . . .
>
> We wear masks and carry a clean vaccination kit into each house, applying gloves once we're inside to draw up and administer the vaccine. We're welcomed with (socially distanced) open arms

and many offers of tea, which we regretfully have to decline. We visit three centenarians, and one is disappointed to learn that he's only the third-oldest person we're vaccinating today. By the end of the afternoon, we've covered more than 100 miles, vaccinating some of the most vulnerable people in our community and spreading a little hope.

Reference

Pulse Practice Jobs, 2021. Working life: administering the COVID vaccine to the housebound in rural Cumbria. www.pulsepracticejobs.com/article/working-life-administering-the-covid-vaccine-to-the-housebound-in-rural-cumbria.

The third consideration, after identifying the populations of interest and understanding that more and different things will need to be done, is to specify where local action by rural practitioners is most likely to make a difference. The obvious and perhaps most pressing example is the threat posed by global warming. This is a very long-term problem with distant risks and rather unpredictable current consequences. It is beyond the scope of local healthcare providers to change policy and reverse climate change—but it is not impossible both to think locally in terms of sustainability and minimising the climate impacts from our work and simultaneously to take seriously the relevant risks (for example, more frequent wildfires) in our current emergency or disaster planning. (See later in this chapter.)

A lot of differences in health and healthcare outcomes are directly correlated to economic status. That, in turn, mediates additional disadvantage through missed educational opportunities and less access to good, well-paid work; housing; nutrition; and social networks. These drivers of health disadvantage require changes to national policy, which, like climate change, will feel hard to influence for rural healthcare providers, and while they can join relevant forums and interest groups to lobby for change and find local solutions to local issues (like better housing and improved social networks for at-risk groups) these policy-based strategies will inevitably be a lower priority than specific interventions where targeted healthcare delivery will make a difference. Rural healthcare providers should never underestimate their authority and influence on local issues and seek partnerships with local public health specialist providers, third-sector providers and their local authorities, but they must also always lead on the public health response within healthcare delivery.

Table 15.2 illustrates how basic public health strategies, such as prevention, protection and service improvement, can apply in a rural setting; nonetheless, different circumstances—from remote island communities to

TABLE 15.2 Basic Strategies for Health

Strategy	Rural Healthcare Examples
Primary prevention (preventing disease or injury before it occurs)	Leading a road safety campaign—using local standing to influence known local risks
	Sponsoring initiatives for good health like Parkrun
	Using every consultation to offer brief interventions in smoking cessation, healthy eating or exercise requirements
Secondary prevention (reducing the impact of existing conditions)	Screening programmes—especially to catch up with non-engaged groups
	Cardiovascular risk reduction—blood pressure treatment, statins, etc.
	Raising awareness of the need for a rapid response to illness (like stroke) among a potentially stoical community; leading by example—being a first responder to accidents and emergencies
Tertiary prevention (easing the impact of long-term illness)	Leading group participation for post-stroke rehabilitation or long-term mental health problems
	Using local knowledge to help people with disability find and cope with suitable work
Protection	Vaccination campaigns—especially to catch up with non-engaged groups
	Keeping personal protection on the agenda of multidisciplinary team meetings (at risk children, people in care, safety of staff, etc.)
Service improvement	Regular audit of all these issues
	Becoming a training practice
	Hosting regular multidisciplinary education meetings, journal clubs, research meetings, community development learning (guest speakers from your community)
	Learning specific improvement techniques (for example, see the Cumbria Learning and Improvement Collaborative at www.theCLIC.org.uk)

prosperous 'home counties'—will dictate different priorities, and all rural practitioners should do their own 'needs assessment' for every group within their population.

Of course, public health is not a linear set of strategies—as in a Venn diagram, components overlap—and as with all complex systems, each component feeds the others.

To disentangle this, we often start with evaluation—indeed, 'audit' is a familiar concept to all healthcare providers—and often our review is spurred on by the complex financial incentives that policy makers have devised. Keeping good records, coding, compiling and reviewing the data extracted from them and then building on 'last year' is a good starting strategy (Table 15.3).

This, then, is a familiar model; we can all be effective public health practitioners. But given the special challenges of rural populations, what should be the priorities? It is too simple and less than professional to merely say, 'We will follow policy' because policy is often defined for urban and large populations, and anyway, policy is never usually sufficient. In the UK, there are clear provider incentives—for example, to pursue secondary prevention measures in heart disease and stroke (manage hypertension effectively in all people with diabetes, all people with previous experience of heart disease, etc.)—but, of course, hitting those targets isn't all we should do, and it is less clear, for example, how local rural healthcare providers should tackle rising and widespread obesity among our patients.[4]

The fourth challenge is complexity. We might have defined and identified our population of interest (for example, everyone who needs a flu vaccination); we have understood our need to intervene unequally to achieve fairly distributed outcomes (not everyone can travel to us so we will have to travel to them); and we have chosen relevant priorities within the scope of our practice (for example, patients identified with frailty). However, it will not be sufficient just to organise home visits to vaccinate our target group. There will be complex interactions that define our population of interest and therefore multiple risks to consider. ('Frailty' is a useful concept that combines age and longstanding disease processes.) For frail elderly people, the risks range from trips and falls to loneliness, inadequate nutrition and hydration, complex medication side effects and exacerbations of underlying conditions—attending to offer a flu vaccination will inevitably lead to a complex assessment and response. Done the wrong way, we have a nightmare of multiple interventions, no efficiency for time-poor practitioners and ever-more-complex care plans for the carers.

And in the rural setting, the whole management of any population group and the management of the interaction of risks are further complicated by each group existing in relatively small numbers and usually being sparsely distributed; the usual tactics for population strategies at the healthcare-provider level are then harder to implement. Specialisation within a small team is harder, focused clinics less easy to operationalise, campaigning and service customising less cost effective and so on. Partnerships with specialist providers may help (for example, with voluntary agencies focused on the priority group identified—say homelessness, certain ethnic groups and indigenous populations, children with special needs and so on), but these are often scarcer in rural settings.

There is a trend in modern healthcare to separate technical medicine from community medicine. More specialists in narrower specialisms. More complex diagnostic technology and more complex interventions—from robots to gene therapy—tending to centralise more and more in larger institutions. Meanwhile, public health as a specialty in itself has moved

TABLE 15.3 Actions for the Rural Healthcare Team, Thinking in a Public Health Way

Action	Purpose
Champion generalism, not specialisation, for all professions	For every consultation, every encounter, to be health improving and protecting, every practitioner has to be multi-skilled and open to opportunistic interventions. The professional backgrounds of the multidisciplinary team bring important perspectives and skills—but they must be shared, not siloed.
Build a high-performing team	Shared vision and common values, clear objectives, clear roles, good employment practices, fabulous communication, continuous improvement, collective leadership.
Work in partnership	Health is not the prerogative of healthcare providers only; work with the whole community and all agencies.
Co-produce services	Every community of interest (from 'everyone with diabetes' to itinerant travellers) has more expertise than you on what will help them the most—pool your technical know-how with their local knowledge.

to be less and less clinically led and more policy driven (and, in the UK, separated completely, both in budget and special workforce terms, from the NHS and placed largely in local authorities). How, in rural healthcare, can we both succeed as expert healthcare providers to families and individuals and deliver better public health thinking and defined population outcomes? The answer, as in the frailty example earlier, is not to have a team nurse do an assessment of nutrition and hydration, a physiotherapist to assess falls risk, a pharmacist to carry out medication reviews and a doctor to give the vaccination. The answer is for the team to share knowledge and skills and provide health-based thinking and care at every opportunity. This will help with completing straightforward challenges (checking blood pressure regularly) but will also stimulate useful ideas for the bigger problems, like what to do about obesity. Even better if the team asks the target population what they need.

CASE HISTORY 2

A young mother attends my surgery: she is clearly dealing with longstanding but largely untreated depression; she is struggling with her children, one of whom has severe and untreated eczema. She doesn't want medication, nor does she want referral. She is hoping for a quick fix for her child's issues. She is part of a large family of travellers who regularly pass through the practice area.

The needs of this complex, disparate group have been well documented and are familiar in both cause (for example, racism, employment and social discrimination, lack of access to services) and effect (significant mental health problems and substance misuse all cause excess in mortality and morbidity, educational underachievement and over representation in the criminal justice system).

What is also clear is that the barriers are not necessarily related to any lack of lay understanding (for example, that children are vulnerable to infectious disease and need immunisation) but getting consistent advice, access, delivery and follow up—all more difficult than they should be, even sometimes led by professionals' discriminatory attitudes.

Evidence of effective healthcare interventions to reduce the poor outcomes in traveller populations is limited, but key features include:

- Greater success for signposting and support to access routine services than providing 'special' services
- Engagement and discussion to 'co-produce' initiatives (for example, in supporting children's education)

- Learning to see the others' point of view: developing understanding of the corrosive effects of discrimination, creating more empathy, perhaps having a few team members develop the necessary skills for outreach

Mainly, my young patient needed to be listened to.

The final piece of the jigsaw for the rural practitioner is genuine engagement with the population of interest. Policy may support the idea of patient participation, but the public health mindset is to share power and control with the group of people we are trying to help—large or small. This is adaptive thinking. The rural practitioner is not the technical expert that a hospital-based specialist colleague who dispenses expert knowledge and skill may be—the rural practitioner knows that they do not always know what will suit their patients best. They know that their expertise is in helping people navigate the messiness and complexity of their risks, their symptoms, their illnesses and their whole social and emotional lives. (See Chapter 3: Role of the generalist.) This applies to groups as well as to individuals. The practitioner cannot know what will help the population in question most, but they can bring their expertise in healthcare to the negotiation about what services would help best and co-produce the most useful answer.

For the time-poor, endlessly demanded-upon rural practitioner, how are these strategies for better health realisable? Of course, we would like the disadvantaged groups in our communities to suffer less from their burdens and for them to achieve the same outcomes in health and well-being as their more advantaged neighbours—and we cannot easily change the financial and social conditions which afflict our patients. Still less can we prevent global warming or stop pandemics. Our team effectiveness is our best hope for finding time to make some difference and both find and apply some priority public health actions. The features of a high-performing team always include continuous improvement.[5] It is a sound principle that 'the problem will be with our processes, not our people', and process improvement—to give us back time to make a difference—is critical to any health improvement goal.

Communicable Disease Control in Rural Settings

COVID-19 has changed both the public and the non-specialist professional perspective on epidemiology and the control of infectious disease. While the last 50 years had seen less interest in the spread of communicable diseases and greater interest in—and knowledge of—the study of chronic, non-communicable diseases like cancer and heart disease, the

TABLE 15.4 Basic Concepts of Communicable Disease Control

Concept	Example
Prevent	Clean water, sanitation, good hygiene (like handwashing) good food preparation practice
Protect	Immunisation
	Personal protective equipment (PPE)
Interrupt transmission	Masks for droplet and aerosol reduction
	Isolating and 'closing down' food sources of infection
Targeting reservoirs/vectors of infection	Screening for TB
	Tracing contacts and rules for isolation
	Control of mosquitoes in malaria areas
Treatment	Identify and treat all cases

appearance of COVID-19, a life-changing pandemic (and before that, new threats like Ebola virus and, of course, HIV; see Lewnard 2018[6]) has refocused everyone's attention on the study of how, why, where and when infectious agents spread across communities. The usual public health strategies of prevention, protection and healthcare delivery apply, together with specific measures to interrupt transmission and the targeting of reservoirs of infection (see Table 15.4), but what is different or special in the rural setting?

Low-density, relatively homogenous populations with relatively low connectivity (for example, fewer centres of commerce and industry) are protected from the easier spread of communicable disease seen in denser urban populations. Some diseases are more specific to or more likely in a rural setting (for example, leptospirosis and orf in the UK, but malaria, TB and HIV worldwide), and the principal challenges are the ones constantly facing the rural practitioner: limited access to expertise and fewer disciplines in smaller teams, all facing dispersed pockets of special risk populations with limited access to services (for example, those with isolated or poor drinking water supply). For some infections, notably sexually transmitted diseases and HIV, the lack of confidentiality and anonymity within smaller rural communities (more usually characterised as providing good networks of support, compared to urban dwellers) can inhibit normal healthcare-seeking behaviour.

It isn't the primary role of rural healthcare providers to manage communicable disease—although spotting outbreaks and engaging the local health protection specialists are clearly rewarding objectives—and the COVID-19 experience has been a clear reminder of the five core principles to follow: protect vulnerable people, treat and support affected people, maintain services for the whole population, protect and support the team and support the mental health needs of the community and the team.[7]

COVID-19 has also been a timely reminder that disaster planning is an essential component of rural healthcare leadership.[8,9] The very remoteness and other special qualities of a rural setting also mean resilience will have to be high; national and regional resources will inevitably be focused on larger urban populations. The core principles of disaster planning apply to pandemics but also work for the healthcare team thinking about more prosaic risks (like fire and flooding) as well as extreme natural disasters such as earthquakes. The four stages of emergency planning will support the team for any future event: prevent, prepare, respond and recover. (See Chapter 9: Emergencies.) So, can we prevent a huge problem (for example, through regular maintenance, IT resilience, etc.)? Are we prepared (from stocking PPE to planning an alternate working site if our premises are lost)? Is our response ready (from simple building evacuation procedures to operating procedures for key staff in each situation—see the five principles mentioned earlier)? What will we require in recovery (clearing a backload of work; additional support, especially for mental health and well-being, to our community and our team; etc.)?

Pandemic planning is a special case, but not different. There is little room or scope for individuals to prevent a pandemic (besides constant vigilance for the 'next outbreak'), but the recent COVID-19 experience will give everyone a spur to prepare better.

SUMMARY: PUBLIC HEALTH FOR THE RURAL HEALTHCARE PROVIDER

There are some very specific rural health disadvantages, like some cancers and male suicide; there are rural expressions of universal health disadvantage from poverty to racism to the presence of hazardous occupations; there are special rural risks like higher accident and trauma incidence; and there is generalised rural healthcare disadvantage, especially in terms of access.

Except in very particular cases (for example, indigenous populations in Australia and black populations in some states in the USA), the rural challenge is less about 'place' and more about specific groups at risk. The availability and distribution of staff and the availability and distribution of services remain a constant headache for rural healthcare planning and delivery, so innovation is required.[10]

The rural practitioner, facing these perennial challenges, has a number of tasks to focus on:

- Thinking in public health way—'all groups of people at risk are my patients, not just the individual in front of me'.
- Acting in a positively discriminating way—unequal interventions will help deliver equal outcomes.
- Building a high-performing team that shares the same values, vision and goals.
- Building partnerships and showing leadership of the healthcare components of those partnerships to meet shared needs.
- Engaging with and sharing the production of the solutions with the groups of people concerned because evidence is often lacking to guide us on the best course of action.

This set of challenges dictates two things: a development need for rural practitioners and a required shift in policy thinking.

The ability to build and lead a high-performing team, for example, may be the antithesis of what an independently minded practitioner wants to do. Leadership for complex adaptive problems, with experimental and delegated solutions, runs counter to the technical and highly 'governanced' scope of modern healthcare practice—and the way we all are trained. Policy makers who set the climate and incentives for the priorities of healthcare delivery need to address why rural healthcare is different—especially to tackle the long-term, worldwide tendency for human resources to be scarce in rural settings. Health promotion and protection, alongside healthcare delivery, require first and foremost the incentives for and training of great teams.

This is not just a public health view of how to deliver healthcare but is also, of course, a 'primary healthcare team' model—and it does challenge the modern, developed world view of healthcare, which is increasingly centralised, specialised and technical. No matter, rural healthcare providers with a public health mindset have the opportunity to champion generalist skills and high-performing teams and real community engagement and, ultimately, to have comfort with messy, complex and often experimental solutions to messy, complex problems.

FURTHER READING

Donaldson, Liam, and Paul Rutter. 2017. *Donaldsons' Essential Public Health.* Abingdon: Routledge.

Warren, Jacob, and Bryant Smalley. Eds. 2014. *Rural Public Health: Best Practices and Preventative Models.* New York: Springer.
Heifetz, Ronald A., Marty Linsky, and Alexander Grashow. 2009. *The Practice of Adaptive Leadership: Tools and Tactics for Changing Your Organization and the World.* Cambridge: Harvard Business Press.

REFERENCES

1   Acheson D (ed.). *Committee of Inquiry into the Future Development of the Public Health Function. Public health in England: Report of the Committee of Inquiry into the Future Development of the Public Health Function* (Cm. 289). London: The Stationery Office, 1988.
2   Smith KB, Humphreys JS, Wilson MGA. Addressing the health disadvantage of rural populations: How does epidemiological evidence inform rural health policies and research? *Aus J Rur Heal.* 2008; 16: 56–66. https://doi.org/10.1111/j.1440–1584.2008.00953.x.
3   Cole AM, Jackson EJ, Doescher M. Urban-rural disparities in colorectal screening: Cross-sectional analysis of 1998–2005 data from the Centers for Disease Control's behavioral risk factor surveillance study. *Can Med.* 2012; 1(3): 350–6. https://doi.org/10.1002/cam4.40.
4   Lombard CB, Harrison CL, Kozica SL, Zoungas S, Keating C, Teede HJ. Effectiveness and implementation of an obesity prevention intervention: The HeLP-her rural cluster randomized controlled trial. *BMC Pub Heal.* 2014; 14: 608. https://doi.org/10.1186/1471–2458–14–608.
5   West M, Eckert R, Steward K, Pasmore B. *Developing Collective Leadership for Healthcare.* London: King's Fund, 2014.
6   Lewnard JA, Reingold AL. Emerging challenges and opportunities in infectious disease epidemiology. *Amer J Epidemiol.* 2019; 188(5): 873–82. https://doi.org/10.1093/aje/kwy264.
7   Kidd MR. Five principles for pandemic preparedness: Lessons from the Australian COVID-19 primary care response. *Br J Gen Pract.* 2020; 70(696): 316–7. https://doi.org/10.3399/bjgp20X710765.
8   O'Sullivan B, Leader J, Couch D, Purnell J. Rural pandemic preparedness: The risk, resilience and response required of primary healthcare. *Risk Manag Heal Pol.* 2020; 13: 1187–94. https://doi.org/10.2147/RMHP.S265610.
9   Willson KA, FitzGerald GJ, Lim D. Disaster management in rural and remote primary health care: A scoping review. *Prehospital Disast Med.* 2021; 36(3): 362–9. https://doi.org/10.1017/S1049023X21000200.
10 Ziller E, Milkowski C. A century later: Rural public health's enduring challenges and opportunities. *Am J Pub Heal.* 2020; 110(11): 1678–86. https://doi.org/10.2105/AJPH.2020.305868.

CHAPTER 16

Rural Social Exclusion

....

Jim Cox

There are many benefits associated with life in rural areas of the UK. Compared with towns and cities, there is more space, the air is cleaner, outdoor recreation is more pleasant, and the pace of life is slower. The impression that people who live in the countryside are fortunate is confirmed by morbidity and mortality statistics. Rural dwellers live an average of two years longer, and their morbidity rates are lower, as are other indicators such as infant mortality.[1,2]

But caution is necessary because rural disadvantage, poverty and social exclusion are often hidden. Advantaged and disadvantaged people, in terms of both income and health, live side by side, particularly in sparsely populated areas. Routine statistics, which aggregate individuals and households

DOI: 10.1201/9781003302438-21

from diverse socio-economic backgrounds, do not distinguish between the 'haves' and the 'have-nots'. Scattered among relatively wealthy landowners, commuters, retirees, second-home owners and professional people are other, less fortunate rural dwellers living on low incomes, with limited access to services. Some, such as small-scale farmers, are capital rich but cash poor. They are invisible in routine statistics yet, like their more obvious urban counterparts, at increased risk of health and social problems.

To understand rural communities, it is important to consider individual people and households.

Data used by government and other policy makers and service providers are broken down by local authority area, electoral ward, postcode or 'output area'. The minimum size of an 'output area', the smallest unit used by the Office for National Statistics[1] for census and other data, is 100 residents in 40 households in England, Wales and Northern Ireland or 50 residents in 20 households in Scotland. Such aggregated data easily hides rural deprivation.

SOCIAL EXCLUSION

The concepts of 'social inclusion' and 'social exclusion' are of multi-dimensional advantage and disadvantage, relating the individual to the society in which he or she lives. The United Nations definition, underpinning its 17 development goals for 2030, is that:

> Social exclusion describes a state in which individuals are unable to participate fully in economic, social, political and cultural life, as well as the process leading to and sustaining such a state.[3]

It is obvious that residents of islands, remote villages and hamlets cannot benefit conveniently from the same range of amenities and services as people in more densely populated areas. For example, in general terms, rural dwellers travel farther to get to work and shops or to enjoy cultural activities.

Despite an increase in the size of many villages in the UK, there has been a decline in rural services including public transport, shops, post offices, schools, banks, police stations and pubs.[4] People without their own transport and those with mobility problems have increasing difficulty in gaining direct access to services and are likely to use those local services that remain. They therefore spend more per item at village stores than those who can drive to supermarkets. The rural rich can economise in ways that their poorer neighbours cannot.

These differences extend to health and social services in which there is a trend towards larger, more centralised doctors' surgeries and teams of community staff with closure of branch surgeries and fewer house calls. The range of services may have improved in quality and quantity, but they have become less accessible. Some services, such as day care or support for 'carers' of elderly or chronically ill people, are simply not available in some isolated areas.

The increased use of smartphones, internet shopping, internet banking and remote healthcare has helped. However, such benefits depend on effective broadband or mobile phone connections, the willingness and ability to learn how to use the technology and support when problems occur. Most starkly, elderly people in high-speed broadband and mobile phone 'not spots' and those without ready access to technical support are unable to benefit. Their disadvantage is compounded.

RURAL POVERTY

The full impact of the COVID-19 pandemic and (at the time of writing) developing international economic turmoil on social exclusion remains to be seen.

Sometimes described as the 'social gradient in health', the link between poverty, ill health and mortality is well known. Dickens described it vividly, as did the authors of the Black report,[5] the Acheson inquiry report,[6] the Marmot review,[7] a Health Scotland review[8] and others. Despite repeated calls to address inequalities, the gap between poor and wealthy people is widening in the UK and worldwide.[9,10,11]

Although the percentage of people living in poverty is lower in rural areas than in urban areas, poverty is not a purely urban problem. In England in 2018–19, 13% of rural households were on absolute low income (based on a level defined in 2010–11, adjusted for inflation) and a further 14% were on relative low income (households with an income below 60% of median income), rising to 17% if housing costs were taken into account.

Again, overall generalised figures can mislead. For example, there was less of a rural-urban divide for pensioners, with 15% of rural households on absolute low income before housing costs in both rural and urban areas.[12]

Comparison of potential financial vulnerability, a composite measure of financial resilience used by the Financial Conduct Authority (FCA), also reveals a different picture. Noting that the average household income of adults living in rural areas of the UK (£41,000) is lower than in urban areas (£48,000) and much lower in remote areas such as Cornwall and the Isles of Scilly (£33,000), Cumbria (£32,000) and West Wales (£31,000), the FCA estimates that 54% of adults in rural areas, compared to 50% of adults in the UK as a whole, show characteristics of potential financial vulnerability.

Low-paid rural residents are more likely to have multiple jobs and, in the absence of an effective rural public transport system, the added expense of running a car. Such people are more financially vulnerable than their better-off neighbours and more likely to suffer if things go wrong.[13]

DEPRIVATION

The UK government's index of multiple deprivation (IMD) is based on seven domains: income, employment, education, health, crime, housing and the living environment. Overall, rural areas are less deprived than urban areas. For example, in England, just 1% of rural dwellers are in the most deprived areas, compared to 12% of urban dwellers.

Once again, analysis reveals a more subtle picture. Deprivation increases as the population becomes sparser. Only 1% of people in the most sparsely populated communities are in the least deprived 10% of the IMD, compared to 4% in rural villages and 18% in rural towns.[12]

Nevertheless, the diversity of rural communities where privilege and deprivation co-exist side by side means that average figures based on indices such as IMD lack granularity. Rural deprivation hides easily behind routine statistics.

MENTAL HEALTH AND DISABILITY

There is a close association between debt and poor mental health and evidence that the welfare benefit system in the UK is insufficiently nimble to deal fairly with volatility and unpredictability. When incomes fluctuate and benefits are underpaid or overpaid, adjustments to benefit payments, up or down, can be slow and stressful. Such challenges are experienced disproportionately by the more vulnerable members of society and exacerbated in rural areas by limited broadband access, centralisation of advice and support services and lack of public transport. Unwell and disabled people may be required to travel long distances to be assessed for their capability to work or access face-to-face support to complete forms or maintain necessary records such as journals of job search activities.[14]

DISTANCE DECAY AND RESOURCE ALLOCATION

Uptake of services is distorted by their availability, their accessibility, the costs to the service users of accessing them and the attitudes of the population to using them. People who live farthest from doctors' surgeries, hospitals and other health and social care providers are least likely to seek attention for comparable problems. The explanation of this phenomenon ('distance decay') is multifactorial: many rural services, including healthcare, are relatively unavailable or inaccessible and people who live in different geographic areas have lower expectations. Many rural dwellers compare their situation with the harsher conditions of the past rather than with the current lifestyles of the majority. The popular image of poor rural dwellers being uncomplaining seems to be true.[15]

Rural health services are relatively under-funded.[16,17] Funding formulae under-reflect the costs of service delivery, including emergency services, hospital trusts and social care.[18] Furthermore, they are generally modelled on proxy calculations of need based on historic activity and expenditure, not on the cost of providing equitable services, thus perpetuating disparities and inequalities. For example, University College London receives 29% more than Royal Cornwall Hospitals for delivering the same unit of care.[19]

Not only are rural areas relatively under-funded but their provision also costs more. Service providers struggle to achieve economies of scale in more remote areas. For example, the travel-related unit costs for domiciliary care in England are more than twice as high in North Yorkshire than in Birmingham, and the average annual mileage of rural occupational therapists (OTs) in Dorset is 4,880 miles, compared with 1,952 miles for urban OTs. The Arbuthnott review of resource allocation in the Scottish NHS found that health visiting and district nursing costs were 3.3% above the national average in rural Argyll and Clyde and 5.3% below the national average in urban Glasgow.

Many social care staff are not paid for the time they spend travelling. Nor is additional travel time always taken into account when planning their work. The unfortunate result is either that quality is compromised—for example, by shortening the duration of visits to compensate for extra travel time—or staff choose to work additional hours at their own expense.

One solution for cash-strapped health and social care providers is to reduce costs by employing cheaper, unregistered support staff such as healthcare assistants, again compromising quality of care.[20] In 2010, more than 37% of all nursing and support staff in rural Taunton and Somerset, Mid-Cheshire and United Lincolnshire NHS Trusts fell into this category—over three times the proportion in London Hospitals.[21] The shortage of nurses in the UK has led to a rapid increase in recruitment of nursing support staff, particularly in community services.[18]

When the free market is left to its own devices in rural areas, the outcome tends to be limited provision as exemplified by the paucity of rural public transport and the closure of village shops, post offices and pubs.

TRANSPORT

People who live in the most rural areas travel almost twice as far per year than those in the most urban areas: 90% of rural households have access to a car or van, compared with only 73% in urban areas; 87% of rural dwellers' travel is by car, compared with 67% in the most urban areas.

Cuts to rural bus subsidies have led to the virtual absence of an effective rural public transport system to enable people to get to and from work or to access services. Local authority expenditure on public transport is significantly lower in rural areas than in urban ones. Even excluding London, where public transport is relatively well funded, urban authorities spend 63% more than rural authorities on bus subsidies and 348% more on concessionary fares.[22]

Although rural car ownership is often a necessity, lack of car ownership is regarded as a characteristic of deprivation in both the Townsend and Carstairs deprivation indices, widely used in the analysis of census data and measurement of deprivation in health, education and crime.[23,24] Resource allocation based on such indices is a 'double whammy' for low-income families in rural areas where car ownership is an expensive necessity and not an indicator of wealth.

EMPLOYMENT

Rural economies are changing. Compared with the past, fewer people are employed in agriculture, horticulture and forestry, and more people are employed in services such as tourism, health, retail and education. Many rural residents work in jobs that are low paid, part time and/or seasonal with volatile or unpredictable incomes and limited opportunities for career progression.

Overall, working-age people who live in rural areas are more likely to be employed and less likely to be registered as unemployed than those in towns and cities. The percentage of 'economically inactive' working-age people, such as students, retirees and sick and disabled people who are unavailable for or not seeking work, is also lower. However, these figures are based on where people live, not where they work. Because many people who live in rural areas work in urban areas in well-paid jobs, average incomes are higher than local wages. (The converse applies in major urban areas, where the earnings of those who work there are higher than the incomes of those who live there.)

Prior to the COVID-19 pandemic when, of necessity, home working increased dramatically, the highest rate of home working (32%) was found in rural hamlets and dispersed areas, compared with only 13% in urban areas. How this trend plays out in the longer term remains to be seen. For many people—for example, carers, cleaners and others who work in services and tourism—home working is not an option.[25]

FUEL POVERTY

Fuel poverty is a serious problem from three perspectives: poverty, health and carbon. Since 2017, fuel poverty, a measure based on household income, energy efficiency and energy prices, has been more prevalent in urban areas of England than in rural areas, a reversal of the situation prior to 2017. But levels of fuel poverty remain high in rural hamlets where older houses with solid walls and poor insulation are not energy efficient and, lacking connection to a gas network ('off-grid' or 'off-gas'), are dependent on more expensive fuels such as oil. The 'fuel poverty gap' (the spending necessary to take the household out of fuel poverty—a measure of the depth of fuel poverty) in more remote areas is twice as high as the average for all fuel-poor households.[26,27,28,29] The impacts of the war in Ukraine and policies in response to the climate crisis remain to be seen.

SAVINGS

Compared with urban adults, rural adults are more likely to have cash savings of £50,000 or more and less likely to use consumer credit, be overdrawn or to use a credit card without paying off the full monthly balance. They are better satisfied with their financial circumstances and less likely to have a negative outlook regarding making ends meet.[30]

Access to financial services is a particular issue in rural areas. Of UK adults who never use the internet, 70% (or 3.7 million people) live in rural areas. Many rural bank branches have closed but the take-up of mobile banking by rural adults is only half that of their urban counterparts. In 2020, internet banking was relatively inaccessible for nearly half (48%) of adults in rural areas compared with only 20% in urban areas.[31]

HOUSING AND HOMELESSNESS

Although predominantly an urban phenomenon, homelessness is a substantial rural problem too. For example, prior to emergency government intervention during the COVID-19 pandemic, 1.4 people per 1,000 households in rural areas were homeless, compared with 2.5 per 1,000 households in urban areas. But the trends differ. From 2018 to 2019, rough sleeping across all of England fell by 9% but rose by 2% in rural areas.[32,33]

Rural homeless people are most commonly families with young children, women expecting babies and those vulnerable through age, disability or illness who can no longer live with parents, relatives or friends. Rented accommodation may only be available during the winter, out of the tourist season.

The availability of affordable housing is compromised by high purchase and rental prices because of competition from wealthy people moving to the countryside on retirement or looking for second (or third or more) homes and the demand for tourist accommodation, including holiday rentals and 'bed and breakfasts'. The result is that, to find affordable housing, younger people move to towns and cities to be replaced by older people with more money migrating in the opposite direction.

In England in 2019–20, the average cheaper house (priced in the lower quartile) was 8.6 times average lower quartile earnings, compared to a ratio of 7.4 in predominantly urban areas, excluding London.[12]

For understandable reasons, the situation is exacerbated by protective planning policies which restrict the building of new houses and conversion of existing properties, such as disused barns, for housing. Rural planners have the unenviable task of balancing conservation and protection of the countryside against the need for additional housing, particularly for affordable housing for young people who wish to remain in their home area or who are employed in the countryside.

As a result, the typical commuting pattern is the reverse of the typical migration pattern. For example, large numbers of residents who can afford houses in the Peak District National Park typically commute to work in Greater Manchester and Sheffield while those on lower incomes, who work in the National Park but can't afford to live there, cross their paths as they commute in the opposite direction.

BROADBAND AND MOBILE PHONE COVERAGE

For society as a whole, 'digital inclusion' is as much a necessity as a dependable supply of electricity or drinking water. The areas missing out are predominantly rural. Unlike urban areas, where businesses and homes generally have fast fibre broadband, many rural properties still have slow connections through copper cables or the mobile phone network. In 2018, 7% of premises in rural areas, rising to 35% in hamlets and isolated dwellings, had ineffective broadband download speeds of less than 10Mbit/s.[34]

Slow broadband access discourages new businesses from setting up in rural areas and is a time-consuming and frustrating problem for existing businesses such as farming, which are required to communicate electronically with the government. It is also a major hurdle for people claiming welfare benefits and creates challenges for online shopping and access to public, private and voluntary sector organisations.

The issue was amplified during the COVID-19 pandemic when many adults and schoolchildren struggled to work from home and is compounded by the closure of public libraries, which previously provided internet access.

ARTS

Culture, including performing arts, visual arts, literature and online arts, make for healthier lives by fostering aspiration, learning and personal development. They play a vital role in building cohesive communities.[35,36]

But, for many rural dwellers, access to the countries' major performers, bands, orchestras, opera, theatre and national museums etc., is expensive, difficult or impossible, particularly when overnight stays are necessary.

In terms of social exclusion, there is a balance. Many rural communities pride themselves in their cultural traditions, which bring people together and raise their spirits. For some, the benefits of local community cultural activities may outweigh the disadvantages of missing out on major concerts etc. Others, particularly young people whose development and well-being would benefit from inspirational art and artists, suffer relative disadvantage. Digital access is increasingly available and welcome, but it is not the same as experiencing the buzz of a live performance or the magic of seeing original fine art.

In recent years, public spending on arts and culture in 'predominantly rural' areas of England has declined faster than elsewhere.[37] Arts Council England has committed to reversing the trend, supporting community activity, touring, rural festivals and libraries.[38]

EDUCATION

Rural school pupils perform better than those living in urban areas. More leave secondary education with English and maths GCSEs at A* to C grade or equivalent. However, the inverse is true for pupils from deprived households where, for the same level of deprivation, the attainment of rural pupils is lower than that of those who live in urban areas.

Despite their better GCSE performance, fewer rural 18-to-20-year-olds enter higher education, and those who do are more likely to study part time.

The figures for vocational qualifications such as National Vocational Qualification (NVQ), Higher National Certificate (HNC) and Higher National Diploma (HND) are more complex. Although the proportion of the working-age population with at least one qualification is higher for people living in rural areas, from a workplace-based perspective, rural residents are less likely than their urban counterparts to have vocational qualifications. One reason for the apparent paradox is that businesses that can benefit from the skills are more likely to be based in urban areas.[12]

CRIME

Figures for reported crime show that average rates and those for violence, sexual offences, robbery, burglary and vehicle offences are lower in rural than in urban areas.[12] Conversely 'rural' crimes such as the theft of tractors, tractor global positioning systems (GPS), quad bikes, all-terrain vehicles (ATVs), livestock and sheepdogs are (not surprisingly!) higher in rural areas. Rural theft cost the UK £54.3 million in 2019, an increase of 9% on the previous year, although it fell in 2020 during the COVID-19 pandemic when, like everyone else's, thieves' movements were restricted. Another pandemic-related trend has been a surge in dog ownership and countryside visits with a 10% rise in dog attacks on farm animals at an annual cost of £1.3 million.[39,40]

Unfortunately, the annual Crime Survey for England and Wales (CSEW), which includes unreported crimes, does not publish rural data.

PUBLIC LIBRARY SERVICES

On average, predominantly rural local authorities' budget 25% less per resident for library services than those in predominantly urban areas. Given the relative lack of provision of rural libraries and the barriers to accessing rural services, it is not surprising that a lower proportion of rural residents (29%) use the service than urban residents (35%). As a response to library closures and threatened closures, many rural library outlets are supported by rural local authorities but run by volunteers.[41]

SUMMARY

Many, perhaps most, of the problems discussed in this chapter are unlikely to be solved by front-line rural healthcare workers not involved in policy decisions. They are important because, to function effectively and provide the best possible care for patients, it is necessary to understand the context of practice. Without an understanding of rural disadvantage, hidden social exclusion, digital inclusion, transport and access to healthcare, it is not possible to address the needs of relatively uncomplaining people in remote or sparsely populated areas.

Solutions to the broader issues are in the hands of healthcare and political leaders.

SUMMARY BOX

- Overall, rural dwellers are generally healthier and less deprived than their urban counterparts.
- But rural communities are diverse. Advantaged and disadvantaged people, in terms of both income and health, are indistinguishable in routine statistics which aggregate individuals and households from diverse socio-economic backgrounds.
- Deprivation increases with population sparsity.
- People who live farthest from doctors' surgeries, hospitals and other health and social care providers are least likely to seek attention for comparable problems ('distance decay').
- Funding formulae for public services, including the NHS and education, are partly based on historic payments, providing less money per individual for those who live in rural areas than for those who live in urban areas.
- Although rural car ownership is often a necessity, lack of car ownership is regarded as a characteristic of deprivation in census analysis and measurement of deprivation in health, education and crime.
- Excess costs of rural service provision include:

  - Travel costs
  - Travel time
  - Lack of economies of scale
  - Rural healthcare employers substitute proportionally more cheaper, unregistered support staff such as healthcare assistants.
  - Many rural dwellers compare their situation with the harsher conditions of the past rather than with the current lifestyles of the majority.

REFERENCES

1 Office for National Statistics (ONS). *Census Geography.* London: Office for National Statistics, 2021. www.ons.gov.uk/methodology/geography/ukgeographies/censusgeography#output-area-oa [Accessed 1 August, 2022].

2 United Nations. *Leaving No One Behind: The Imperative of Inclusive Development. Report on the World Social Situation 2016.* New York: United Nations, 2016. www.un.org/esa/socdev/rwss/2016/full-report.pdf [Accessed 1 August, 2022].

3 Ibid.

4 Rural England. *State of Rural Services.* Tavistock: Rural England, 2019. https://ruralengland.org/wp-content/uploads/2019/02/SORS18-Summary-Hi-Res-screen-version.pdf [Accessed 1 August, 2022].

5 Black D, Morris J, Smith C, Townsend P. *Inequalities in Health: Report of a Research Working Group.* London: Department of Health and Social Security, 1980.

6 Acheson D. *Independent Inquiry into Inequalities in Health.* London: HMSO, 1998. https://assets.publishing.service.gov.uk/government/uploads/system/uploads/attachment_data/file/265503/ih.pdf [Accessed 1 August, 2022].

7 Marmot, M. *Fair Society, Healthy Lives: Strategic Review of Health Inequalities in England Post 2010.* London: Marmot Review, 2010. www.parliament.uk/globalassets/documents/fair-society-healthy-lives-full-report.pdf [Accessed 1 August, 2022].

8 Health Scotland. *Health Inequalities: What Are They? How Do We Reduce Them?* Edinburgh: Health Scotland, 2015. www.healthscotland.scot/media/1086/health-inequalities-what-are-they-how-do-we-reduce-them-mar16.pdf [Accessed 1 August, 2022].

9 Office for National Statistics (ONS). *Health Inequalities.* London: Office for National Statistics, 2021. www.ons.gov.uk/peoplepopulationandcommunity/healthandsocialcare/healthinequalities [Accessed 1 August, 2022].

10 Williams E, Buck D, Babalola G, Maguire D. *What Are Health Inequalities?* London: King's Fund, 2020. www.kingsfund.org.uk/publications/what-are-health-inequalities [Accessed 1 August, 2022].

11 Marmot, M, Allen, J, Boyce, T, Goldblatt, P, Morrison, J. *Health Equity in England: The Marmot Review Ten Years On.* London: Institute of Health Equity, 2020. www.health.org.uk/publications/reports/the-marmot-review-10-years-on [Accessed 1 August, 2022].

12 Department for Environment, Food and Rural Affairs (DEFRA). *Statistical Digest of Rural England.* London: DEFRA, 2021. www.gov.uk/government/statistics/statistical-digest-of-rural-england [Accessed 1 August, 2022].

13 Financial Conduct Authority (FCA). *The Financial Lives of Consumers Across the UK: Key Findings from the FCA's Financial Lives Survey 2017, Updated January 2020.* London: Financial Conduct Authority. www.fca.org.uk/publication/research/financial-lives-consumers-across-uk.pdf [Accessed 1 August, 2022].

14 Shucksmith M, Chapman P, Glass J, Atterton J. *Rural Lives: Understanding Financial Hardship and Vulnerability in Rural Areas.* Newcastle: Newcastle University, 2021. https://pure.sruc.ac.uk/en/publications/rural-lives-understanding-financial-hardship-and-vulnerability-in [Accessed 1 August, 2022].

15 Joseph Rowntree Foundation. *Disadvantage in Rural Scotland: Social Policy Research 62*. York: Joseph Rowntree Foundation, 1994. www.rurallives.co.uk/uploads/1/2/7/3/127324359/disadvantage_in_rural_scotland_findings_sp62.pdf [Accessed 1 August, 2022].

16 All-Party Parliamentary Group on Rural Health & Care. *Parliamentary Inquiry*. London: National Centre for Rural Health and Care, 2022. http://roseregeneration.co.uk/wp-content/uploads/2022/02/Rural-Health-and-Care-APPG-Inquiry-Report.pdf [Accessed 1 August, 2022].

17 All-Party Parliamentary Group on Rural Services. *The Implications of National Funding Formulae for Rural Health and Education Provision: Summary Report*. London: Rural Services Network, 2010. www.rsnonline.org.uk/images/files/appgfunding-summary-260310.pdf [Accessed 1 August, 2022].

18 Buchan J, Gershlick B, Charlesworth A, Secombe I. *Falling Short: The NHS Workforce Challenge*. London: Health Foundation, 2019. www.health.org.uk/publications/reports/falling-short-the-nhs-workforce-challenge [Accessed 1 August, 2022].

19 Palmer B, Appleby J, Spencer J. *Rural Health Care: A Rapid Review of the Impact of Rurality on the Costs of Delivering Health Care*. London: Nuffield Trust, 2019. www.nuffieldtrust.org.uk/research/rural-health-care [Accessed 1 August, 2022].

20 Buchan J, Gershlick B, Charlesworth A, Secombe I. *Falling Short: The NHS Workforce Challenge*. London: Health Foundation, 2019. www.health.org.uk/publications/reports/falling-short-the-nhs-workforce-challenge [Accessed 1 August, 2022].

21 Asthana S, Gibson A. *Police Funding Arrangements in England and Wales; Report to the NRCN*. National Rural Crime Network, 2016. www.nationalruralcrimenetwork.net/content/uploads/2016/07/Fair-funding-for-rural-policing-Dr-Alex-Gibson.pdf [Accessed 1 August, 2022].

22 Rural England. *State of Rural Services*. Tavistock: Rural England, 2019. https://ruralengland.org/wp-content/uploads/2019/02/SORS18-Summary-Hi-Res-screen-version.pdf [Accessed 1 August, 2022].

23 Yousaf S, Bonsall A. *UK Townsend Deprivation Scores from 2011 Census Data*. UK Data Service, 2017. http://s3-eu-west-1.amazonaws.com/statistics.digitalresources.jisc.ac.uk/dkan/files/Townsend_Deprivation_Scores/UK%20Townsend%20Deprivation%20Scores%20from%202011%20census%20data.pdf [Accessed 1 August, 2022].

24 Office of National Statistics (ONS), National Records of Scotland, Northern Ireland Statistics and Research Agency, UK Data Service. *2011 UK Townsend Deprivation Scores*. London: ONS, 2017. http://dx.doi.org/10.5257/census/aggregate-2011-2 [Accessed 1 August, 2022].

25 Department for Environment, Food and Rural Affairs (DEFRA). *Statistical Digest of Rural England*. London: DEFRA, 2021. www.gov.uk/government/statistics/statistical-digest-of-rural-england [Accessed 1 August, 2022].

26 Department for Environment, Food and Rural Affairs (DEFRA). *Statistical Digest of Rural England*. London: DEFRA, 2021. www.gov.uk/government/statistics/statistical-digest-of-rural-england [Accessed 1 August, 2022].

27   Hills J. *Getting the Measure of Fuel Poverty.* London: Centre for Analysis
     of Social Exclusion, 2012. https://sticerd.lse.ac.uk/dps/case/cr/CASEreport72.
     pdf [Accessed 1 August, 2022].
28   Department for Business, Energy and Industrial Strategy. *Annual Poverty
     Statistics in England.* London: Department for Business, Energy and
     Industrial Strategy, 2021. https://assets.publishing.service.gov.uk/government/
     uploads/system/uploads/attachment_data/file/966509/Annual_Fuel_Poverty_
     Statistics_LILEE_Report_2021__2019_data_.pdf [Accessed 1 August, 2022].
29   Department for Environment, Food and Rural Affairs (DEFRA). *Fuel Poverty
     in Rural Areas.* London: DEFRA, 2020. https://assets.publishing.service.gov.
     uk/government/uploads/system/uploads/attachment_data/file/969870/Fuel_
     Poverty_August_2020__2018_Data__accessible_version_CC_checked.pdf
     [Accessed 1 August, 2022].
30   Financial Conduct Authority (FCA). *Financial Lives 2020 Survey: The Impact
     of Coronavirus.* London: Financial Conduct Authority, 2021. www.fca.org.
     uk/publication/research/financial-lives-survey-2020.pdf [Accessed 1 August,
     2022].
31   Financial Conduct Authority (FCA). *The Financial Lives of Consumers
     Across the UK: Key Findings from the FCA's Financial Lives Survey 2017,
     Updated January 2020.* London: Financial Conduct Authority. www.fca.org.
     uk/publication/research/financial-lives-consumers-across-uk.pdf [Accessed 1
     August, 2022].
32   Department for Environment, Food and Rural Affairs (DEFRA). *Statistical
     Digest of Rural England.* London: DEFRA, 2021. www.gov.uk/government/
     statistics/statistical-digest-of-rural-england [Accessed 1 August, 2022].
33   Weal R. *Out of the Woods? Tackling Homelessness in Rural Communities.*
     St Mungo's, 2021. www.mungos.org/out-of-the-woods-tackling-homelessness-
     in-rural-communities/ [Accessed 1 August, 2022].
34   Department for Environment, Food and Rural Affairs (DEFRA). *Statistical
     Digest of Rural England.* London: DEFRA, 2021. www.gov.uk/government/
     statistics/statistical-digest-of-rural-england [Accessed 1 August, 2022].
35   World Health Organization (WHO) Europe. *Health Evidence Network
     Synthesis Report 67: What Is the Evidence on the Role of the Arts in Improving
     Health and Well-Being?* Copenhagen: WHO, 2019. https://apps.who.int/
     iris/bitstream/handle/10665/329834/9789289054553-eng.pdf [Accessed 1
     August, 2022].
36   Arts Council England (ACE). *Arts, Culture and Rural Communities – How the
     Arts Council Works in Rural England.* London: ACE, 2020. www.artscouncil.
     org.uk/community-and-place/rural-positioning#section-1 [Accessed 1 August,
     2022].
37   Arts Council England (ACE). *Arts, Culture and Rural Communities – How the
     Arts Council Works in Rural England.* London: ACE, 2020. www.artscouncil.
     org.uk/community-and-place/rural-positioning#section-1 [Accessed 1 August,
     2022].
38   Arts Council England (ACE). *Let's Create.* London: ACE, 2020. www.
     artscouncil.org.uk/letscreate [Accessed 1 August, 2022].
39   NFU Mutual. *A Challenging Time for the Countryside: Rural Crime Report
     2020.* Stratford upon Avon: NFU, 2020.

40 NFU Mutual. *The Impact on Our Communities: Rural Crime Report 2021.* Stratford upon Avon: NFU, 2021. www.nfumutual.co.uk/globalassets/farming/rural-crime/2021/rural-crime-report-2021.pdf [Accessed 1 August, 2022].

41 Rural England. *State of Rural Services.* Tavistock: Rural England, 2019. https://ruralengland.org/wp-content/uploads/2019/02/SORS18-Summary-Hi-Res-screen-version.pdf [Accessed 1 August, 2022].

CHAPTER 17

Research

....

Christopher E. Clark

General practice is often described as an art, as well as a science. Debating this tension is beyond the scope of this chapter, but a multitude of guidelines exist to shape primary care treatment of conditions. Such guidelines can only be practical and applicable if they are grounded in and supported by evidence derived from populations representative of our primary care patients. This chapter sets out an argument for the importance and relevance of primary care research in rural and remote settings. It also offers ideas as to how an individual or practice team may start to engage with the research process and suggests useful resources for further guidance.

WHY RESEARCH IN PRIMARY CARE?

Randomised controlled trials (RCTs) guide us in choosing new treatments over established ones, but it is well recognised that when study inclusion criteria are restricted, the results may not be applicable to our primary care practice populations. For example, the much-publicised 2015 SPRINT trial of intensive blood pressure lowering excluded people with diabetes, previous stroke, heart failure and cognitive impairment, as well as those living in nursing care or 'too far from the study clinic site'—an example of all too common exclusion of rural participants from research.[1] SPRINT remains a landmark trial that has contributed to a lowering of blood pressure targets in European and American hypertension guidelines.[2,3] However, multimorbidity—the presence of two or more long-term conditions—occurs in 78% of those with hypertension, so many patients would not have met

DOI: 10.1201/9781003302438-22

the inclusion criteria for SPRINT. Does the evidence, therefore, really support more intensive blood pressure lowering in a hypertensive primary care population?[4, 5] In practice, multimorbidity is associated with less intensive blood pressure–lowering treatment. In other words, current data on intensive blood pressure lowering are not generalisable for many people seen in primary care with hypertension.[6] This is one reason for the apparently more lenient blood pressure targets set in current UK National Institute for Health and Care (NICE) guidance, which encourages practitioners to use clinical judgement in the presence of multimorbidity.[7] Gaps in evidence such as this can only be overcome by including representative primary care populations. This requires engagement with the research process by primary care teams.

Julian Tudor Hart 1927–2018
Glyncorrwg, Glamorgan

A ground-breaking pioneer of preventive healthcare based on epidemiological research.

Julian Tudor Hart was born into a medical family in London, both his parents being politically left-wing doctors. After education at Dartington Hall and Pickering College, Ontario, where he was evacuated during the Second World War, he read medicine at Queen's College, Cambridge. and St George's Hospital, London.

He began work in general practice in a deprived area of west London before undertaking epidemiological research as a registrar to Richard Doll at the London School of Hygiene and Tropical Medicine, then moving to Cardiff in 1960 to work for Archie Cochrane at the Welsh National School of Medicine.

In 1961, he returned to general practice, this time in Glyncorrwg, a small mining village in the Afan Valley. The stability of the community and cooperation and trust of his patients allowed him to make long-term observations of his patients' blood pressure, the value of blood pressure monitoring, the role of dietary salt and the value of warfarin as preventive medication.

He was the first UK general practitioner to routinely measure blood pressure, and Glyncorrwg became the Medical Research Council's first research practice. His writing and publications on preventive and anticipatory care were influential throughout the world. Most famously, he described the 'inverse care law' in *The Lancet* in 1971:

The availability of good medical care tends to vary inversely with the need for it in the population served. This inverse care law operates more completely where medical care is most exposed to market forces, and less so where such exposure is reduced.

> He had strong political affiliations, standing as a Communist Party candidate in three general elections. Later he was a member of the Labour Party.
> Tudor Hart, Julian. 1971. *The inverse care law. Lancet* 297:405–12.
>
> — Philip Evans

Without evidence applicable to our patients, we cannot interpret trial evidence on their behalf. A recent review suggested that only 18% of recommendations in primary care were based on high-quality, patient-orientated evidence.[8] It is argued that empiricism, the application of population-based evidence to the individual, has taken on too large a role in the practice of primary care.[9] Nevertheless, future care seems unlikely to improve significantly without a growth in the evidence base for primary care practice. So, in order to successfully practice evidence-based primary care (rural or not), we need evidence grounded in the populations we seek to serve.[10, 11] Even if we do not undertake research ourselves, we need an appreciation of the research process in order to find and appraise such evidence to guide our discussions with patients.[12] The unique nature of every consultation dictates that we will never have a guideline for every circumstance (nor should we—an ability to address every unique presentation is a key attribute of medical generalism—see Chapter 3: Role of the Generalist), but our patients bring us evidence from an ever-widening range of sources. An ability to weigh and place such information in an appropriate and holistic context is a necessary skill for modern practice.

There are several reasons a rural healthcare professional might wish to engage with primary care research during their career. Many areas of practice are only amenable to study within primary care: for example, the study of aspects of the consultation process itself. (See Chapter 14: Technology.) This is why it is vital that research does take place in primary care.

RELEVANCE TO RURAL PRACTICE

Rural primary care can be isolating for multidisciplinary team members.[13] Engaging in research allows us to step out of the clinical setting, offering new perspectives on a service or therapeutic intervention that we would not otherwise consider. By bringing our patient experiences to bear on research questions, we can identify opportunities to improve care without just working harder in the same rut.[14] Primary care research is a multidisciplinary activity which can bring the benefits of closer teamworking towards a shared goal to the practice, in turn contributing to improved staff satisfaction and retention.[15, 16] It also offers wider networking outside relatively small rural primary care teams, leading us to interact with new colleagues external to the practice, with a different range of skills such as trial managers, statisticians or public and patient representatives, among others.

Research into rural issues or health is most relevant if the research team involves rural expertise, which may reside with nurses, other allied health professional team members, non-clinical staff or doctors, as well as service users. For example, a study of the potential for the integration of community pharmacies into the care of people living with long-term conditions would have lacked credibility without the strong engagement of both rural pharmacists and primary care teams.[17] There are some notable exemplars of historic rural primary care–based research. (See boxes in this chapter.)

In the era of big data, what can a small rural practice contribute? Apart from ensuring the relevance of findings to rural practice, there are specific attributes of our populations, such as the relative stability of cohorts, that lend themselves to long-term studies and successful repeated follow up.[18–20]

Similarly, research into rural diseases (see Chapter 4: Rural Diseases) is clearly best informed with the support and participation of rural practices.

William Norman Pickles 1885–1969
Aysgarth, Yorkshire

A world-class epidemiologist and the first president of the Royal College of General Practitioners.

Born in Leeds, Yorkshire, he attended grammar school and medical school in the city, graduating in 1910 and proceeding to a doctorate, MD, in 1918. He was one of six brothers who all became doctors, four of them general practitioners.

Following service in the First World War as a surgeon lieutenant in the Royal Naval Reserve, he practised in Wensleydale for more than 50 years. Here, he demonstrated that rural doctors had unrivalled opportunities to observe and record illness and disease.

Two influences on his career and work were William Budd and the general practitioner and cardiologist James Mackenzie (1853–1925), who devised a 'polygraph' to study cardiac rhythm, first described atrial fibrillation, furthered understanding of the role of digitalis and famously wrote that 'a heart is what a heart can do'.

> In the *British Medical Journal*, Pickles published papers on 'catarrhal jaundice' (viral hepatitis) and the first detailed description of Bornholm disease. Later, in *Epidemiology in Country Practice*, published in 1939, he described his meticulous observations of common infectious diseases including jaundice, chicken pox and measles, clearly demonstrating, for example, that the incubation period of measles is 12 days and that patients are only infectious for a short period so that no more than 7 days isolation is necessary. Similarly, he showed that the incubation period of 'catarrhal jaundice' was 26 to 35 days, a shorter window than previously believed.
>
> As a result of the originality and scope of his work, he was honoured by many institutions, including the Royal College of Physicians, the BMA, Harvard University and the Royal College of General Practitioners, which elected him as their first president in 1952.
>
> — Philip Evans

Practice research has wider benefits for the primary healthcare team and for patients. The relationships between research engagement and quality are complex and hard to define but suggest a link between such engagement and improved care.[21] Allied healthcare professionals perceive improved approaches to patient care when engaging in research.[22] Research activity in acute NHS trusts is associated with lower mortality for acute admissions and higher CQC ratings, and there are also signals that this is the case for primary care.[23-25]

LEVELS OF ENGAGEMENT

Practice teams or individual members can meaningfully engage with research on a number of levels which do not require individual expertise or research leadership. Opportunities exist for all professionals to gain experience of the research world and to influence research priorities and subject-led research calls. For example, the National Institute for Health Research (NIHR) and the James Lind Alliance operate priority-setting mechanisms. Research questions are also generated by NICE through guideline committees which regularly advertise for primary care members.

HOW TO GET GOING IN RESEARCH

There follow some further suggestions of ways to get started in research and opportunities for further career development. See the Further Reading section at the end of this chapter for links to the resources mentioned.

- Practices may contribute routine data in an automatic or semi-automatic way to large datasets such as the Clinical Practice Research Datalink (which has led to over 3,000 peer-reviewed publications over the last 30 years). Participation ensures that findings include, and are therefore relevant to, rural primary care populations.
- The Royal College of General Practitioners (RCGP) offers education about and accreditation for research through its Research Ready programme. This is a good starting point, helping practices develop a research culture and ethos and promoting teamwork and engagement. The RCGP also offers a range of small grants through its Scientific Foundation Board; these can support first steps in personal research funding.[26]
- Practices in England may engage with their local NIHR primary care clinical research networks (CRNs), which have expertise in recruitment to and delivery of research projects. CRNs promote opportunities to take part in clinical research, supporting recruitment of the public, patients or staff to local or national studies and ensuring that participation is adequately remunerated.
- Many charitable and industrial organisations provide specific financial support and engagement. Contact with a local university primary care department can help find the most appropriate resources.

Engaging in research requires personal drive and interest. Every patient contact may generate PUNs (patient's unmet needs) pointing to DENs (doctor's educational needs).[27] Despite the nomenclature, a DEN can, of course, apply to any member of the primary healthcare team; it is not doctor specific. Some DENs cannot be met through usual resources because the required information does not exist, making the DEN a potential audit or research question. Clinical audit is a way of finding out whether you are doing what you should be doing, measuring performance against recognised best practice. Research, on the other hand, evaluates practice or compares alternative practices, seeking to establish what you should be doing: i.e. what best practice might be. Making this distinction is important because practices usually audit their processes without external reference, whereas research generally requires approval of an ethics committee and other regulatory bodies. The Medical Research Council offer useful guidance for determining the difference. (See Further Reading.)

William Brownrigg 1712–1800
Cumberland

Following apprenticeships with a local Cumbrian apothecary and a London barber-surgeon, Brownrigg gained his medical degree at the prestigious University of Leiden in the Netherlands. Returning home, he set up practice in Whitehaven, a busy port and mining area. In a surviving case book, largely written in Latin, he describes the range of conditions he encountered, including 'gaol fever' (typhus), puerperal sepsis, urinary calculus and haemorrhoids. His reputation took him to see patients on horseback throughout Cumberland.

Following the death of 22 miners in an explosion at Whitehaven Colliery in 1737, he embarked on an investigation into noxious and explosive gases, persuading the owner, Sir James Lowther, to contribute to an onsite laboratory with pipes connected to underground mine workings and bladders to contain poisonous gases. Brownrigg was able to demonstrate that impure air led to asphyxiation and that explosions occurred more commonly during periods of low atmospheric pressure. His work on gases led to a series of papers to the Royal Society, fellowship (FRS) in 1742 and the award of the Royal Society's Copley Medal in 1766 for an investigation of spa water.

His other discoveries included the use of super-heated steam in steam engines and a novel method for boiling large volumes of sea water to manufacture salt, an important commodity for the preservation of food. With his brother-in-law, Charles Wood, he described the physical properties of platinum.

In the summer of 1772, at his home, Ormathwaite Hall near Keswick, Brownrigg entertained Benjamin Franklin, fellow scientist and one of the founding fathers of the USA, and Sir John Pringle, president of the Royal Society. As well as visiting coal mines, they ventured on to Derwentwater in a small boat where, using a small quantity of oil kept by Brownrigg in the hollow upper joint of his bamboo cane, they studied the wave-calming effect of 'oil on troubled waters'. Better known by sailors than scientists, the phenomenon was deemed worthy of a paper read to the Royal Society in June 1774 and a later publication in *Philosophical Transactions*.

Brownrigg's work on gases paralleled that of Black, Priestley and Cavendish. Had he moved to London instead of remaining in his home county of Cumberland, his name would surely be as well known.

Beckett, J V. 1977. "Dr William Brownrigg FRS: physician, chemist and country gentleman." *Notes and Records of the Royal Society of London*. 31(2):255–71. https://royalsocietypublishing.org/doi/10.1098/rsnr.1977.0016.

Mertens, Joost. 2006. "Oil on troubled waters: Benjamin Franklin and the honor of Dutch seamen." *Physics Today*. 59(1):36. https://physicstoday.scitation.org/doi/10.1063/1.2180175.

— Philip J Sykes

It is generally a long journey from an initial question to a clearly focused research idea, developing and funding a study, then analysing results and generating findings. (See the case study later in this chapter.) There is still much to do beyond generating research findings, especially around the need for successful publication and dissemination. The impact of research is also relevant—how it is cited, taken up and used for the benefit of patients. Research impact not only improves patient care and is personally satisfying, but it is also important for the research careers of colleagues and for university institutions, whose performance is regularly assessed in the Research Excellence Framework. (See Further Reading.)

The process of clinical research should come full circle back to changed or improved care for patients. It will also raise further questions, so a new cycle develops. This process can offer a great degree of personal satisfaction. Indeed, this is a pre-requisite because each step may take longer than anticipated. Journeys from ideas to publication usually take some years, and personal drive is needed to see them through. While research endeavour may be seen as an 'ivory tower' activity, those living in that tower realise just how much effort, energy and tenacity is required to see a research idea through from initial conceptualisation in a clinical setting to delivery of relevant, potentially impactful data and findings. The journey has been conceptualised as being similar to Bunyan's *Pilgrims Progress*, starting from the 'City of Hope' and ending at the 'Delta of Editors' in a journey traversing the serendipity mine, the canyon of despair, the great funding desert and the data analysis jungle.[28]

Funding streams exist to support research. CRNs ensure that participating practices should not be out of pocket when conducting studies. A major component of most research funding bids is usually staff costs and making time for the research, although this is not likely to be a highly remunerative aspect of primary care. Consequently, interest in and capacity to undertake research always needs to be balanced with personal and family commitments and other competing primary care activities (such as managing the recent COVID-19 pandemic).[29]

The landmark researchers described in the boxes would probably struggle now to perform their studies, working largely alone as they did, without the current complexities of research ethics and governance and competitive funding calls. Taking the early steps from an idea to defining and funding a research proposal can be some of the hardest stages of a research career. The case study from Professor Hayes Dalal (see box) exemplifies many of the steps needed to successfully turn a consulting room question into a change in clinical practice. Hayes got the idea for his research question from a patient who was not keen to attend hospital-based cardiac rehabilitation classes.

BOX: CASE STUDY

In the early 2000s, Dr Hayes Dalal, a GP in Cornwall, became interested in helping his patients better access cardiac rehabilitation following a heart attack or diagnosis of heart failure. He wanted patients to be able to choose a home-based intervention, overcoming some of the barriers to attending centre-based classes—the standard form of delivery at the time. Attendance rates were low, and difficulties in accessing centralised services are a familiar challenge in rural practice.

Hayes sought advice and guidance from local primary care academics. Working with them, he undertook some background research to establish the scope of, and existing evidence for, his research ideas. They also helped him source local research funding from the NHS Executive Southwest, with which he trialled home-based rehabilitation after myocardial infarction using *The Heart Manual*, an existing programme, and found it to be as effective as rehabilitation delivered through his local hospital.[30, 31] He went on to apply for a programme development grant (PDG) from the NIHR to extend the project to include home-based rehabilitation for heart failure. PDGs enable research teams to carry out preparatory work and apply for a competitive (and much more costly) programme grant for applied research (PGfAR).

The PDG funded a survey to explore heart failure patients' attitudes, beliefs and expectations and examine why so few took part in cardiac rehabilitation.[32] The research group also reviewed the evidence for exercise training in patients with heart failure.[33] Their published findings were instrumental in making a robust case for Hayes's subsequent PGfAR application. This secured a £2 million funding award for the Rehabilitation Enablement in Chronic Heart Failure (REACH-HF) study, a facilitated, home-based, accessible rehabilitation programme for people with heart failure and their caregivers which included tailored exercise and wellbeing interventions.

The award funded up to five years of research activity. Hayes's team (which now included statisticians, qualitative researchers, health behaviourists, academic general practitioners and heart failure experts, among others) developed, piloted and trialled the REACH-HF intervention.

The team first conducted a RCT to assess the feasibility of a full trial of the clinical effectiveness and cost effectiveness of the intervention. This work confirmed that the rehabilitation programme improved quality of life at 12 months compared with usual care alone and showed that it was cost effective.[34]

Following the success of this research, the REACH-HF programme was rolled out into everyday clinical practice in four other localities as an additional option for patients with heart failure.

In 2021, the team successfully applied for a new PDG to fund developing a digital version of the REACH-HF training programme, maximising its accessibility and minimising its cost. The shift from a three-day, face-to-face course to a two-day online course allowed convenient access to training for NHS staff, avoiding travel and reducing cost.

The team's evidence-based rehabilitation programme extends the availability and uptake of cardiac rehabilitation for people with heart failure, a key objective of the NHS Long-Term Plan.[35]

When first considering a research project, there are ample opportunities to get deflected onto tangential questions, spending time and energy in the wrong directions and getting disheartened in the process. It is also easy to feel overwhelmed by the apparent gulf between how you see your (simple) research idea and the complex series of steps and stages (which may feel like barriers being erected) that are precursors to the study you are itching to undertake. Seeking early advice from colleagues in an academic department of primary care helped Hayes minimise the risk of wasted effort, and getting 'buy-in' and support from practice colleagues helped him get started successfully.

Preliminary work, including assessing the existing evidence, gaining an understanding of what potential funders may be looking for and mapping out a clear, logical and feasible research plan in as much detail as possible, is vital for a successful funding proposal. Hayes also published a letter in the *BMJ* establishing some credentials in the topic area to help in gaining funding.[36]

While an evidence-based background section is an important justification for any research proposal, developing it can also generate an early win with a 'stand-alone' publication; evidence synthesis, such as systematic reviewing of the literature, sits high in the hierarchy of evidence.[37]

An evidence review is a good way to start when resources and time are limited because it can be undertaken in small steps (although working to an agreed and feasible timetable is important). It also builds on the now-common training experience of most health undergraduates in synthesising published research evidence. A thesis for a higher degree usually includes an evidence synthesis as an early chapter. In Hayes's case, the evidence review was published as a Cochrane review and led to a significant separate body of research.[33, 38]

Waiting long months between submission and peer review before responding, sometimes rapidly; coping with rejection; and being prepared to revise and resubmit are essential attributes for researchers. In 2021, the NIHR success rates for PDGs and PGfARs were 44% and 25%, respectively.[39] Writing an unsuccessful research application takes just as much effort as writing a successful one, so it really pays to use the time, advice and support available to maximise your chances of success.

William Budd 1811–1880
Devon and Bristol

William Budd began his medical career as an apprentice to his father, a rural general practitioner in North Tawton, Devon, followed by four years studying in Paris. There, he developed an interest in 'putrid fever', known in Britain as typhoid fever, still sometimes confused with typhus.

After further study in Edinburgh, where he gained an MD and a gold medal for a study on acute rheumatism, he served on the HMS *Dreadnought*, a hospital ship for merchant seamen moored near Greenwich. Here, his interest in typhoid fever became personal when he suffered a near-fatal attack of the disease.

He returned home to practise in North Tawton where, in 1839, typhoid fever broke out in a village of 1,300 people, most of whom were his patients. It seemed that the patients did not have any connection with each other until Budd observed that when three people returned to their homes some miles away 'as soon as they began to droop', the disease spread locally. He also noted that a friend of one of the patients, who had visited him at his worst, not only developed typhoid fever but also went on to infect others.

Budd entered his observations in a writing competition organised by the Provincial Medical and Surgical Association, later to become the BMA, but his entry was unsuccessful, and the paper was not published.

In 1847, now practising in Bristol, he observed another typhoid epidemic. His careful observations revealed that all the cases occurred in 13 houses drawing water from the same well, while the other 21 houses, which used a different well, were unaffected.

He concluded that typhoid fever could be spread both by water and from person to person, that there was a 'latent' (incubation) period between infection and the onset of symptoms and that an attack of typhoid conferred 'exemption' (immunity) from future attacks. After a delay of several years, he published his observations in *The Lancet* in 1859.

His 'contagionist' proposition that typhoid could spread from person to person was supported by other rural doctors who had observed the epidemiology of the disease in their own villages and come to the same conclusion. However, it met significant opposition from 'anti-contagionist' doctors in towns and cities, who supported the popular explanation that the infection was acquired from 'miasma': noxious fumes of bad air from rotting organic matter and poor drainage.

Convinced that he was right, Budd taught and wrote about the importance of sanitation and the use of disinfectants to prevent the spread of both typhoid and cholera, eventually publishing his major work, *Typhoid Fever*, in 1873. Gradually, his views gained acceptance, supported by the 1854 findings of John Snow, who famously aborted a cholera outbreak in Broad Street, Soho, by removing a water pump handle.

Budd, William. 1873. *Typhoid Fever: Its Nature, Mode of Spreading, and Prevention*. London: Longmans, Green.

Moorhead, Robert. 2002. 'William Budd and typhoid fever'. *Journal of the Royal Society of Medicine* 95: 561–4.

— Philip Evans

The biggest barriers to Hayes' research journey were predominantly the early ones—getting a primary care nurse to work in the local hospital for his first big study[30] and gaining permission from local trusts and research ethics committees. Later on, he cites the hard work involved in getting published in a high-impact journal—a potentially important support for further funding. His story covers 20 years of research, charting the steps through local engagement and support, assessing existing evidence and building the platform for successfully gaining substantial competitive funding. This is not an uncommon time span from an initial idea to a successfully implemented change in clinical practice. Research is without doubt a marathon, not a sprint. Enthusiasm rises and falls during so long a period. Events such as publication successes or funding rejections are waypoints, and being part of a research team who can support and perhaps perpetuate a programme of research is important to stay the course.

Publicising and disseminating research findings are necessary, but the journey does not end with the publication of a successful trial. The major challenge at the end is often to bridge the gap between evidence generation and implementation.

CONCLUSIONS

The UK is a global leader in primary care research. Research continues to be needed to guide implementation of effective and cost-effective improvement to models of care, but challenges exist. The rising demands of clinical workloads threaten the availability of research time.[40] Postgraduate study to MSc and preferably PhD levels is an essential step in a research career. Protected time for research can be funded by NIHR personal awards and fellowships at many career levels; other organisations and charities also offer such support, but all these awards are competitive. The constraints of short-term funding and lack of tenured mid-career positions do, however, threaten the development of adequate numbers of future primary care research leaders.[41] Encouraging the next generation of researchers is vital if we are to continue to guide policy makers in improving care. This chapter aims to offer insight into and ideas about the research process and how one may become involved with it. Space does not permit a full treatment of the topic, but if it has offered inspiration, this can be followed up through the further reading suggested here. Local academic departments of primary care are also key resources for support in understanding the research landscape, development of research ideas and academic career advice for all healthcare professionals.

FURTHER READING

The following organisations offer useful resources and advice on setting out on or developing an idea for or a career in primary care research:

Clinical Practice Research Datalink: https://cprd.com.

General Medical Council: Good practice in research: www.gmc-uk.org/ethical-guidance/ethical-guidance-for-doctors/good-practice-in-research.

James Lind Alliance: www.jla.nihr.ac.uk/.

Medical Research Council: Is my study research? www.hra-decisiontools.org.uk/research/.

NICE: Join a committee: www.nice.org.uk/get-involved/our-committees/join-a-committee.

NIHR: Embedding a research culture: www.nihr.ac.uk/health-and-care-professionals/engagement-and-participation-in-research/embedding-a-research-culture.htm#one.

NIHR: Integrated academic training, describing academic clinical fellowships and clinical lectureships: www.nihr.ac.uk/explore-nihr/academy-programmes/integrated-academic-training.htm.

NIHR: How our journey through NIHR funding has improved care for people with heart failure: www.nihr.ac.uk/blog/how-our-journey-through-nihr-funding-has-improved-care-for-people-with-heart-failure/28394.

NIHR: Identifying research needs: www.nihr.ac.uk/partners-and-industry/charities/identify-research-needs.htm.

NIHR Primary Care Network: www.nihr.ac.uk/explore-nihr/specialties/primary-care.htm.

NIHR School for Primary Care Research: www.spcr.nihr.ac.uk/.

North American Primary Care Research Group: www.napcrg.org/resources/getting-started-in-primary-care-research/.

Research Excellence Framework: www.ref.ac.uk/.

Royal College of General Practitioners—Research Ready and Scientific Foundation Board: www.rcgp.org.uk/clinical-and-research/our-programmes/research-at-rcgp/support.aspx#research-ready.

UK Society for Academic Primary Care: https://sapc.ac.uk/.

REFERENCES

1. The SPRINT Research Group. A randomized trial of intensive versus standard blood-pressure control. *N Eng J Med.* 2015;373(22):2103–16.
2. Arnett DK, Blumenthal RS, Albert MA, Buroker AB, Goldberger ZD, Hahn EJ, et al. 2019 ACC/AHA guideline on the primary prevention of cardiovascular disease. *A report of the American College of Cardiology/American Heart Association Task Force on Clinical Practice Guidelines.* 2019;74(10):e177–e232. Doi: 10.1016/j.jacc.2019.03.010
3. Williams B, Mancia G, Spiering W, Agabiti Rosei E, Azizi M, Burnier M, et al. 2018 ESC/ESH guidelines for the management of arterial hypertension. *Eur Heart J.* 2018;39(33):3021–104.
4. Guthrie B, Payne K, Alderson P, McMurdo ME, Mercer SW. Adapting clinical guidelines to take account of multimorbidity. *BMJ.* 2012;345:e6341.

5. Barnett K, Mercer SW, Norbury M, Watt G, Wyke S, Guthrie B. Epidemiology of multimorbidity and implications for health care, research, and medical education: A cross-sectional study. *Lancet.* 2012;380(9836):37–43.

6. Camafort M, Redón J, Pyun WB, Coca A. Intensive blood pressure lowering: A practical review. *Clin Hyper.* 2020;26(1):21.

7. Turner BJ, Hollenbeak CS, Weiner M, Ten Have T, Tang SS. Effect of unrelated comorbid conditions on hypertension management. *Ann Intern Med.* 2008;148(8):578–86.

8. Ebell MH, Sokol R, Lee A, Simons C, Early J. How good is the evidence to support primary care practice? *Evid Based Med.* 2017;22(3):88–92.

9. Gillies JC. Getting it right in the consultation: Hippocrates' problem; Aristotle's answer. *Occas Pap R Coll Gen Pract.* 2005(86):5–35.

10. Hobbs R. Is primary care research important and relevant to GPs? *Br J Gen Pract.* 2019;69(686):424–5.

11. Hypertension in adults: Diagnosis and management (NG 136) [Internet], 2022. www.nice.org.uk/guidance/ng136 [Accessed 28 August 2019].

12. Onion CW. Evidence-based medicine in primary care. *Occas Pap R Coll Gen Pract.* 2001;(80):1–23.

13. Williams MA. Rural professional isolation: An integrative review. *On J Rur Nurs Heal Care.* 2012;12:3+.

14. Shelley B, Kessler D, Mughal F, Creswell C. Why GPs need to be involved in mental health research. *Br J Gen Pract.* 2021;71(709):365.

15. Helfrich CD, Dolan ED, Simonetti J, Reid RJ, Joos S, Wakefield BJ, et al. Elements of team-based care in a patient-centered medical home are associated with lower burnout among VA primary care employees. *J Gen Intern Med.* 2014;29(Suppl 2):S659–66.

16. Lemieux-Charles L, McGuire WL. What do we know about health care team effectiveness? A review of the literature. *Med Care Res Rev.* 2006;63(3):263–300.

17. Hindi AMK, Schafheutle EI, Jacobs S. Community pharmacy integration within the primary care pathway for people with long-term conditions: A focus group study of patients', pharmacists' and GPs' experiences and expectations. *BMC Fam Pract.* 2019;20(1):26.

18. Clark CE, Powell RJ. The differential blood pressure sign in general practice: Prevalence and prognostic value. *Fam Pract.* 2002;19(5):439–41.

19. Clark CE, Powell RJ, Campbell JL. The interarm blood pressure difference as predictor of cardiovascular events in patients with hypertension in primary care: Cohort study. *J Hum Hypertens.* 2007;21:633–6.

20. Clark CE, Taylor RS, Shore AC, Campbell JL. The difference in blood pressure readings between arms and survival: Primary care cohort study. *BMJ.* 2012;344:e1327.

21. Boaz A, Hanney S, Jones T, Soper B. Does the engagement of clinicians and organisations in research improve healthcare performance: A three-stage review. *BMJ Open.* 2015;5(12):e009415.

22. Newington L, Alexander CM, Wells M. Impacts of clinical academic activity: Qualitative interviews with healthcare managers and research-active nurses, midwives, allied health professionals and pharmacists. *BMJ Open.* 2021;11(10).

23. Ozdemir BA, Karthikesalingam A, Sinha S, Poloniecki JD, Hinchliffe RJ, Thompson MM, et al. Research activity and the association with mortality. *PLoS One.* 2015;10(2):e0118253.

24. Jonker L, Fisher SJ. The correlation between National Health Service trusts' clinical trial activity and both mortality rates and care quality commission ratings: A retrospective cross-sectional study. *Public Heal.* 2018;157:1–6.

25. Riding H, Haining S, Robinson L. Research activity and quality indicators in primary care—An explorative qualitative interview study. *Br J Gen Pract.* 2018;68(suppl 1).

26. Clark CE, Smith LFP, Taylor RS, Campbell JL. Nurse led interventions to improve control of blood pressure in people with hypertension: Systematic review and meta-analysis. *BMJ.* 2010;341:c3995.

27. Eve E. PUNs and DENs: A model for reflective learning. *InnovAiT.* 2020;13(3):189–90.

28. Agnew NM, Pyke SW. *The science game: An introduction to research in the behavioral and social sciences.* 7th ed. Don Mills, ON: Oxford University Press, 2007.

29. Mughal F, Khunti K, Mallen CD. The impact of COVID-19 on primary care: Insights from the National Health Service (NHS) and future recommendations. *J Fam Med Prim Care.* 2021;10(12):4345–9.

30. Dalal HM, Evans PH, Campbell JL, Taylor RS, Watt A, Read KLQ, et al. Home-based versus hospital-based rehabilitation after myocardial infarction: A randomized trial with preference arms—Cornwall Heart Attack Rehabilitation Management Study (CHARMS). *Int J Cardiol.* 2007;119(2):202–11.

31. NHS Lothian. The Heart Manual 2022. https://services.nhslothian.scot/TheHeartManual/Pages/default.aspx [Accessed 27 June 2022].

32. Dalal HM, Wingham J, Palmer J, Taylor R, Petre C, Lewin R, et al. Why do so few patients with heart failure participate in cardiac rehabilitation? A cross-sectional survey from England, Wales and Northern Ireland. *BMJ Open.* 2012;2(2):e000787.

33. Taylor RS, Dalal H, Jolly K, Moxham T, Zawada A. Home-based versus centre-based cardiac rehabilitation. *Cochr Database Syst Rev.* 2010(1):Cd007130

34. Dalal HM, Taylor RS, Jolly K, Davis RC, Doherty P, Miles J, et al. The effects and costs of home-based rehabilitation for heart failure with reduced ejection fraction: The REACH-HF multicentre randomized controlled trial. *Eur J Prev Cardiol.* 2020;26(3):262–72.

35. NHS England. The NHS long term plan 2019. www.longtermplan.nhs.uk/wp-content/uploads/2019/08/nhs-long-term-plan-version-1.2.pdf.

36. Dalal H. Don't forget rehabilitation. *BMJ.* 2010;341:c4286.

37. Murad MH, Asi N, Alsawas M, Alahdab F. New evidence pyramid. *Evid Based Med.* 2016;21(4):125–127.

38. Taylor RS, Walker S, Smart NA, Piepoli MF, Warren FC, Ciani O, et al. Impact of exercise-based cardiac rehabilitation in patients with heart failure (ExTraMATCH II) on mortality and hospitalisation: An individual patient data meta-analysis of randomised trials. *Eur J Heart Fail.* 2018;20(12):1735–43.

39. National Institute for Health Research. Programme grants for applied research and programme development grants—success rates 2021. www.nihr.ac.uk/documents/pgfar-and-pdg-success-rates/21325 [Accessed 1 April 2021].
40. Hobbs FD, Bankhead C, Mukhtar T, Stevens S, Perera-Salazar R, Holt T, et al. Clinical workload in UK primary care: A retrospective analysis of 100 million consultations in England, 2007–14. *Lancet.* 2016;387(10035):2323–30.
41. Cheraghi-Sohi S, Perry M, Wallace E, Wallis KA, Geraghty AW, Joling KJ, et al. A future in primary care research: A view from the middle. *Br J Gen Pract.* 2018;68(674):440–1.

Index

Printed in the United States
by Baker & Taylor Publisher Services